Making Climate Policy Work

Making Climate Policy Work

Danny Cullenward
David G. Victor

polity

First published in 2020 by Polity Press

Polity Press
65 Bridge Street
Cambridge CB2 1UR, UK

Polity Press
101 Station Landing
Suite 300
Medford, MA 02155, USA

ISBN-13: 978-1-5095-4179-9
ISBN-13: 978-1-5095-4180-5 (pb)

A catalogue record for this book is available from the British Library.

Typeset in 10.5 on 12pt Sabon
by Fakenham Prepress Solutions, Fakenham, Norfolk NR21 8NL
Printed and bound in Great Britain by TJ Books Limited

For further information on Polity, visit our website:
politybooks.com

Contents

Figures and tables

Figures

Tables

Preface

We are two scholars who have spent nearly all of our professional lives intersecting with the problem of climate change. For Danny, that has meant a career at the nexus of law, economics, and engineering, looking at how energy systems might evolve in the future. For David, that has meant a career trained in political science and focused on how industrial transformations actually occur. When you spend this much time on one big issue that keeps getting worse, you live a life of constant reminder that the climate problem is really hard to solve.

Realism about the scale of the challenge is often discouraged in climate policy circles because it is easy to confuse with pessimism. Precisely because the climate problem has proven so stubborn, the whole ecosystem of climate activism and scholarship spends a lot of time painting stiff smiles on inconvenient facts. Yet any serious analysis must start by understanding climate solutions for what they are: requirements for profound industrial change that are difficult to initiate, sustain, and run to completion. The river of industrial investment and climate pollution runs deep and fast with powerful incumbents. Elements of change are becoming visible, but most to date are minnows swimming against that strong current.

This level of difficulty, we think, is a call not for pessimism but for realism about solutions. Because it is so hard to make

deep cuts in global emissions – deep decarbonization, as it is
called – effective solutions require clear thinking and strategy.
Efforts spent tilting at ephemeral, magical policy solutions
waste scarce resources that should instead be invested in
things that work.

For the last decade, both of us have observed a rapidly
growing disconnect between the solutions that are most
popular among policy and academic elites and the facts
on the ground. Conventional wisdom in elite circles holds
that market-based solutions work best; decades of policy
advocacy and design within this paradigm have produced a
network of fledgling cap-and-trade systems that portend to
lay foundations for solutions. In a few places, carbon taxes
have emerged as well. These pockets of market-based action
have been created, in part, with the belief that they will
spread – ultimately to global coverage and with big leverage
on emissions. The realities are different, however. Those who
are watching closely know those promises are largely failing
and, we argue, will continue to fail.

What drew us together as collaborators is that while
both of us are rooted in academia – and thus steeped in
debates around which policy instruments are best from the
perspective of theory – we spend much of our professional
lives elsewhere. We work with governments, regulators,
NGOs, firms, and investors – institutions whose leaders
are all grappling in practical terms with the challenges of
deep decarbonization. Everyone is asking about the theory
of change. "What moves the needle?" is a common refrain.
Outside of the academy we see policymakers and CEOs
talking a lot about market-based strategies to address climate
change. Yet when they actually do something that moves
the needle – such as adopt a policy that makes a big dent in
emissions, redirect investment toward low-carbon solutions,
or craft a business strategy based on the reality that deep
cuts in emissions are essential – they make those choices
without much attention to abstract market forces such as
carbon pricing. Rather, they respond to policy and political
pressures rooted in other concerns – such as fear of losing
access to vital markets, rising social opposition to their
business models, or regulatory requirements and industrial
policies that require big changes in behavior. From Davos to

Washington DC, Sacramento, and Brussels, most elites who talk about the climate crisis from an altitude of 30,000 feet are talking about markets. Meanwhile, at sea level, pretty much all the serious work of deep decarbonization is being done by industrial policy and strategy.

This book is about that disconnect.

Our goal is to explain why market-oriented climate policies have fallen far short. This is not an accident, we argue, but a reflection of the political structure of the climate problem and the administrative tools that modern governments can apply in response. Reducing emissions in the world as it is requires understanding that world. It requires understanding why, after thirty years of diplomatic meetings – most of them tilting at market-oriented policy – we haven't made more progress. That failure is rooted in the difficulty of the challenges of industrial transformation. It is also rooted partly in the fact that policy elites, business leaders, and even some environmental groups that want serious action have imagined they live in a world where the massive changes required for deep decarbonization will emerge with a technocratic nudge from the market's invisible hand.

It is vital that policy designers and advocates start making a sharper distinction between the world as it is and a fantasy in which market policies could do most of the work in creating deep decarbonization. Failure to grapple with that difference means that growing pressure to act on climate change can't be channeled in the most productive ways. Many parts of the world are, plausibly, on the cusp of a huge surge of interest in and action on climate change. Nearly all the evidence from climate science is dark – warming is happening faster than expected, impacts such as rising seas are looking more dire than initially forecast – and a catalog of unknowns mostly points darker. Growing public awareness and concern among corporate leaders and politicians is not leading to swift action everywhere, but it is leading already to a lot more action in some places. The global effort is deepening and widening. Yet most of the key actors pushing for a coherent strategy are pushing a playbook we believe is outdated and ineffective. Market-based strategies haven't just fallen short in the past, but they will keep failing to deliver the elements of deep decarbonization that will be demanded as awareness of the climate crisis grows. We explain why and offer alternatives.

We come to this project from very different political backgrounds.

For Danny, insights into the climate problem are intertwined with understanding how the left wing of American politics is pushing the country to get serious – whether on economic policy, financial regulation, or energy system transitions. Time and time again the left has expressed a prescient understanding of climate policy dysfunction. The environmental justice community, for example, has sounded the alarm about offsets and other failures of carbon markets much more loudly and accurately than practically any other segment of the political debate. Yet many of the same voices have struggled to articulate alternative policy strategies that are practical to implement at scale. In recent years Danny has been active in Sacramento, participating in regulatory processes, testifying at legislative oversight hearings, and serving on an expert advisory panel focused on California's carbon market. If most of the action on climate change is happening in a few places like California that are willing and able to invest heavily in solutions, how do these leaders channel their resources into actions that really matter for deep decarbonization?

For David, the climate problem began as a topic to be understood through the lens of effective international cooperation and viable corporate strategy. Most of the global climate efforts to date have failed because they were disconnected from facts on the ground – from what governments and firms were willing and able to do. From that perspective, David's career has involved bouncing between the worlds of industrial incumbents (such as electric power companies) and the worlds of Silicon Valley (which is all about disruption, innovation, and dethroning incumbents). If the climate problem is largely about industrial transformation, what really guides the process?

Starting from these two different perspectives, we puzzled through the questions surrounding how to seed and nurture the technological and political transformations needed to address climate change. Many of these conversations were, frankly, a litany of vents. In our different worlds we separately observed a lot of talk about solutions that didn't seem to solve much. We also saw a lot of actual problem-solving – real companies and governments investing in risky new technologies and building new lines of business – that didn't seem to follow any of the standard academic prescriptions for "first-best" climate policy that relied on simple market signals.

The journey from catharsis to synthesis began when we realized a lot of the conventional wisdom had the story backwards. In a globalizing world where markets seemed to be triumphing over states, we saw serious solutions to the climate crisis rooted in the opposite approach – where the state was playing a much bigger role. And if the state could play an even larger role, so too would firms. That realization is bad news for governments and political parties that have spent a lot of time de-skilling or trashing the state. Firms, left to their own devices, aren't going to decarbonize the world. Governments without the capability to lead transformations won't steward much change. Incumbents are perfectly happy to stay the course.

The standard wisdom about the role of markets will, we think, be shaken badly by the facts. We will show that market forces can help optimize the allocation of resources, but they aren't that good at leading massive industrial transformation. Yet it is exactly that kind of transformation that's needed. This is one of many areas where the left – especially the deeper, more ecological left of the "Green New Deal" and other visions of massive state intervention – has been more accurate than most of the rest of the political spectrum. At the same time, however, accuracy in the diagnosis has also come with deep misunderstandings about how transformation will be organized and can unfold, once compelled to begin. On that front, the practical corporate industrial community has been more accurate than most other groups that are active in the climate policy debate. Demonizing firms just because they are firms or incumbents ignores the reality that these enterprises will steward much of the innovation, transformation, and infrastructure investments needed for climate solutions.

Pragmatists who see existing firms as vital to practical solutions on climate change have failed to appreciate that most of the political energy for reform comes from the left, where suspicions about incumbency and compromise run deep. What politics must do is create the incentives for industrial transformation so that firms will invest both technologically and politically in a decarbonized future. With successful investment and expanding social movements, those incentives will grow and the forces that want deep decarbonization will become more powerful. That process will happen only if pragmatists and activists recognize the vital roles that each plays in this process of creating broader and deeper political pressure for decarbonization. Successful decarbonization will help lower costs and increase confidence in climate policy, ultimately creating a political dynamic that will accelerate decarbonization and make it more self-sustaining.

Most of this book was written over a six-month period starting in the fall of 2019. As often happens, once a new way of thinking about things emerges, old facts don't disappear so much as fall into new places. The approach we take in this book aims to organize the data on markets' increasingly visible shortcomings into a coherent narrative – one that offers a new interpretation of what is feasible with markets and thus what must be achieved with other policy strategies. We lay out the standard prescriptions for market-oriented policy and then show how the facts actually fit a different pattern. Explaining that pattern requires a theory of politics and some willingness to think differently about what really works, all of which we cover in chapter 1. If you want to read just one chapter, that's the one.

As we completed this manuscript in February 2020, the world was descending into a global economic lockdown. In those rare moments when a huge shock hits, it is tempting to think that everything has changed, but we decided to change nothing in this book as a result of the pandemic. Our aim has been to write a book about the fundamental politics that determine climate policy effectiveness, particularly with respect to market-based policy instruments. Our ideas should be judged by whether we get those fundamentals right. Rather than chase the twists and turns of the pandemic and government policy responses – by May 2020, when the final editing wrapped up, the top ten economies had committed $7 trillion in stimulus spending and counting – we decided the crisis is another opportunity to ask: can market-based instruments, in the real world, cause the needed transformation in industrial decarbonization? Our answer before the pandemic was no; after the pandemic, we expect the evidence will be even stronger.

On two fronts, the pandemic is revealing how politics affects policies and the industrial action needed for deep decarbonization. First, carbon prices in nearly all of the world's cap-and-trade systems have fallen in line with economic upheaval – and with them, the revenues governments collect from these programs. Carbon markets amplify macroeconomic shocks because they are fundamentally pro-cyclical policies, which is why we are so keen to convince governments to move away from instruments whose practical impact is so flaky and toward other policy instruments, like industrial policy, that can more readily be kept in line with the public's demands and the signals firms need to invest.

Second, the pandemic has transformed political priorities. Abstract global amenities are on the wane, with immediate employment, economic recovery, and public health at the front of all policy agendas. This shift will test the political commitment to cutting climate pollution, with effects that vary by economic sector. In places where the decarbonization agenda is aligned with employment, we expect the public's willingness to invest in deep decarbonization will grow. In other sectors, the opposite patterns may appear. We draw from this a lesson already offered in this book: policy instruments that link together all sectors in a common, transparent effort to impose a single price on carbon fundamentally misread political reality.

In telling the story of how market-based climate policy works in the real world, we adopt the premise that idealized markets would be desirable if they were feasible. We hope this choice allows us to reach readers who identify strongly with the power of market forces, since we hope to change their minds. We want them to understand how political forces constrain what market-based policies can do, especially at the early stages of deep decarbonization, because wishing those forces away isn't practical and hasn't worked. We also seek readers among the many who have long ago rejected markets. We hope they will read on as well, as our critique will help offer a systematic logic for many of their concerns – new arguments in support of familiar positions – while providing a framework for better policy strategies. What matters most to us – and the planet – is whether a policy works, not which ideological camp claims a notch in its belt.

We wrote this book in our spare time with no grants or other financial support. Our strong suspicion is that had we gone out looking for help, funders would not have been interested. Too much of the support for writing and thinking on the politics of the climate crisis is, in fact, support for advocacy around familiar policy strategies. While climate advocacy comes in many flavors, it is largely rooted in the idea that an elite group of climate intelligentsia knows all the right answers – the right policies, the right technologies, and the right political strategies to deliver the goods. Yet the biggest follies in climate policy strategy over the last few decades all emerged from an uncritical reliance on untested theories of change. Major industrial transformations don't lend themselves to easy planning with existing policy tools – that is why they are transformations. All of us know less than we think, ourselves included. Yet overconfidence abounds, including in policy advocacy. Interest in questioning accepted wisdoms is scarce. Groupthink reigns.

Our book is an effort not just to rattle the climate commentariat, but also to explain why any rigid theory of change is likely to become brittle as circumstances evolve. We hope it leads more groups to reflect on what really works and to anchor their reflections in research. Indeed, many of the key questions around the efficacy of different policy instruments should be addressable with hypotheses and data. What has been most disturbing to us in this project is that the data needed for serious analysis of market-based policies are strikingly scarce, rarely collected together, and usually of low quality. Even where there are legal or fiduciary obligations to report data – such as around where money raised by market-based systems gets spent, or whether carbon offset schemes actually reduce emissions – most information is shrouded in opacity and complexity. More research will help, but in some cases the analytical *terra incognita* is by design. Many climate policy systems that have been created at huge financial and political expense are designed not to reveal their failures. We call out some of the most egregious examples in the hope that those who want to understand what really works will press harder for both transparency and analysis.

Although we worked without grant support, no project that probes widely into whether the status quo is working could happen without many colleagues who have helped with ideas, data, and constructive disagreements.

There's a world of difference between a book in principle and a book in reality. Louise Knight and her colleagues at Polity sit at the center of that difference. For years Louise has asked about a possible book, and as these ideas came together, she, Inès Boxman, and Justin Dyer – along with a group of insightful external reviewers – played an essential role in turning them into an actual manuscript.

We are particularly grateful to several people who read drafts. Among them, Jeremy Freeman, Peter Gourevitch, Jess Green, Michael Grubb, Lars Gulbrandsen, Justin Gundlach, Matto Mildenberger, Arild Underdal, and Jørgen Wettestad. In tandem, we had many conversations with people about our ideas as they emerged: Grayson Badgley, Ross Brown, Dallas Burtraw, Chris Busch, Geoffroy Dolphin, Meredith Fowlie, Matthew Freedman, Oliver Geden, Larry Goulder, Barbara Haya, Dan Jacobson, Bruce Jones, Jonathan Koomey, Vanessa Pinsky, Ric Redman, Chuck Sabel, Dianne Saxe, Katie Valenzuela, Michael Wara, and David Weiskopf. A special thanks to the many people who helped us with data: Jeremy Carl, (again) Geoffroy Dolphin, David Fedor, David Hytha, Quentin Perrier, and Marissa Santikarn.

In tandem with writing this project, both of us have been working on many other projects that have shaped our thinking – with ideas reflected on these pages.

Danny is grateful first and foremost to his partner, Nina, with whom he is raising twins Adela and Oscar. Nina and Danny's sister, Laurie, spent countless nights and weekends caring for the babies so that Danny could write or field calls at odd times from wherever in the world David happened to be that week. With help from Debbie Sivas, Amy Applebaum, Pam Matson, and Anjana Richards, Danny has been teaching energy and climate policy at Stanford, where several of our ideas began in dialog with curious students. Danny's research in California would not have been possible without selfless support from Karen Fries and José Carmona – not to mention his collaborators Michael Mastrandrea and Mason Inman, who helped cut through so much of the opacity. Finally, Danny thanks the civil servants, policy advisors, and policymakers who work tirelessly to advance climate progress in California and gave generously of their time to help him learn the ins and outs of state policy – especially Kip Lipper. Special thanks to California Senate President *Pro Tem* Emeritus Kevin de León and Senator Bob Wieckowski for their leadership and for appointing Danny to California's cap-and-trade advisory board.

David thanks four long-time collaborations that have facilitated conversations and ideas that had a big impact on this project. First is joint work with Bob Keohane around the factors that explain the politics of international cooperation – work that has, increasingly, emphasized the national and transnational factors that condition what is possible in the international system. A second is a big book project with Chuck Sabel (slated for publication in 2021) on Experimentalist Governance: that is, on how societies solve problems when there is strong pressure for action but nobody, frankly, knows exactly what to do. Working with Chuck has sharply refined our thinking about the incentives that affect when and how firms invest in new technologies and how societies learn which policy strategies actually work. Third is a collaboration with Frank Geels and Simon Sharpe to look at how the insights from the history of technological change and the history of international cooperation could guide new sector-by-sector strategies for deep decarbonization. That study, released in December 2019 in Madrid, helped us sharpen our thinking about the degree of technological innovation still needed in nearly every sector. It also builds on work that Bruce Jones and David have been leading for several years at the Brookings Institution, one of the publishers of the Madrid study. Finally, every effort to study technological change, for David, involves voices from early mentors on that topic: Jesse Ausubel, Arnulf Grübler, and Nebojša Nakićenović. They – and the International Institute for Applied Systems Analysis (IIASA), where we all worked at various times – have shaped a world view for the better. Although they sometimes arrive at very different conclusions, David has learned a lot from his colleagues in economics who study market design: Larry Goulder, Rob Stavins, Gernot Wagner, and the late Marty Weitzman. And a special thanks from David to his family – Emilie Hafner-Burton in particular – who were steady supporters even as he was in remote corners of the world on the phone with Danny.

1
A turn toward markets?

In the late 1980s, global attention started to focus on the problem of climate change caused by pollution from carbon dioxide (CO_2) and other greenhouse gases. In tandem, analysts and policymakers argued that the best strategy for dealing with pollutants that harmed the whole planet would be to create environmental markets that also spanned the globe. These market schemes would, in theory, create strong price incentives to cut emissions anywhere and everywhere. The scale of the policy response, it was thought, must be matched to the scale of the problem. And beyond scale, powerful market forces would help ensure that cuts in pollution were achieved at the lowest economic cost. The use of markets became the watchword for smart, efficient climate change policy.

Although the use of markets to control carbon pollution has never been without controversy, its dominance in the climate policy debate is hard to overstate. Market-based strategies were built into every major international agreement on climate change and formed the rhetorical core of the most ambitious countries' climate strategies. Most of these schemes envisioned setting caps on emissions and allowing firms and governments to trade credits – policies known as carbon markets or "cap-and-trade" programs. Governments would negotiate the desired pace and extent of emission reductions by setting pollution caps. Through trading, the collective genius of the market would discover the best allocation of effort. Many of the world's biggest emitters – starting first in the West, and now spreading to South Korea, China, and other emerging economies – have considered or adopted cap-and-trade programs. A few countries have taken a different market-based climate strategy and set prices directly via carbon taxes. Whereas cap-and-trade fixes the quantity and lets the market find the cost of emitting pollution, carbon taxation does the opposite: it specifies the price and lets the market discover the volume of pollution that aligns.

Market-based policies on a planetary scale, the theory goes, would empower firms and governments with the flexibility to focus investment on the least expensive options for controlling emissions. Flexibility would reduce costs, allowing more environmental protection with fewer resources; in turn, frugality would make it easier to mobilize business and voter support for ever-deeper climate pollution reductions. Ever since the early 1990s, when active efforts to develop climate policy began, the politics of crafting and sustaining policies needed for achieving deep cuts in emissions have been stymied by concerns that deep decarbonization – as the transformation to a climate-friendly future is known – would be expensive, difficult, and could even harm economic competitiveness. That's why policy strategies to keep costs as low as possible were seen not just as good for the economy, but also as essential to mustering political support to protect the planet.

Today, the original vision of a globally coordinated, market-based policy solution lies in tatters.

Many pollution markets exist, but nearly all are smoke-screens that create the impression that market forces are cutting emissions when, in fact, other policies are doing most of the real work of decarbonization. Almost everywhere that market systems are in place they operate at prices that are so low as to have little impact on key decisions such as whether to invest in or deploy new technologies. After thirty years of policy attention to climate change and twenty years of active efforts to design market systems, jurisdictions with reasonably ambitious carbon prices – say, $40 per ton of CO_2-equivalent[1] – account for less than 1% of global emissions (Figure 1.1). Those with carbon prices approaching $100 per ton of CO_2-equivalent – a strong signal more consistent with the level of effort the best new science suggests is needed for deep decarbonization – are an even tinier sliver of the global picture.

In a few places, carbon prices from market-based policies have been powerful enough to induce some changes in emission patterns – such as when firms decide whether to produce electricity from high-emission coal plants or lower-emission rivals. Those impacts, however, have nearly always involved commercially mature technologies competing in stable environments and under other highly restrictive conditions. In the United Kingdom, for example, a climate policy strategy that included carbon pricing accelerated the extinction of coal from electric power because other technologies, notably cleaner natural gas and renewables, were readily available and much more competitive when coal-fired power plants were required to pay the extra cost of their emissions.[2] Those are important roles for markets,

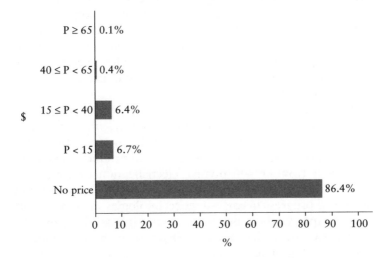

Figure 1.1 Carbon prices around the world in 2019

Source: Figure redrawn with permission from Jesse Jenkins, "Why Carbon Pricing Falls Short and What to Do About It," Kleinman Center for Energy Policy, University of Pennsylvania (Apr. 24, 2019); underlying data from World Bank, "State and Trends of Carbon Pricing" (2019).

but those roles are not central to the challenge of creating a global transition to near-zero emissions.

Nearly all the real challenges of deep decarbonization require incentives for governments and firms to back novel, risky, and untested technological systems – not simply to deploy known, proven options that are sitting on a shelf ready for use. In 2019 a team of scholars supported by the Energy Transitions Commission took a fresh look at exactly where the world stands with respect to deep decarbonization. The results, summarized in Figure 1.2, use the standard S-shaped curve for explaining the emergence, diffusion, and then reconfiguration of infrastructure that is typical of technological change. Strikingly, in nearly all of the ten sectors that account for the bulk of climate pollution, technological progress on deep decarbonization is in the very early stages – when, typically, the best choices are unknown, risks for investors are high, and active policy support is essential. The power sector is furthest along (at least in some countries), which is precisely why marginal market incentives have been able to achieve significant impacts in some contexts by affecting choices of known, proven technologies in that sector. But even the power sector requires comprehensive transformation with new technologies and investments – such as in advanced control systems, building electrification strategies, and bigger electric grids – that carbon pricing, alone, is unlikely to deliver.

What's needed nearly everywhere in the world is to test and deploy novel technologies energy, industrial, and agricultural systems. Even in electricity – where there has been a lot of progress in developing clean production systems – the next frontier will involve electrification of many end uses, including space heating and cooling, which requires continued progress in early-stage technologies such as reliable heat pumps. Carbon prices, even at high levels, won't be enough to induce the necessary investment in and adoption of novel technologies.

In addition to having little impact at home, the world's efforts to create market forces that encourage decarbonization have generated almost none of their promised international benefits. Despite nearly three decades of diplomatic and other policy efforts, no global carbon market exists today.

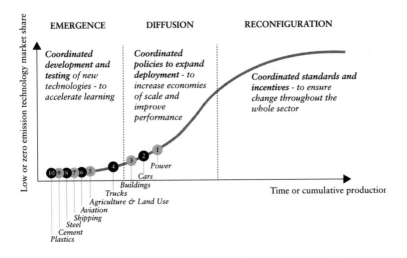

Figure 1.2 The state of decarbonization technology by sector

Source: Redrawn with permission from David G. Victor, Frank W. Geels, and Simon Sharpe, "Accelerating the Low Carbon Transition: The Case for Stronger, More Targeted and Coordinated International Action," Energy Transitions Commission and Brookings Institution (2019), based on assessments of technological development that rely heavily on the work of the Energy Transitions Commission (*http://www.energy-transitions.org/*).

Interregional emissions trading is a footnote in climate policy, not the main attraction. Various efforts to create regional carbon markets – such as in the European Union, across subnational governments in North America, and within private firms – remain inspired by the vision that these decentralized markets will become stitched together in time as the coverage of markets broadens and climate ambitions deepen. Yet in the real world there has been little stitching together and almost zero deepening.[3]

The most visible example of market links – the joint trading program involving California, Québec, and Ontario – recently shrank, with a conservative Ontarian government pulling out of cap-and-trade after winning power in 2018. Years earlier, nascent links between the Australian and EU markets dissolved as soon as Australia abandoned emissions trading. China, meanwhile, is in the middle of an opaque and years-long effort to develop a national emissions trading program in the power sector, where a small number of powerful state-owned firms dominate, environmental regulators have struggled for influence, and the state planning system has historically been much more potent than marginal market incentives in determining investment and environmental outcomes. Only one integrated international market has proved sustainable – the market for pollution across the European nations – because that market is built on top of a powerful superstructure of common European economic institutions, common rule of law and administrative procedure, and common confidence that the superstructure is robust. Those are highly demanding conditions to meet and unlikely to be seen anywhere else in the world anytime soon. This success within the EU bodes well for Europe, but the continent's share of global emissions is only about 9% and shrinking. As a leader, what it does is relevant to the global problem of climate change primarily if its leadership inspires and directs followership in the places where emissions are rising.[4]

As the sheen of markets dulls, it has also become clear that the world is making little progress on decarbonization. Since around 1990, when diplomacy to address global climate change first began on a sustained basis, world emissions have risen by two-thirds.[5] In only one sector (electric power) and one group of countries (the Western industrial democracies) have emissions declined a bit. Most of that is due to fortuitous changes in fuel markets, the decline in the cost of wind and solar power, and policies that have mandated a shift away from coal toward cleaner sources. In the United States, the shale gas revolution has crushed coal and cut CO_2 emissions along the way (even as evidence grows that needless methane leakage from the gas system undermines the climate benefits from replacing coal with gas). In places where gas is costlier – notably, continental Europe – renewables have been more important in cutting emissions. In most other sectors, such as transportation, emissions keep rising.

The unfortunate truth is that many governments around the world are ignoring the problem of greenhouse gas emissions, focusing, instead, on other priorities. That's why, in Figure 1.1, nearly all world emissions are priced at zero. Even the leaders – the EU, Nordic countries, Japan, and parts of the United States – have until recently been mostly tinkering at the margins, with market-based policies targeted mainly in sectors where technology has already advanced and costs are low. The best studies suggest that a few percent of global gross domestic product (GDP) should be allocated to controlling emissions – an investment on the scale of recent war and defense-related expenditures, yet requiring sustenance over decades.[6] So far, almost no major economy – except perhaps Germany, and with German leadership the rest of Europe as it contemplates a "European Green Deal" to accelerate deep decarbonization – has stepped up to the challenge. Collectively, the global level of effort is perhaps two to three orders of magnitude lower than needed.

The inconvenient problems of politics

These two profound problems – the failure of efforts to create effective market-based climate policies, and the failure to make significant progress in reducing global emissions – are inexorably linked. Massive political resources have been mobilized to push market forces as the central mechanism for cutting emissions. That mobilization, we will argue in this book, has largely failed and will keep failing. Its failure is not rooted in the economic logic of markets. Nor is it rooted in the idea that resources must be devoted efficiently, so that more protection from the ravages of global climate change can be obtained at lower economic cost.

Rather, the problem with markets is political.

The attractive academic logic of markets has become misaligned with the political realities of the climate problem on two fronts.

One front, most crucial, is that successful climate policy requires building and sustaining political coalitions to support policies that will transform all the major emitting sectors of the economy: electric power, transportation, industry, buildings, agriculture, and so on. Studies that look closely at these political processes show that every sector is different, with varied organization and authority of interest groups.[7] For academics, markets offer the prospect of economy-wide prices and transparency so that, ideally, all sectors are treated equally. Unfortunately, that feature of markets is toxic to policymakers and climate policy advocates, who must tackle political barriers and opportunities one step at a time, one sector at a time.[8] In some sectors, key political constituencies (such as voters) are highly sensitive to visible policy impacts on prominent carbon-emitting products (such as gasoline). In other sectors, industrial production is oriented around highly competitive, tradeable commodities – like steel – and firms are well organized politically to block policies that would harm their price-sensitive and trade-exposed industries. And so on – a string of problems, all rooted in the political organization and influence of powerful interests, each of which requires a tailored political solution. A market perspective on the climate problem emphasizes that resources and effort are fungible across every economy and around the world. A political perspective sees each sector as a separate challenge that requires bespoke solutions. Because textbook market-based policies treat all sectors with the same price, applying that textbook without an eye to political reality creates markets for which the overall effort is restrained to the lowest common denominator.

On another front, what markets do best – creating transparent, marginal price signals that encourage firms and households to optimize their choices – is misaligned with the industrial challenges facing deep decarbonization today. In most sectors the world is not far along with deep decarbonization: key technologies, demonstration projects, and the emergence of new firms to back low-carbon technologies are fledgling at best (see Figure 1.2).[9] Industrial firms and consumers aren't waiting for a faint, marginal signal from markets to nudge their behavior. Instead, they need active programs to mobilize and apply resources to new technologies that, with time and effort, will launch the global process of deep decarbonization and displace incumbent industries. The incumbents are powerful.[10] The new entrants are not.[11] Well-designed market signals, at best, are good at encouraging optimization when technologies are commercially mature and strategic choices are clear – such as when the UK electricity market had a signal to select mature renewable energy technologies and gas instead of coal. The hardest challenges of deep decarbonization involve redirecting investment toward technologies and businesses that are the opposite: beset with risk and danger for first movers. Creating those new industries requires a policy strategy – industrial policy, in effect – that is focused on the problem at hand, rather than inducing marginal changes in behavior with known technologies and production methods.[12]

Climate change presents an extremely difficult political problem that pits the diffuse public interests of the future – where everyone, to varying degrees, benefits from protecting the planet – against the private concerns of the present. Relying on markets to redirect those political forces takes a hard problem and makes it even harder to solve.

This book develops the argument that market-based strategies have, on balance, gotten in the way of building politically viable climate policy in three ways.

First, we offer a diagnosis for what has gone wrong. Our central contribution is to explain how political forces affect the design and operation of every major aspect of pollution markets. We focus heavily on cap-and-trade systems because they account for so much of the real-world effort to use market forces to cut carbon, but many of our insights apply to tax systems as well. We explain why idealized, "first-best" designs for pollution markets envision systems that produce high carbon prices as a powerful incentive for change. In the real world, the outcome has been the opposite: prices are low and often volatile, which undercuts the incentive to invest in ambitious new technologies and to make changes in production methods beyond those that are straightforward with few risks. First-best visions for pollution markets also imagine that markets should cover many sectors simultaneously, allow extensive interconnection with markets overseas, raise large amounts of revenue, and spend those revenues efficiently to offset distortions in the economy. On every front the real world has produced outcomes that are the opposite from theory: markets are fragmented, links are few, sectoral coverage mostly is narrow, and revenues raised are small.[13]

When policymakers do choose market-based instruments – as they have in countries or states that account for about one-fifth of global emissions[14] – those policies are designed to have little impact. The industrial enterprises whose emissions would be subject to market signals have found ways to ensure that market prices stay low through excessive allocation of emission credits, liberal emission credit banking schemes, and generous but environmentally dubious carbon offset programs. The full extent of this disaster has not been apparent because all of these cap-and-trade systems have been implemented on top of other regulatory policies that, compared with market policies, have a more potent impact on cutting emissions. Cap-and-trade systems, in effect, trade the residual emission reductions left over after more potent regulatory instruments have done their work.

The outcome resembles the Potemkin villages in imperial Russia that were supposedly constructed to give Catherine the Great the impression of economic renewal when in fact, behind the façade, very little was going on. Potemkin markets create the impression that costs are low and markets are performing well, even as most of the real work of emission control is done through regulatory instruments.[15]

Second, we offer a playbook for how to reform market-based policy systems to make them more effective. Some reforms are needed to make market signals more reliable – an outcome that requires shifting away from cap-and-trade systems, where market structures create volatile prices, and toward systems where prices are managed within narrow bands. In effect, cap-and-trade systems can be made more effective when they are designed to behave more like taxes; it is no accident that the few jurisdictions with the highest prices and the greatest level of effort use taxes, not cap-and-trade. More stable prices will make it easier for firms to invest in anticipation of market signals and to build political coalitions that are supportive of that investment. Systems that are designed like taxes also perform better in the real world where market policies are implemented alongside other regulatory programs. In that setting, cap-and-trade schemes merely trade the residual and get little work done in cutting emissions – they are Potemkin markets. Tax approaches, by contrast, create a clear incentive for change (the specified tax level), which persists even as other policy instruments have big impacts on behavior as well.[16]

Our playbook for market reform offers some insights into why so many of the visions for market-oriented climate policy won't happen under real-world political conditions. For example, many advocates for market-based policies imagine that the adoption of market schemes will occur alongside massive policy reforms that roll back regulation. We explain why, politically and administratively, those regulatory and industrial policies are not easily rolled back. Moreover, we explain why pushing for that outcome would be a bad idea – since those other regulatory policies, in fact, are doing most of the serious work in cutting emissions.

One of the most important contributions of markets is among the least appreciated today: well-designed market schemes can raise revenue. A politically savvy strategy for market reforms requires paying closer attention to how program revenues are spent – and specifically to allocating funds to activities that will build experience with new technologies and thus also catalyze new interest groups that are supportive of accelerating deep decarbonization.[17]

Careful reforms can make markets more effective, but even more important is recognizing that in nearly all societies markets will play only a small role in overall decarbonization efforts – especially in the early stages of developing and deploying new technologies. We call this "rightsizing" markets.

Third, having diagnosed what has gone wrong with markets and offered a vision for reform, we look at what else is needed. The key is to channel resources into the sectors that are critical for deep decarbonization. Rather than link all sectors together into a common market system, each must be treated independently because each has its own political economy and state of technology. In sectors where technologies are immature, industrial policy should focus on research, development, and demonstration (RD&D) in a diverse array of options – an approach that yields knowledge and also builds political coalitions around new low-carbon industries.

Foreign policy plays a key role because early investments in low-carbon technologies – such as low-carbon steel or plastics, and electric power from renewables – need reliable sources of demand for the products they support. International coordination can enlarge the pool of consumers for these new technologies, creating more experience and learning, better performance, and politically stronger interest groups. Industrial policy and foreign policy must go hand-in-hand because the logic of deep decarbonization is ultimately a global logic. Emissions are diffused throughout the world and thus the level of climate change experienced anywhere is the result ultimately of efforts everywhere. We expect that the readers of this book – people looking for better climate policies – are mainly in the places of the world that are already doing a lot to lead on climate policy. These jurisdictions can work together in small like-minded groups ("climate clubs") that can transform industries sector-by-sector toward low emissions. But the leaders must not forget that today they account for a small and shrinking fraction of the global total of emissions. Their leadership must be designed to generate followership.

The need for followership is why a political eye to climate policy design is so important. Followers, who are much warier about the disruptions of climate policy, can be coaxed along by leaders who invest in new low-carbon industries, develop programs that scale applications and drive down costs, and provide credible new information about the real-world performance of low-carbon technologies. All else being equal, climate followers – places like the emerging economies, or the middle of the United States – are less committed to action on global warming and thus even more sensitive to getting the politics wrong. These political challenges will only grow as the world gets serious about cutting emissions. Public interest groups and the voters they mobilize will expect governments to adopt costlier and more decisive policies that have bigger effects on economic competitiveness. Policy elites who press for and design climate policies will advocate the same. The outcome of these political processes will generate greater risks for firms and workers. Green leaders from strong economies may be able to paper over these – for example, by implementing generous social welfare programs – but followers will be more skittish. Realigning the politics is essential to success that is ultimately needed at a global scale; doubling down on market-based strategies that magnify the political challenges and strategic risks to industrial transformation will only slow international progress.

Throughout this book, we argue that troubles with creating effective market-based strategies for cutting carbon do not reflect policymakers' failure to understand how markets work. What's missing in climate policy discussions isn't more understanding about market design that can be advanced with more data, better PowerPoint presentations, blue-ribbon commissions, and the like. Political leaders were not sleeping through economics 101 when the subjects of externalities and market incentives for internalizing external costs were taught. They were wide awake, know what they heard, and are explicitly choosing alternative policies – or, when they do adopt market-based policies, implementation strategies that keep these systems from functioning as theory envisions. Doing better requires recognizing the structural limits to what is achievable with market-based approaches – limits that are rooted in how the politics and technological opportunities are organized in each sector.

A theory of politics

Our study is not the first to look at the politics of using markets to address warming pollution. Some scholars have been documenting the many ways that carbon pricing – both through cap-and-trade schemes and through emission taxes – are falling short.[18] Even more than scholars, journalists have long been exposing an array of flaws in how carbon markets function in the real world.[19] Mindful of this evidence, some scholars and advocates have suggested that it will be politically easier to achieve deep decarbonization if climate policy is linked to other policy objectives such as employment or reduction of inequality, perhaps under the umbrella of a "Green New Deal."[20] Indeed, a European Green Deal is gaining traction and, at this writing, may be poised to become the defining climate change strategy for that region.[21] Still others who are more firmly inclined to advocate for market-based strategies have begun to explore why, in the real world of politics, those strategies often produce designs that are far from optimal.[22] All these studies rely on theories of politics to explain what they observe in the real world; often, however, those theories are highly divergent in the factors they think matter.

What's new in this book is not attention to politics. Rather, it is our effort to organize "politics" into a simple set of key variables and to show how those variables facilitate a comprehensive set of insights about the limits to market-based strategies. That same theory provides a grounded basis for market reforms and the need to pursue other policy strategies for deep decarbonization. It is easy to say, "the problem with markets is the politics," but that answer does not offer much insight into exactly how politics shapes reality. Nor does it offer much guidance for how policy reforms could rewire the politics.

Our simple model of politics relies on two major clusters of political variables (see Table 1.1). The real world is complex, of course, but these two factors offer the best way to start organizing that complexity into a coherent set of patterns.

The first and most important cluster is the organization of interest groups. Our model of politics has five interest groups, although throughout this book we will show that only two or three have a regular impact on the design and implementation of market-based policies:

- **Voters and the broader public.** The public matters because it is the ultimate source of authority in democratic countries. However, the mass public is

Table 1.1   Key political variables

Interest groups	Institutions
Voters and the broader public	Adoption rules
	What kind of vote or action
	is required to make the policy
Emitting industries	*become legally binding?*
Low-carbon industries	Administrative capacity
	How effectively can policy-
Civil society	*makers accommodate powerful*
	interests?
Political leaders	*How competent are*
	government agencies?

highly diffuse and not automatically well organized in political terms. Much of what happens in politics is not visible to them; public attitudes point in many directions. In the United States, public concerns about climate change appear to be rising as visible evidence of the problem grows,[23] but only a small segment of the public links climate concerns to behaviors such as voting and donating time and money to political candidates and parties.[24] Thus we focus on one central aspect of the broader public: do they notice the cost of climate policy?[25] While the benefits of climate action are abstract and diffused, some costs are apparent.[26] This disdain for visible policy costs – even as voters demand cuts in pollution – is exemplified by perennial complaints about gasoline taxes in the United States (where they are among the lowest in the world) and the yellow vests protests in France (where an ambitious carbon tax has drawn opposition from the *gilets jaunes*).[27]

• **Emitting industries.** These firms are highly organized because they already engage in activities that are the subject of policy intervention: for example, the production and combustion of fossil fuels, which has a myriad of impacts on land use, local air pollution, and the like. While these firms may be numerous, compared with voters they are very small in number and relatively easy to organize politically. Big firms, in particular, have a disproportionately large stake in policy outcomes and therefore have strong self-interest in organizing whole industries.[28] While these firms and their industry associations are highly informed about policy, whether policy proposals actually affect their interests depends on industrial structure. Some industries have high "trade sensitivity" – meaning that the cost of their factors of production, such as energy, has a big impact on the cost of their final goods and services, and those goods and services must compete in global markets where there are other jurisdictions whose firms may not bear such costs.[29] Firms and industries that are highly trade-sensitive care a lot about climate policy because differential policy treatment across global markets leads to leakage: a flow of trade, investment, and emissions away from the firms that bear higher costs due to climate policy and toward their overseas competitors. Those exposed firms are highly motivated to make sure that climate policy is impotent, or at least designed to protect them from the ill effects of competition with firms that don't bear climate policy burdens.

• **Low-carbon industries.** In principle, low-carbon interest groups are the political antidote to high-carbon incumbents. In most of our story, however, these interest groups don't figure prominently because they are small, poorly organized, and politically weak. Often, they don't exist at all – at least not yet. In our story, these industries appear mainly in sectors where the low-carbon industry has begun to take hold or incumbents can readily switch technologies – electric power, in particular. With successful decarbonization, such firms will become larger, gain access to more revenues and jobs, and become better able to influence the policies needed for deeper cuts in carbon. Indeed, in countries that have long histories of adopting the policies consistent with decarbonization – for example, the active German *Energiewende* that created a German renewable industry (until that industry was crushed by Chinese competition) – exactly this political dynamic is evident.[30] For the most part, however, powerful coalitions of low-carbon industries are a topic for the future, not today.

• **Civil society.** We distinguish civil society from voters by the degree of organization. Voters, as noted above, are not reliably organized around climate policy – and thus their voice is heard, usually, when policy affects something they notice *en masse*, such as higher energy prices. Civil society is the organized variation of public interest – reflected, on the matter of climate change, by environmental NGOs. In theory, organized groups within civil society should figure prominently in our story. They are mobilizers of latent public forces and progressive firms that want action on climate change; their mission is to provide public goods. What will be striking, however, is how rarely these groups are decisive in the design and operation of effective market-based systems. Some NGOs have pursued particularized interests: forestry-oriented NGOs channel resources to forests, NGOs of the energy persuasion push for efficiency and renewables, and environmental justice groups focus on policies to benefit historically marginalized communities. Some even contribute to the dysfunction at the core of our theory by backing ideas for market reforms that don't work politically. But NGOs that would advance broad public goods – which in our story would mean mobilizing pressure to correct the errors in design of market-based policies – are scarce. The design and operation of market-based strategies is the world of specialists and incumbent industrialists.

• **Political leaders.** Finally, our simple model of politics treats leaders as an independent political force. Their goal is obtaining and retaining political authority, which means devising policies that are politically responsive to relevant interest groups.[31] Political leaders find solutions to opposing political forces by taking advantage of the fact that voters value visible action over real action and favor hidden costs over palpable new expenses; existing industries favor protection for existing interests; and new industries, for now, favor actions that benefit new entrants in particular. Political leaders balance these competing interests by identifying places where political opposition would be debilitating and deploy methods to respond to those organized interests.

In the real world there are lots of other interest groups as well, of course. We will introduce them as they become important to our story and will argue that their importance can be understood within the context of our three main driving groups. Organized labor plays important roles that vary depending on whether unions back incumbents or bet on new entrants. Indigenous groups and communities living next to major polluters are usually the first to feel the impact of environmental problems and are prominent in efforts to resolve them – efforts that, increasingly, correlate with actions on climate change. Scientists and other intellectual entrepreneurs matter as well, although the purveyors of ideas typically gain force only when they resonate with the interests of organized groups.

While mindful of the fuller array of stakeholders whose voices matter in climate policy, we aim to convince you that most of what is observed with market-based climate policies is principally the product of a subset of organized groups' interactions. And three of these groups – voters paying close attention to visible costs; incumbent high-carbon industries; and political leaders – explain most of what we observe in politics around carbon markets, most of the time.

The second cluster of political variables is institutional. By that, we mean networks of expectations about how politically organized actors will interact. Those networks include formal legal structures, like constitutional rules, within which governments and other political actors make and implement decisions. Much of the work of these informal and formal expectations is framed in the mandates of organizations: for example, regulatory bodies and their missions. Institutions are important because politics is not merely a free-for-all where the best-organized group that has the most resources determines outcomes. Instead, institutional rules and arrangements mediate between organized political interests and actual political and policy outcomes.[32] The importance of these rules is seen all the time. For example, one of the last major controversies under the 2015 Paris Agreement concerns how to implement a provision called Article 6 – a much-debated text seen by many as the rules that will govern which international emission credits and international trading systems will be seen as allowable under the Agreement.[33] Resolution on Article 6 has been elusive because organized interest groups disagree massively, yet the formal organizational rules for making decisions require diplomatic consensus.

There is an extensive academic literature on the importance of institutions. We focus on two main institutional factors:

• **Adoption rules.** The creation of a market-based policy involves the creation of novel structures, which frequently requires legislative action. Some legislative measures can be enacted by simple majorities; sometimes market-based policies can be shoe-horned into existing legislative authority. By contrast, tax instruments – including pollution taxes – are typically treated as fiscal or budgetary items that, in many political systems, require special qualified or supermajority votes. In the early 1990s, Europe's attempt to pass a carbon tax failed because it could not attract near-universal support among its member states. After that failure, it shifted to a cap-and-trade scheme – the policy that persists today – partly because political leaders could treat cap-and-trade as an environmental measure, which does not require the near-unanimous support of all European member states.

• **Administrative capacity.** When organized interests mobilize for state action, they must look not only at the rules for adopting the action, but also at the skills of the state in putting that action into practice. Most modern states are highly skilled at implementing regulatory and other measures that determine – typically jointly with industry – which technologies to adopt and how to allocate costs. By contrast, managing a pollution market is often just as complex but requires very different skills from those in the environmental agencies that are typically tasked with administering climate policy – expertise that is more akin to financial regulation. This observation helps explain two phenomena that will loom large in this book. One is that environmental markets are often poorly administered, at least initially, but can improve with robust support and adequate legal authority. The other is that governments vary in their ability to respond to politically organized groups that require special treatment for their sector.

Institutions help explain why early choices have lock-in effects. Initial policy choices constrain what is possible in the future because major policies are hard to unwind once in place.[34] Poorly crafted beginnings can thus impede reform, which is why much more care is needed in the early stages of policy design than pragmatic incrementalism would normally prescribe. Institutions also explain why a variety of exogenous shocks can be particularly helpful in policy reforms: for example, electoral shocks that cause a major member to exit a trading system, or salient information about how a trading system has undermined the goals of a critical interest group. Shocks help reopen old decisions and realign interest groups and choices related to policy design – windows of opportunity that, if reformers are armed with the right tools, can become opportunities for change. Outside those windows, however, it is very difficult to effect change.

In the real world, a full-blown theory of institutional behavior would have many other complex elements. It would include the role of ideas, for example – for just as new ideas and information about climate impacts or about climate policy design can affect politics, they can also affect institutional design and the default policies that policy elites think work best. A complete analysis would include close attention to where and how social movements can form so that political support for policy is much deeper than just elites and parties.[35] A full-blown theory would also reflect the fact that constitutional and other constraints on decision-making vary across countries because electoral rules and other institutional factors that affect collective choice vary.[36] As these examples illustrate, systematic theorizing and empirical testing are still needed to fill in the details beyond the broad contours we outline here.

In the chapters to follow, we will apply this simple model of politics to every major aspect of climate policy design. It will help us understand why the roles for markets are smaller than expected decades ago and why direct regulation will be bigger (and less costly) than expected.

The evidence

To illustrate our story, we will draw from examples of pollution markets anywhere and everywhere that policy-makers and firms have created to address climate change.

We focus in particular on the experience in three carbon markets: the European Union's Emissions Trading System (EU ETS), the Western Climate Initiative (WCI) linking California and Québec, and the northeastern United States' Regional Greenhouse Gas Initiative (RGGI). These three programs have the longest and most relevant track records and are, by far, the best documented. What we argue here will be highly controversial, but an advantage of relying on well-documented and established policy programs is that the evidence is available to everyone. Our simple theory of politics can't explain everything that is observed across these three touchstone cases, but it will explain more of what has been observed in the real world and more systematically than other efforts to explain these policy systems to date.

Looking across these three systems, we see three radically different visions of how markets can work when viewed through the lens of political realities rather than theoretical ideals.

RGGI's vision is the most realistic and generally applicable precisely because it is the most pragmatic about what is able to be achieved. The program encompasses states with varied political interests around climate change, ranging from the highly ambitious to the cautiously engaged. It covers only the electricity sector – where the technologies for cutting emissions are most mature – with transparent and predictable program rules. Even in the power sector, however, RGGI is not the only or even main show in decarbonizing its participating states' electric grids. Other policy programs are having a bigger impact, including state renewable portfolio standards; subsidies that keep nuclear power plants, which are prodigious suppliers of zero-carbon power, from shutting down; and other government-managed regulatory and procurement efforts all aimed at making the RGGI states' power infrastructure less carbon-intensive. In many respects, the RGGI system represents the high-water mark for what subnational markets can do: RGGI supports the broader goal of deep decarbonization, generates discretionary revenue streams for participating governments, and increases the static economic efficiency of a policy portfolio – all in a single sector. Its benefits are clear and relatively modest. Among purists, RGGI is often mocked because its prices are low (about $5–6 per metric ton of CO_2 emissions in 2019) and coverage is limited to just one sector. We see the experience through a completely different lens: RGGI works because its architects knew what they were doing and designed a system that is politically feasible and durable. The EU ETS represents an effort at the opposite extreme: a hope for a more ambitious, yet still limited, role for markets. Part of the reason for optimism is that the EU ETS is built on a powerful EU institutional foundation. The European Union has reliably been the main leader in the global fight to slow climate change and has been willing to invest in the administrative systems needed to make a market work within the limits of what markets can do. Its efforts to create a cap-and-trade system began in the context of failure to pass a carbon tax in the early 1990s and the need, later in the decade, to implement the 1997 Kyoto Protocol – a treaty that put caps on emissions for all industrialized countries. (The United States never joined and never capped.[37]) Even so, creating the EU ETS was not easy – the system originated in a series of political compromises that left it impotent for a long period. Gaining initial political support required allocating an excessive number of pollution permits to politically well-organized industries that sent the spot market's carbon price to zero in the program's pilot phase (2005–7). Although prices recovered briefly in the market's second period (2008–12), they cratered and remained too low to make much of a difference for many years thereafter.[38]

A series of reforms beginning in the mid-2010s have pushed European carbon prices to the level where they could plausibly make a significant difference in the two main sectors covered by the program: electricity and industrial emitters. Strong European institutions, which were the key to those reforms, make it possible to do in Europe what has not been observed in any other pollution market so far. First, European climate policymakers became, in effect, central bankers: their reforms automatically adjust the supply of permits to create some scarcity, but not too much. These reforms, by raising prices in predictable ways, have increased the program's climate benefits and also partly model what we will recommend in this book: the transformation of trading systems into price-like systems that better resemble taxes in their function and therefore provide greater predictability and political stability. (Legally, the EU ETS likely needs to remain an environmental trading program and thus can't become too tax-like, lest it require unanimity among EU member states.) A central ongoing challenge in Europe has been that the EU itself has few mechanisms that allow it to be responsive to the political needs of each sector included in the ETS and is, understandably, particularly fearful of imposing costs on export-oriented industrial firms. The only real mechanism available has been awarding those firms free allocations to blunt the practical effect of the ETS (and help them remain competitive). Now that ETS prices are rising and free allocations are becoming constrained, the EU must find other mechanisms – such as border carbon adjustments or other trade measures.

The least successful of these three examples is the WCI. It pretends to be an EU-ETS-like market, but its architects have not grappled with the reality that none of the institutional conditions that exist in the EU ETS are present within the WCI. The WCI's anchor jurisdiction, California, is widely celebrated as a climate policy leader. Historically, the state relied on regulations to drive reductions in warming emissions (and many local air pollutants), but recently reversed strategic course: California's official climate policy now relies on its cap-and-trade program to deliver nearly half of the reductions needed to achieve its ambitious and legally binding emissions limit for 2030.[39] Unlike RGGI (which covers only the electricity sector) and the EU ETS (which covers both electricity and industry), California includes electricity, industrial emitters, and transportation fuels under its program cap. This expansion in coverage is based on the beautiful economic logic of covering all sectors and letting the market do the work, but has been plagued by the political liabilities created when voters notice the cost of a policy program without seeing tangible benefits – particularly when it comes to impacts on transportation fuel prices. That visibility has unleashed demands for special treatment and excess allocations, to which policymakers have responded. California is now stuck with an emissions trading system that is supposed to be central to the state's deep decarbonization plans, yet program administrators have not altered any of the market design features that explain why the market is faltering. By linking multiple sectors together under a single program, California exemplifies the problem our theory predicts will plague broad-based carbon markets: all the sectors, together, must follow the politics of the least ambitious sector. Fixing the problem would require separating the sectors – a politically herculean task because that would involve unraveling the WCI market. The best approach is to double down on industrial policy, and that need will grow as California aims for even greater ambition.

While we rely heavily on those three core markets, we draw on other experiences around the world. They include the active market in South Korea – one that has proved hard to study because so many of its key elements are opaque.[40] In New Zealand a carbon trading system has emerged that is, basically, a system for crediting reductions achieved outside of the energy system, and, in particular, in the country's prominent forestry sector.[41] China has run pilot emission trading in eight provinces and is now rolling out a scheme for the whole country, beginning in the power sector – although the rollout has been slow and it is hard to see how a Chinese pollution market will interact with more powerful state planning tools.[42]

While we focus on cap-and-trade because these policies account for the majority of the experience with market-based climate policies, many of our arguments apply to carbon tax systems as well – such as those in France, Sweden, and Norway. The experiences with these systems are relevant for our core focus, too, because tax-oriented reforms can play a big role in making markets more effective.

As is customary in studies of market-based strategies, we show the prices that have emerged from these six cap-and-trade systems over time in Figure 1.3: the three core markets that we rely on most heavily, plus three newer ones (South Korea, New Zealand, and the Shanghai pilot scheme as an example of China's approach). These prices are frequently offered as evidence that markets are working, with variation in prices implying that there are big gains from trade to be had from linking markets and helping firms find the most efficient places to concentrate their effort. Throughout this

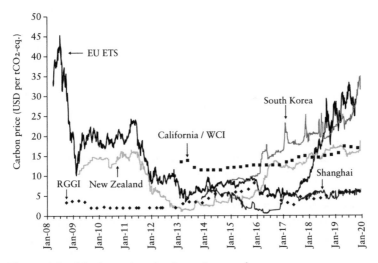

Figure 1.3 Market prices in six major markets
Source: Redrawn from data accessed via the International Carbon Action Partnership (ICAP), *https://icapcarbonaction.com/en/ets-prices*. Data for the WCI and RGGI programs are quarterly because there are no public secondary market prices available.

book, however, we will show that most of what all of us thought was right about markets is misleading. Prices do not reveal real effort; the evidence that these schemes are working is thin; and the gains from trade that seem to scream from the variation in prices are illusory.

A roadmap

Our analysis proceeds over eight more chapters.

Chapters 2 through 6 are the core of the book. Over these chapters we look at the five major attributes of market-based policies and explain why, in every case, real-world outcomes have been different from theory.

In chapter 2 we look at ambition. The theory of markets suggests that because market policies are more efficient economically they will be the catalysts of ambition. Chapter 2 shows why, instead, no political jurisdiction has relied on markets for its most ambitious policies. The logic of Potemkin markets reigns.

Chapter 3 explains how the sectoral coverage of market policies varies and why that matters. Originally, the case for market-based policies – cap-and-trade in particular – was oriented around the ability to create markets with economy-wide coverage of all major emitting sectors that could eventually link together all major emitting economies around the world. That approach would ensure that all emissions are exposed to similar incentives for reductions. Chapter 3 explains why, in practice, every sector covered by a cap-and-trade program is treated differently – including in how policymakers allocate emission credits. Heterogeneity in sectoral treatment is a critical factor that helps explain why neither global nor serious international markets have emerged.

Chapter 4 is about money. Market-based policies generate revenues, and they have the potential to generate a lot more. While the potential for generating revenue is huge, the politics of creating markets has led, at least initially, to much more modest outcomes. Actual revenues are dramatically smaller than theoretical potentials, and tax systems have proven much more effective at raising funds under real-world political conditions when compared with cap-and-trade. Chapter 4 explains that outcome – why the money, so far, has been small – along with how the money gets spent. Well-organized environmental groups and a few clean energy industries have advocated channeling funds to favored purposes. That's why so many market-based systems use a "green spending" model: revenues are appropriated to projects that claim to achieve additional emission reductions as well as important political and economic benefits. Green spending is a good idea – it can, in principle, become the backbone of a green industrial policy – but in practice much of the money ends up spent as "green pork." Concentrated interest groups, and political actors who control the institutions that allocate funds, direct these funds to pet purposes without much oversight. Chapter 4 explains the politics of why this outcome – a bad one for the planet – has emerged and persisted. (Improving the cost-effectiveness of political and environmental spending requires new institutional rules, which we discuss later, in chapter 7.)

Chapters 5 and 6 are about how markets interact with the outside world via offsets and direct market linkages. Offsets are credits that reflect emission reductions purportedly achieved in other jurisdictions and imported into a cap-and-trade scheme. For example, California envisions that it can protect North American forests by crediting actions that purport to change the harvesting practices large landowners employ. The climate benefits of such actions, once calculated, become usable tender in California's cap-and-trade system. Chapter 5 shows why there are powerful constituencies that want to create as many offsets as possible; it also shows why the experience with offsets is nearly uniformly negative. The powerful coalition that favors generous offsets policies, in effect, seeks the right to print money – legal tender that can dampen the cost of compliance with cap-and-trade obligations. The political interests that favor generous offsets is easy to understand; what is harder and more disturbing is why there is no constituency for quality. In the real world almost every activity that might, in theory, be worthy of earning an offset is nearly impossible to monitor remotely in ways that can guarantee that the offset credits rewarded reflect real changes in behavior. We also show how the geographic reach of offsets tends to shrink over time – local interests, which are better organized and more powerful politically in a home market, outweigh the aspiration (and all the theory) that says offsets should be allowed globally. The outcome is an offsets regime that is focused locally, even when local costs are higher. Finally, our darkest observation is that offsets create perverse incentives for firms to oppose the expansion of legally binding climate policy – and thus rather than offer a path to policy proliferation, offsets end up supporting incumbent firms' entrenchment.

Chapter 6 explains what is probably the biggest real-world disappointment for market-based policies. The chief economic value in creating market approaches to controlling pollution involves merging "unlike" markets: that is, connecting markets where there is a high willingness to pay for emission control (generally in the rich Western democracies) to those where there are many low-cost opportunities for cutting emissions (generally in the emerging economies). By maximizing the gains from trade, the economic value of market-based approaches would be maximized through linkage. The problem is that markets that are unlike in their politics and emission control opportunities are also unlike in terms of the sector-specific accommodations policymakers provide to key domestic stakeholders. Links between unlike markets threaten to destabilize those arrangements. Because links between similar markets don't threaten those outcomes, they are more feasible – but they also produce few gains and therefore create few consequences when they come undone. This is why links forged even between highly similar markets – for example, between New Jersey and its neighboring states, or between Ontario and California – can be undone easily when parties divorce. Because their gains are limited, so too are economic consequences when links fall apart. Deeper and more economically salient links are possible only when administrative systems are strong and shared between cooperating jurisdictions – a condition observed to date only in the European Union.

Chapters 7 and 8 are about solutions.

Chapter 7 focuses on how to reform markets. Our main message is that efforts to make markets more effective must begin by understanding the limitations of market-based strategies. Rather than seeking markets that have high prices that drive big changes in behavior, in nearly all political jurisdictions markets will lack much ambition. Prices will be low. Rather than trying to create globally linked market systems that cover all sectors, progress will come from doing the opposite: narrowing the scope of market policies and focusing them on sectors and places where administrative and political systems allow effective outcomes. Offsets and nearly all forms of cross-border linkages are not only bound to fail but actually impede the environmental goal of deep decarbonization because they flood the market with credits that do not reflect genuine reductions.

Market policies must be redesigned so that they aren't irrelevant Potemkin markets but, instead, have impacts on behavior even as regulatory and other industrial policy instruments actually do most of the heavy lifting. That redesign involves stripping away excess allocations of emission credits – allocations that were needed politically to create market instruments in the first place. (This process of stripping away what many firms see as assets is politically fraught, but the experience in Europe shows how it can be done when administrators are given the skills and legal authority.) Reform requires eliminating problematic offsets and accommodating the interests they once served via less damaging means. It also requires policies such as administrative price collars that shift cap-and-trade systems away from high-volatility credit schemes and toward systems that have more reliable price trajectories: that is, to make them look and operate more like carbon taxes. Reforms won't be easy, but we outline a strategy that is politically coherent. It is also a limited vision. Successful reforms will enable market policies to play supporting roles in deep decarbonization, not the lead.

Chapter 8 is about how, with rightsized markets, governments can make a big dent in the carbon problem. Because our assessment of market policies is so damning, and our reform strategy involves sharply constraining where and how markets are used, a book that radically narrows the proper role for markets must also offer a vision for other approaches that would be more effective. Thus, in chapter 8, we tour the academic literature along with the real-world policy experience to show that, in fact, many governments are already using highly effective policy instruments. These include smart, adaptive regulations designed to experiment in places where key facts are unknown and to learn from that experience. They also include direct government support for fledgling technologies – branded, negatively, in the United States as industrial policy, but actually highly effective in places where market forces on their own can't generate needed outcomes, such as investment in new deep decarbonization technologies. Smart strategy includes, as well, dealing with what is the central political challenge for first movers and deep cuts in emissions: the impact on competition in a global economy. This problem, we show in chapter 8, can be solved by governments working directly with other governments to create more level playing fields. The tools they have available are numerous – including coordination of investment and procurement policies, as well as border tariff adjustments. Grappling with these realities requires new thinking about trade policy, which, for decades, has been focused on lowering barriers to trade as a means of creating bigger markets and more prosperity. In a world that gets serious about climate change, a different strategy will be needed – one that can threaten and raise barriers to penalize laggards so that leadership on deep decarbonization leads to global decarbonization and not just dead ends.

Finally, chapter 9 concludes with a brief review of our overall argument. It also points to some important unknowns – areas that we did not explore in this book that are useful places for additional research and policy experimentation.

2
Ambition

In theory, the flexibility and economic efficiency of carbon markets should make them ideal for maximizing the effort to control carbon pollution. Markets can be ratcheted tighter as society's willingness to address the climate problem grows more acute, and the fact that market policies put less of a drag on the economy means that more resources can be devoted to cutting carbon. This chapter explains why carbon markets fall short of those promises.

Carbon markets are never allowed to work according to textbook theory – instead, they always operate as subsidiary to far more ambitious regulatory programs. Even where political leaders are pursuing cap-and-trade or carbon tax policies, regulations, not market policies, continue to dominate the overall effort to control emissions. Rather than lead the charge on climate policy, markets end up weak in practice and feature low prices that fail to reflect what society is willing to spend on reducing emissions.

Political and institutional forces explain these outcomes. The primary reason is deeply rooted in the politics of controlling emissions. Carbon pricing policies require policy-makers to impose visible and politically costly price increases on consumer-facing products such as electricity, gasoline, and diesel fuels. In contrast, regulatory policies like energy efficiency standards or renewable energy mandates are stealthier in their impacts. Consumers, who in democracies are also voters, rarely know much about what they cost – even when those costs are significant. Firms in highly organized industries are much more aware of the costs imposed by regulation, but those firms often favor regulation over simple market-based strategies because it confers many benefits: regulation can create barriers to entry (making it harder for new firms to compete, to the benefit of incumbents) and stabilize expectations (reducing the risk of long-term investments). As a result, policymakers generally face lower resistance when pursuing pollution reductions through relatively opaque and more predictable regulatory measures.

The interaction between markets and regulations only exacerbates this dynamic. Because regulations dominate initial climate policy portfolios, cap-and-trade schemes end up trading only a residual share of emission reductions. Rather than determine effort, they clean up whatever is left over after regulations do their work. When a regulation requires a firm that is also subject to a cap-and-trade program to reduce its emissions – even at a relatively high cost – those emission reductions also act to reduce demand for allowances in the cap-and-trade program.[1] Two effects follow. First, the market price ends up significantly lower than the marginal cost of controlling emissions, an outcome that enables policymakers and environmental groups to promote the appearance of low costs. Second, over time the market price also becomes subject to greater volatility as program ambition deepens. Because uncertainty over macroeconomic trends and technological change is large and markets are thin, the range of possible market-clearing prices widens[2] – increasing the odds that, if the going gets tough, carbon prices could rise to politically unacceptable levels. These risks further reduce policymakers' interest in relying on carbon markets to control emissions, even as political pressure mounts for greater climate policy ambition.

In addition to these core political forces, the institutions through which policies are designed and implemented are tilted against making full use of market-based strategies. Market policies often require high institutional barriers to political choice. For example, legislators in California needed to secure a two-thirds supermajority vote to extend the state's cap-and-trade program through 2030;[3] a similar state constitutional requirement in Oregon proved too difficult a political barrier for a 2019 cap-and-trade bill to surmount. In Europe, part of the reason the region's cap-and-trade system was adopted is because it was branded an environmental measure – and thus could be adopted by a qualified majority – whereas fiscal measures like carbon taxes require unanimity. Meanwhile, regulatory programs are often much easier to adopt. Existing statutes give policymakers some authorities they can use through administrative action; other existing laws, in many settings, can be expanded from their original purposes (such as addressing local air pollution) to address some warming emissions. New laws to enable new regulations generally require only simple majority votes to enact. Thus, even when market-based policies are adopted, they are layered on top of popular regulations that were developed first, remain anchored in place, and are more readily supplemented with new regulations. Many clever analysts imagine the potential for grand bargains – where comprehensive market-based strategies replace all conflicting and distorting regulations – yet these kinds of deals are not observed in the real world of climate policy and will be resisted mightily by interest groups that know that such regulations actually get most of the work done.

Together, political and institutional forces combine to produce markets that are thin and feature mostly low carbon prices that mask a society's real ambition to cut emissions – what we call Potemkin markets. Potemkin markets work on the surface of the economy even as other forces – notably regulation and industrial policy – are much more important to the realities of emission patterns and investment in new technologies that lay the foundation for deeper emission cuts in the future. They also create the impression that policy costs are low and markets are performing well, even as most of the real work of emission control is done through regulatory instruments that impose higher costs and deliver greater benefits.

Understanding why cap-and-trade programs tend to become Potemkin markets is an essential first step from which the rest of our analysis follows. This chapter takes that step by explaining why politicians prefer regulation despite all the good theoretical arguments that markets are better policy, why institutional barriers make it even harder to adopt markets, and thus why these political and institutional forces produce Potemkin markets. Our argument is not that market instruments are an inherently rare species; rather, it is that structural incentives produce Potemkin-market outcomes that largely fail, on their own, to have much impact on emissions.

Why politicians prefer regulation

Textbook academic theory offers a straightforward economic prescription for climate change. Climate change is a global market failure caused by greenhouse gas emissions. People and firms pollute excessively because pollution is costless – these harms are "externalized" on others, including future generations, who face the bulk of climate impacts. If policy could instead "internalize" these costs by making polluters (and those who buy their products) pay for their emissions, pollution would fall and intergenerational well-being would improve.[4]

There are two ways to internalize climate externalities. One is to control the quantity of pollution and let the market figure out a price – a policy called cap-and-trade or emissions trading, which creates a carbon market. The other is to control the price of pollution and let the market figure out the quantity – a carbon tax.

A cap-and-trade program puts a price on carbon by creating the limited, tradeable right to pollute. In theory a cap-and-trade program could stand alone, doing all of the work necessary to achieve a jurisdiction's climate goals. Prices would emerge from the market to reflect society's choices about the severity of the problem (as defined through the level of the cap), in tandem with the cost of technologies and behavioral changes required to reduce pollution. This market-oriented approach would provide a number of benefits. Unlike direct regulation, which could be relatively more expensive because government administrators may not have the knowledge or incentive to order the least costly choices, a carbon market would create the private incentive to find and select the cheapest emission reductions. In contrast to a cap-and-trade program, carbon taxes set the price polluters must pay and let the market sort out the consequences. Although taxes provide perfect clarity on price impacts, pollution outcomes under taxes can't be known in advance, only estimated. Many policymakers and environmental NGOs seize on these differences and purport to prefer cap-and-trade programs because these instruments set firm limits on the total pollution. Not only does that not turn out to be true – cap-and-trade systems are easily gamed, such as by issuing low-quality offsets (chapter 5) – but these preferences have as much to do with politics as substance. Because a carbon tax requires the policymaker to identify a specific price for pollution, it also paints a target on the policymaker's back: anti-tax opponents can easily finger exactly how much the policy would raise everyday people's utility or gasoline bills. Since the polling data suggest that the public are wary about policies that have visible costs even when they want the more abstract benefits – they want both "cheap and clean," as the title of one of the best books on public opinion polling around energy topics proclaims[5] – this attribute of direct taxation is a huge political liability. (It has proven even more difficult to enact carbon taxes than carbon markets in all but a few jurisdictions, likely owing to the perception that emissions trading is more of an environmentally beneficial program than a politically toxic tax. To the extent those perceptions make it easier to enact a market instead of a tax, however, they raise similar political challenges on implementation. A stringent market leads to high carbon prices, just like a meaningful carbon tax.)

The theory of market-based climate policies promises low overall economic costs for society as a whole. But what matters to the political leaders who design policies – especially leaders who are attentive to the perspective of voters – is whether the costs are visible. They care about political viability first, and economic optimality later (if ever). If a benevolent philosopher-king would pursue first-best economic policies, the self-interested politician first considers political risks and opportunities. Regulatory policies that might impose higher overall economic costs on the economy usually present lower visible costs than would be the case under a carbon pricing policy. That pattern is a feature, not a bug, to politicians who are wary of over-stepping on climate policy. Only a few jurisdictions, such as many of the Nordic countries, enjoy overwhelming political support for ambitious climate policy and thus can tolerate the high visible costs it can entail. (Even there, the costs are less visible because regulation gets used for the most expensive policies.) For others, the fundamental political incentive to avoid visible cost impacts tilts the playing field against carbon pricing policies and toward regulatory instruments. Those disparities are further reinforced by positive feedbacks in the political economy of regulation. When executed well, regulations provide larger and more reliable benefits to clean energy industries and their supporters – even in polities that enact high visible prices from market-based instruments.

So if visibility of costs drives the political economy of instrument choice, what counts as a visible price impact? The answer depends on who is affected, the level of consumer awareness, and whether or not there is a tangible alternative against which to compare price impacts. In sectors such as transportation fuels, the costs of policies are highly visible to consumers; in highly regulated industries such as electric power, by contrast, consumers often don't know what they pay for goods and services that cause emissions. While consumer awareness varies considerably, large commercial or industrial customers almost always know how policies are likely to affect their costs and are already well organized politically – factors make them better positioned to advocate for their self-interest as a result. Variation in awareness of cost impacts affects the feasible choice of policy instruments in different sectors.

Many of the most ambitious climate regulations apply to the electricity industry. Consider a utility mandate to procure a certain amount or share of renewable energy. If the cost of renewable energy is more expensive than conventional fossil fuels (ignoring pollution and other important but opaque social impacts), then the price of electricity might rise as a result of the regulatory mandate. But very few residential customers are aware of the price they pay for each kilowatt-hour of electricity. They might not be indifferent to costs – if they knew – but most are neither interested in nor informed about what determines utility bills. Indeed, by design, utility bills do not provide information about the counterfactual costs of relying on a more polluting resource mix, so only truly engaged consumers who wish to calculate these matters for themselves will make much headway in understanding how much they are paying to reduce climate pollution. In contrast to residential customers, many industrial or large commercial customers pay close attention to utility rate regulation, are sensitive to price increases, and organize politically to oppose costly action. Regulators know this and can differentiate costs by sector in the design of utility rates, shifting costs around to reflect both economic and political pressures. Regulated utility models therefore allow policymakers capacity to accommodate price impacts across interest groups and customer segments, potentially reducing overall political opposition.

The transportation sector provides additional examples of how the visibility of price impacts shapes policy outcomes. Consider climate pollution standards for cars and trucks. Many governments have standards that require automakers to achieve certain fleet-wide pollution metrics in each sales year. These standards have the effect of raising costs for vehicles. If utility bills make a big difference in many people's lives because they can eat up a significant share of low-income households' expenditures, buying cars and trucks is a major decision for practically all but the very wealthiest households. One would therefore expect that consumers are highly attuned to price impacts from pollution standards in this sector. As with the electricity example, however, there simply is no obvious counterfactual price against which to compare real-world policy costs. Professional economists can readily calculate (and then debate) these cost impacts, but consumers generally cannot. Further complicating matters is that higher upfront costs are frequently offset by lower operating costs owing to higher fuel efficiency or reliance on alternative fuels like electricity.

Many consumers might not notice the effect of fuel economy standards, but the vast majority are highly attuned to the price of gasoline and diesel fuels they regularly pump into their vehicles. Gas stations advertise the price down to the decimal point, competing for business and anchoring drivers on a daily basis to the prices of these fuels. For many living on limited budgets, the weekly expense of driving to work or shuttling kids to school is a regular reminder of both the marginal price and total operating costs of the family vehicle. As a result, policies that directly increase the price of gasoline can be easily translated by policy opponents into simple terms that most people monitor and care about. (Europe has levied significantly higher taxes on transportation fuels since the 1970s, resulting in total consumer fuel costs that are approximately double the level in the United States. It would be tempting to suggest that European consumers are therefore immune to concerns about transportation fuel price increases that dominate US policy discussions. We see those facts differently: after years of taxation, there simply is no low-tax reference point against which consumers compare current fuel prices in Europe. This does not mean that consumers in Europe are indifferent to higher fuel prices, but rather that they are anchored to a different reference point and may be just as sensitive to changes against that reference point. When that reference point changes, political support for the offending policy can come unglued – as the French yellow vests movement illustrates.)

Few politicians are knowledgeable enough to discuss the marginal cost of carbon required to implement one climate policy or another, but nearly all elected officials want to know if a policy will drive up gasoline prices. Policies that create visible impacts on transportation fuels are arguably the hardest around which to organize political coalitions because they affect low-information voters most directly. An economy-wide carbon market might well reduce costs to consumers relative to an abstract suite of alternative regulatory policies, but it potentially makes every associated politician liable for the consequences of its impact on visible fuel prices. Most regulations – particularly those that target other sectors – simply don't face these real-world barriers.

Regulatory paradigms also give policymakers greater control over the incidence of costs and benefits among regulated industries. In an ideal market-based policy, private forces, not government decisions, should determine the allocation of costs and benefits according to the logic of economic competition. While that may be a virtue to market proponents, it can be a liability to politicians because most political behavior is not indifferent to the allocation of resources – politics is mainly about who wins and who loses, and thus political systems are extremely sensitive to questions of resource allocation.

By concentrating benefits on a preferred subset of actors and shifting cost away from politically well-organized groups, regulations create greater political stability and help sustain broad, supportive constituencies. Compared to the potentially disruptive forces shaping market outcomes, these dynamics prove to be more resilient to political change and therefore more self-reinforcing.

The benefits that regulations and fiscal policies create tend to amplify the political preference for low-visibility cost impacts. Because much more ambitious regulations are politically easier to achieve at first, interest groups that benefit from climate policy tend to focus their limited resources on further strengthening those efforts. The best example is the renewable electricity industry. In most jurisdictions, utilities signed renewable energy contracts because regulatory mandates required them to; these mandates, along with direct price supports like tax incentives, drove early investments in clean energy. While a carbon price could help make renewables' competitors more expensive – and thus accelerate renewables' deployment – the value of direct subsidies and renewable mandates has been far more impactful than real-world carbon prices. No wonder, then, that renewable energy companies rarely focus on carbon pricing policies even though they are one of the constituencies that would benefit from higher carbon prices.

Because regulations are relatively popular and easy to enact, they are also more credible. The US transportation sector illustrates how these political dynamics lead to greater overall support for climate progress, even when a change in leadership allows for regulatory rollbacks. During the Obama Administration, the United States and California agreed on a set of relatively ambitious climate pollution standards for new cars and trucks.[6] With a regulatory agreement codified in law, some manufacturers invested capital in supply chains designed to produce low- and zero-emission vehicles. The subsequent election of Donald Trump promised the fossil

fuel industry extraordinary opportunities to roll back regulations.[7] When presented with the option of flatlining vehicle
emissions standards, however, several major manufacturers
balked and preferred to sign on to only a modest weakening
of the existing standards – a compromise position put
forward by the California climate regulator.[8] Some firms may
have already committed significant investments in getting
part, if not all, of the way toward the ambitious Obama-era
standards; some may have decided to make big bets on a bright
future for zero-emission vehicles; and others may have been
concerned that a future Democratic administration would
impose tough requirements against recalcitrant manufacturers. By creating stable expectations to guide investment
decisions, regulation created strong ongoing incentives for
some regulated industries to cooperate – or at least negotiate
– even when the political context shifted.

A similar dynamic can be seen in the US oil and gas sector.
A modest Obama-era climate policy required oil and gas
developers to control methane emissions from fossil fuel
production.[9] Once again, the Trump Administration sought
a complete rollback of the Obama rules and received a mixed
reaction from industry. Not only did some large oil and gas
firms appreciate that a stable regulatory environment would
allow them to make long-term strategic plans, but some also
saw a competitiveness advantage in their ability to set up a
cost-effective national compliance regime – something not all
firms are necessarily well prepared to do.

As both examples illustrate, industry knows a lot about
what policies cost. But when regulations are at stake,
powerful incumbent firms are also keen to ensure stability
– and, where possible, to use regulation to cement their
competitive position. The same cannot be said for carbon
pricing programs. These policies tend to produce low and
volatile prices, not stability. When rolled back, they tend
not to return under new leadership because imposing carbon
pricing policies is politically costly and difficult – a fact that
Australian political leaders learned when, having unwound
an unpopular carbon market scheme, they were unable
to create a new one even though Australian voters had
become much more concerned about climate change. All the
key political actors involved in choosing and implementing

policy instruments have learned these lessons, which is why regulatory interventions are so much more durable and effective than markets.

Why real-world institutions constrain policy choices

Institutional decision rules increase real-world barriers to effective carbon pricing. We focus on two here. First, carbon pricing policies often face supermajority voting requirements that impede their adoption or necessitate political deals that weaken their implementation. Second, the prominence of subnational actors in climate policy is often celebrated for the fact that these actors exhibit a level of policy ambition that exceeds that of their national counterparts, but subnational governments typically lack the institutional capacity and legal authorities needed to make ambitious multilateral markets work in practice. Both institutional attributes constrain the real-world potential for carbon pricing policies.

Supermajority voting rules are an essential but largely overlooked element of the history of carbon pricing policies. Although the details vary across democratic polities, many governments operate under constitutional or other legal regimes that create specific barriers to market-based policies.

Europe famously adopted the world's largest cap-and-trade program for greenhouse gases, but it is widely understood that the choice between market-based policies – that is, between carbon markets and carbon taxes – could only have led to a market owing to the legal authority of the European order.[10] The European Union's legal powers are limited, reflecting decades of treaties and political negotiations between member states. What holds Europe together (mostly) is a compromise between the need for some central authority and much national autonomy. Under EU law, fiscal policy measures, such as EU-wide taxes, require unanimity among member states, whereas activities in a few other areas, such as environmental regulation, require only a majority vote. Environment is different because it is the one area where Europe has learned to speak, more or less, with a common voice. Thus, while a carbon tax offers price stability and creates interactions with regulatory policies that are much more straightforward than is the case with carbon markets, taxes were not a realistic option when Europe stepped up to lead on climate policy in the early 2000s.

In contrast, a carbon market could be designated an environmental measure because of its focus on setting up a program to regulate the limited right to pollute – albeit at the cost of unpredictable and potentially volatile carbon prices. Political leaders knew that setting up a market would be difficult, so when they passed the enabling legislation in 2003 they framed the effort in phases. An initial pilot phase (2005–7) would establish the market. A second phase (2008–12) would align with the Kyoto Protocol. Phases 3 (2013–20) and 4 (2021–30) would align the market's design with European climate goals for 2020 and 2030, respectively.

The initial phase of Europe's market was famously overallocated. While Europe used majoritarian rules that were favorable for adopting environmental measures, the political and administrative capacity of environmental regulators in Brussels was highly limited at first. To get the system going, the individual member states were permitted to establish their own allowance budgets in phase 1 – an important political compromise that brought more members along. Not surprisingly, however, the collective result was that members printed too many permits and spot market prices fell to zero once the extent of overallocation became clear.[11] In phase 2, which began with fresh allocations, prices stayed higher because, over time, European regulators won the right to set EU-wide emissions budgets in more of a centralized manner and with greater oversight of market-wide outcomes. In short, EU climate regulators gained authority and learned how to use that authority effectively.

The Western Climate Initiative – a partnership between subnational markets in California and Québec (see chapter 1) – also reflects institutional barriers to carbon pricing. California's claims to climate leadership are well known, but what is less well known is that the state is also home to conservative anti-tax movements. Since the 1970s, popular ballot initiatives have amended the state constitution to impose supermajority voting requirements on legislative initiatives that raise taxes.[12] A carbon market that auctions pollution allowances to private parties, like California's does, could be said to raise taxes – and, indeed, such a lawsuit was brought against the program.[13] Although the state regulator ultimately prevailed in court, a newer constitutional amendment foreclosed the regulator's initial legal theory, which was valid only through the end of 2020. A market crisis arose when it became clear that the program was overallocated on that same time horizon and could not credibly be extended to reach the state's 2030 emissions goal without a supermajority legislative vote.[14] Eventually, state leaders came together to negotiate an extension in 2017, but had to make serious concessions to the oil industry and other incumbent stakeholders to secure a legislative supermajority.[15] These political compromises rolled back state and local regulatory authority over oil and gas emissions while perpetuating an overallocation problem that keeps the market ineffective, despite its rhetorical prominence in state policy strategy.

Ironically, earlier legislation that established California's ambitious 2030 greenhouse gas limit and provided complete legal authority to develop non-market regulations to meet this goal required only a simple majority vote. But because the state constitution raises the bar for legislative action that involves revenue-raising mechanisms – even if all of the revenue were returned to taxpayers or used to reduce sales or income tax – it was much more difficult in practice to enact market-based policies, despite growing demand for climate action from California voters.[16] Whereas in Europe institutional rules have, over time, allowed and encouraged a more powerful central regulator that has made cap-and-trade more effective, institutional rules in California led to political outcomes that diminished the climate regulator's powers.

California is arguably the most prominent example of this phenomenon, but is not the only polity with supermajority voting restrictions. A number of other subnational jurisdictions in the United States have similar requirements. Oregon was poised in 2019 to adopt cap-and-trade legislation to link with California's program, but Republican legislators literally fled the state to prevent a legislative quorum and the Democratic leadership ultimately dropped the bill in response.[17] Had the bill been legally viable on a simple majority basis, Oregon might now be on a path to linking a new carbon market with California and Québec.

A second set of constraints affects subnational governments. These jurisdictions are often the most ambitious when it comes to climate policy, yet they also have specific institutional attributes that make it hard to meet their goals. For one thing, few subnational governments have large and technically sophisticated regulators; California is arguably the rare outlier in this regard.[18] Yet even in California, a large and sophisticated regulatory apparatus has learned that running a market takes different skills from crafting regulatory mandates and technology programs that address conventional air pollutants. When it comes to managing multilateral markets between subnational governments, that challenge is exacerbated because subnational governments lack the legal authority and political power to negotiate treaties.[19]

Consider the case of the Western Climate Initiative (WCI). When California and Québec linked their carbon markets together to form the WCI, they drafted an agreement in 2013 that provides a series of procedural and substantive commitments each party makes with respect to one another. In 2017 Ontario signed a similar document and joined the WCI as well. By their own terms, however, these documents are not treaties. They do not create any formal, legally binding obligations because subnational governments lack the legal authority to write treaties.[20] Just like the 2015 Paris Agreement, there is no formal legal mechanism to enforce cross-border promises that are made but not kept in the WCI program. That may be all that is feasible at the global level, but when it comes to intergovernmental relations dictating the terms of multi-billion-dollar carbon markets, legally unenforceable is not a particularly credible standard. When the politics of emissions trading came unglued in Ontario under a new, conservative government, the province pulled out of the WCI without following even the superficial terms of the joint agreement its predecessor government had signed.[21] There was no significant impact on the market because all players knew that Ontario could withdraw and, indeed, once the provincial elections took place, would almost certainly withdraw. That the market could anticipate and price these impacts is no small comfort – all this tells us is that the market knew Ontario's promise to remain in the WCI program was unenforceable and therefore not credible. A similar set of patterns can be seen in the north-eastern United States' Regional Greenhouse Gas Initiative (RGGI). Originally comprised of ten states that set up a linked cap-and-trade program for electricity sector emissions, RGGI wobbled slightly when a Republican administration in New Jersey decided to withdraw. Litigation and public relations campaigns aimed to keep New Jersey in the trading program,[22] but what eventually brought the state back in was the very force that precipitated its departure: political regime change.[23] Firms and governments participating in RGGI know that states may come or go, with the consequences managed through an informal political process rather than a legal one.

However disappointing the examples of Ontario and New Jersey might be, they show how there is no legal recourse for withdrawal from subnational multilateral cap-and-trade programs. Multilateral market links operated by subnational governments have limited credibility because market participants know that if political fortunes change in one jurisdiction, there are few options remaining jurisdictions have to enforce their commitments. That is not to say that these markets are incapable of delivering climate benefits, but rather that they cannot effectively constrain their linked partners' behaviors and therefore can't be too ambitious. National governments face similar challenges in keeping multilateral efforts together, as we discuss later in the book, but they have more tools at their disposal, including treaties, other forms of law, and significantly greater capacity to use trade and other policy instruments to reinforce their preferred political outcomes. In contrast, the only multilateral market links that can be formed by subnational governments are relatively fragile and thin.

The logic of Potemkin markets

The political advantages of regulation combine with the institutional barriers to ambitious market-based policies to yield what we call Potemkin markets. Governments that pursue climate policies end up relying primarily on regulations to advance the goals of clean energy and reductions of greenhouse gas emissions. Those that also deploy carbon markets end up in a common situation, at least at first: markets with low prices and weak environmental outcomes. Regulation ends up doing most of the real work in cutting emissions and the markets trade what is left over. This tendency is not an accident, but rather a feature built into the political logic of policy processes that select cap-and-trade systems. And because Potemkin markets trade a residual share of emission reductions via a highly visible and politically sensitive policy instrument, policymakers keep them perennially oversupplied to avoid surprise political shocks. As a result, the apparent costs of a market program – as seen in the price of emission credits – is much lower than the real cost of serious climate policy. The market looks like a beautiful, low-cost program for achieving environmental goals. Yet, in reality, what's behind the market – behind the façade – is what is really cutting emissions.[24]

Like the fabled Imperial Russian villages, a visiting official on a quick tour would be left with the impression that all was well. Potemkin markets feature low prices and play minimal roles in the actual decarbonization efforts of their sponsoring government. They give the politically useful – but frequently misleading – impression that a government's climate policy is simple, cost-effective, and ready for broad emulation. Fundamentally, they mask the economic and political dynamics at work under the surface of a complex policy structure.

The key to understanding Potemkin markets lies in the interaction between regulations and market. Consider a utility company that needs to acquire allowances to cover its greenhouse gas emissions under a cap-and-trade program and is also subject to a renewable energy regulatory mandate.

The mandate might require the utility to procure relatively expensive clean energy for its customers, which creates costs that the utility has to assume no matter what else is going on in the carbon market. Thus, from the narrow perspective of the market's supply–demand balance, the regulation provides a zero-cost supply of emission reductions. The utility reduces its emissions because of the clean energy mandate, so it demands fewer allowances in the carbon market and therefore pays less to comply with market rules, even if it pays more overall as a result of the regulation's costs. In turn, a reduction in demand for allowances leads to lower market-wide prices, even if the total social cost of the regulation and market compliance costs are higher in the end. As a result, markets end up "thin": they trade only the residual emission reductions required after regulations take effect.

Because regulations depress market prices and ambitious regulations are far more readily adopted than strict markets, core political forces strongly favor Potemkin market outcomes. And once markets launch in Potemkin conditions, two related forces work to keep them that way. Reforms are possible, as we address later in the book, but the political pressures that create Potemkin outcomes don't abate and therefore need to be understood.

The first reinforcing factor is a simple extension of the relative political advantage regulations enjoy over markets. Once policymakers create a market that operates alongside regulations, those regulations will reduce the carbon price below what it would be if the market stood alone. From the perspective of economically optimal policy design, the regulations may no longer be needed. Politically, however, regulation persists because there is no powerful constituency for its removal. Existing (and even new) regulations added on top of existing markets both deliver concentrated benefits to specific stakeholder communities and have the advantage of reducing the visible carbon price that applies more broadly. As policymakers contemplate deeper emission cuts, the logic for regulation multiplies in power because direct regulation helps policymakers keep carbon prices from rising to politically unsustainable levels. Regulation offers stability that is extremely valuable – as seen, above, when industries have organized to block regulatory rollbacks.

The second factor is the political value of market oversupply or overallocation, a concept that is as pernicious as it is technical. Polluters put a high value on excess allocations because uncertainty about the future means these extra credits can be a hedge. But in the market, the effect of these excess allowances accumulating in private accounts is to depress market prices and create a surplus stock of pollution rights.[25]

Some analysts see this as merely a transient problem – a necessary initial payoff to powerful interests. However, oversupply in a program's initial years propagates over time through a concept called allowance banking. Markets typically feature generous or unlimited banking rules for allowances. Firms that acquire allowances they don't need for immediate compliance purposes can "bank" them for future use.

The idea behind banking flows directly from economic theory, but runs head-first into political practice. A market leaves it up to private parties to decide where, when, and how to reduce emissions. A firm that can cut its emissions cheaply will want to lower its demand for allowances and, if the firm already received its allowances from the government for free, sell its extra allowances to others. Once faced with a market-based incentive to cut emissions, some firms may even move to cut emissions early and save up unused allowances for future years when costs will be higher. Others might want to accumulate unused allowances to help them weather variable compliance costs. For example, electricity sector emissions will be lower in years with abundant rainfall and therefore greater hydropower production, but higher during droughts. Thus, a utility company might wish to save some extra allowances during rainy years and save those allowances in anticipation of drier weather periods. But once a large bank develops, any effort to clear it up would impose additional visible costs on market participants. As a result, the tendency to enable early oversupply conditions via early giveaways creates a problem that only becomes more difficult to manage over time.

Not all banking is bad. A moderate amount of allowance banking reduces market price volatility and facilitates early emission reductions. Moreover, in the mind of analysts, banking aligns with the geophysical properties of carbon pollution. What matters is control on *cumulative* emissions. Cap-and-trade systems can limit those emissions by fixing the total number of allowances added up across every year of the program – an approach that offers flexibility around when emissions are cut but tells us nothing about when emissions will occur. However, nearly every government's climate target is expressed on an *annual* basis: that is, a government will promise to cut emissions by a certain calendar year. The technical relationship between cumulative program caps and annual policy goals is complicated, opaque, and easily manipulated to serve the short-term optics of a political decision to commit to big goals without implementing the policies necessary to achieve them.

Oversupply of pollution rights has proved to be a large problem because the political demands of firms for compensation in the form of excess allocations are amplified by uncertainty. Setting limits on pollution that are ambitious but not excessively costly requires regulators to make predictions about future emissions, which they need in order to set caps that are lower (but not too much lower) than these levels.[26] Unfortunately, predictions like this are almost always wrong and may be getting even more uncertain as the pace of technological change increases in the energy system.[27] When layered on top of strong regulations and designed in the face of significant uncertainty about macroeconomic conditions and technological change, thin markets tend to produce volatile outcomes: that is, the odds are good that they will end up either cheap or expensive, but rarely in between.[28] In the face of deep uncertainty and with the prospect of politically implausible high price outcomes, policymakers will generally prefer lax program caps over those that could create politically implausible prices.

Other exogenous forces can exacerbate these trends. Most notably, the great recession of the late 2000s and early 2010s led to significantly lower-than-expected economic growth across Europe and North America, which hosted all of the major carbon markets at the time. Each of these markets experienced an exogenous drop in demand when emissions fell owing to poor macroeconomic conditions, and not as a result of either carbon market or regulatory incentives. The supply of allowances remained fixed, however, and contributed to growing allowance surpluses in each program. Climate policymakers have no direct control over macroeconomic conditions, and thus the structure of classic cap-and-trade programs creates an asymmetric political bias in favor of oversupply conditions: when recessions occur, demand falls but supply stays fixed. Efforts to remedy the impacts require policymakers to take actions that can be directly trans-lated into visible and politically unpopular price impacts on electricity and transportation fuels. Worse, implementation of any such reforms needs to consider, as a practical political matter, the timing between visible energy price increases and macroeconomic recovery.

Allowance banking exacerbates all of these political challenges by propagating any errors from one trading period to the next. This is one reason why European policymakers prevented banking from phase 1 into phase 2 – banking overallocated allowances from phase 1 would have diluted the impact of phase 2 and possibly made it harder for the EU to comply with its Kyoto obligations. Because banking was not allowed, spot prices in the market's initial, overallocated phase crashed to zero. This example is often cited as a warning about what happens when there is no allowance banking because the price crash was embarrassing and cast doubt on the program's future performance. That perspective is entirely understandable as a matter of public relations, but exactly the wrong lesson to draw. Rather, the EU's wise decision to disallow banking meant that the program's initial overallocation problem was fully contained in the experi-mental pilot phase.[29]

Finally, oversupply conditions can be intentional as well as accidental. Politicians can take advantage of the fact that few people are capable of understanding when oversupply causes a cap-and-trade program to fall short of what society is willing to invest to address the climate problem. At times, oversight by environmental NGOs, which should be mobilized to avoid those outcomes, ends up lax as well – with some groups too steeped in political compromise to see how the overall system is undermining their environmental goals.

Conclusion

Regulations offer political advantages over market-based policies like cap-and-trade or carbon taxes because the costs they impose are less visible to the voting public. Better still, regulatory costs can be targeted to avoid policymakers' most organized opponents. Because regulations are more popular with politicians and the public, they are more credible and therefore provide greater advantages to emerging industries and their supporters – including the development of guaranteed demand for low-carbon products and barriers to market entry that benefit incumbent firms. Meanwhile, the rules that govern institutional decision-making create powerful barriers against adopting effective market-based policies. These forces combine to produce Potemkin markets: thin programs that are subsidiary to strong regulations and price only the residual emissions left over after regulations do their work. Potemkin outcomes are not transient but built into the structure defined by the political and institutional factors we identified in chapter 1. Political leaders have strong incentives to maintain overallocation conditions, which keep prices low and avoid political resistance from organized industries and from voters when market systems affect goods and services whose costs are highly visible. Overallocation comes at the expense of watering down climate benefits. Lax markets risk getting stuck in low gear as oversupply conditions propagate through generous allowance banking rules. Potemkin markets create the appearance of low-cost policy outcomes while obscuring the more significant regulatory efforts that, although costing more, accomplish much more, too.

3
Coverage and allocation

According to theory, a carbon market should cover as many sectors as administratively feasible, and include as large a geographical territory as possible – ideally global in nature. The greater the sectoral and geographical extent of the program, the more opportunities there are to identify least-cost emission reduction opportunities. In addition to universal coverage, an ideal market would also allocate allowances in an even-handed way. Incumbents and new entrants, in the purest visions for markets, would be required to buy their pollution allowances from the government at auction. Even-handedness is necessary so that the allocation of valuable allowances doesn't distort competition. A giveaway to incumbents might allow them simply to ignore the potential impact of the market scheme on their behavior – enabling them to keep on polluting, especially if they thought they could keep getting more giveaways as time goes on. Excess generosity might even allow them to use the windfall to entrench their position and slow the rate at which society cuts emissions.

In theory, a market designed according to these principles – featuring broad sectoral and geographical coverage, along with benign allocations – would unleash powerful incentives for firms and households to find the cheapest way to control emissions regardless of sector or activity. Each participating sector would face the same marginal cost of complying with the program, with maximum economic efficiency for the economy as a whole.

The real world is completely different. When policy-makers design cap-and-trade programs, they adopt highly uneven and usually narrow sectoral coverage. Moreover, they develop allocation rules that are often highly distortionary and explicitly designed to blunt the impact of carbon prices on the most competitive sectors of the economy: those that are exposed to international trade. Although these interventions are intended to reduce incumbents' political opposition to carbon pricing and accommodate legitimate competitiveness concerns, free allocations can metastasize to the point of *de facto* exemptions that "grandfather" legacy polluters' economic positions – effectively relieving them of the obligation to make major emission cuts. Worse still, they send a clear message that market rules are endogenous to politics. Rather than constitute one-time compromises necessary to get a system off the ground, excessively generous handouts signal that market rules are up for continuous negotiations that favor incumbents.

These real-world approaches – pockmarked with warts from the perspective of ideal market policy design – reflect powerful political and institutional forces at work. This chapter explains why, in the real world, policymakers struggle to design markets that cover multiple sectors and why the sectors they do cover receive differential treatment. (We address geographical coverage later, in chapters 5 and 6, and explain why politicians make choices in that domain that are also so different from the theoretical ideal.) Looking at sectors, we answer two questions in this chapter: what determines which sectors get covered by cap-and-trade programs, and why are sectors treated so differently in practice?

The answer to both questions turns on how the variables introduced in chapter 1 cause outcomes in the real world that vary radically from theoretical ideals. We think of these dynamics in terms of the demand for accommodation from affected stakeholder groups and the supply of policy strategies that adequately respond to those demands.

One cluster of important variables is the political organization of interest groups that are affected by carbon prices.

These forces determine the demand placed on policymakers to respond with accommodations. Both consumer and business concerns play a critical role here.

Consumers' concerns turn on the visibility of price impacts. The more visible the market's impact on the price of consumer-facing goods, such as gasoline, the less likely the policy will earn consent or support from consumers (that is, the voting public). By contrast, businesses' concerns derive primarily from the impact of higher prices on their competitiveness, which we refer to as their trade sensitivity. Firms that use a lot of energy to make goods that face commodity competition – for example, refineries that make gasoline and diesel fuels – will be more sensitive to energy price impacts than others in the services sector for whom higher energy costs aren't a significant drag on corporate profits, such as software companies. Firms that are in export-oriented commodity businesses are especially sensitive to policy because even a small shift in costs can affect global competitiveness; by contrast, firms whose products trade only within the local jurisdiction are less sensitive to these differential costs. Together, the energy intensity and trade exposure of a firm determines its overall trade sensitivity.

These factors – the visibility of consumer price impacts and the trade sensitivity of affected firms – determine the degree of political resistance to policies, which will vary by sector. Of course, resistance does not mean that policies fail. Political leaders under strong pressure to act on climate change might be able to overrule powerful dissenting voices yet survive (or even thrive) politically – a situation that prevails in much of Europe today and is plausibly extending to some parts of the United States like California and New York. But to the extent that political leaders must take dissent seriously, even in jurisdictions with favorable politics, they must turn to various mechanisms they can use to respond to the concerns of voters and industry.

A second cluster of variables concerns the government's institutional capacity to be politically responsive to these organized voices. In highly regulated sectors, such as electricity, regulators can structure rebating mechanisms to alter the incidence of compliance costs across customer classes as the politics demand. Where that scalpel-like capacity to alter impacts does not exist, then blunter instruments may be needed – including provision of free allowance allocations to highly organized, trade-exposed industries. Free allocation programs, in turn, can be based on careful empirical analysis of competitiveness risks, where governments have that capacity; or they can end up more as a reflection of the political power of organized interest groups when government capacity is lower. The greater the government's capacity to manage impacts on competitiveness and other attributes that politically organized groups care about (such as environmental justice concerns over the distribution of local air quality impacts), the more likely a cap-and-trade program will be able to include that sector.

While the real world is even more complex, this chapter will argue that these two clusters of factors – the demand from consumer and business interests to mitigate price impacts, and the capacity of government to be politically responsive to those demands – explain much of what is observed with regard to which sectors are covered by market systems and why their treatment varies.

Which sectors get covered

Firms differ in their sensitivity to the cost of climate policy – with the greatest sensitivity in industries where higher costs of production are hard to pass along. Consumers (voters) also vary, but are principally concerned with visible costs. These two types of political sensitivity lead to demands on political leaders, who can respond, as we argued in chapter 1, within the limits of their administrative capabilities.

In parts of the world where political leaders have powerful incentives to address the climate crisis, they might be able to ignore much of the political opposition they encounter and adopt aggressive climate policies. There are few examples today. As discussed in Figure 1.1, Jesse Jenkins at Princeton University looked at the fraction of world emissions under different pricing regimes and found that only a tiny fraction (less than 0.1%) faced carbon prices consistent with a substantial effort on climate change (around $100 per ton

CO_2-equivalent).[1] Those places – such as Sweden – are pioneer providers of global public goods, and the planet is better for their actions. But they account for a tiny and shrinking part of the total problem.

Even in places where the public is deeply committed to action, political leaders can't operate in ways that are insulated from politically powerful groups' dissenting views. Instead, they must find ways to manage the costs of their policies that are most debilitating in political terms. That requires making tough choices about which groups are most powerful politically. It also requires looking to a variety of mechanisms that program administrators can use to manage political and economic impacts. In effect, political leaders guide the process of designing and administering market systems to manipulate sectoral accommodations in ways that are responsive to the concerns of politically organized and powerful stakeholders. That arsenal of capabilities includes direct control over prices in sectors where those prices are regulated (and where firms, to a point, can continue to operate and tolerate price control). In the extreme, debilitating political pressure can lead politicians simply to exclude the sector from the market's coverage.

The convergence of political forces and the varied institutional capabilities of government to respond to those forces explains the scattered sectoral coverage of real-world cap-and-trade systems. Empirically, that can be seen by assessing how real-world systems have varied in their sectoral coverage and treatment from two different angles.

One angle is to look at the effective price of carbon in a society. If a society adopts a carbon market that generates a nominal price of $100 per ton of CO_2 emissions (or a tax scheme with the same price) and all major sectors of the economy are included, then its weighted average carbon price is $100. If some sectors are excluded, however, then the weighted average price drops. Figure 3.1 shows this difference between the highest nominal price and the weighted average price, thanks to an extraordinary data set compiled by Geoffroy Dolphin and his co-authors that reports carbon prices in fifteen sectors for each country and thus allows a granular look at the political and administrative choices made by governments when they decide which sectors to include.[2] Each country's highest nominal carbon price is shown by the grey dots and line in the figure But the highest nominal carbon price tells only part of the story because in every country there is at least one major sector that is exempt completely, and often many more – even in countries that are highly committed to action, such as Norway and Sweden.[3] One can also look at a country's effective price of carbon by weighting each sector's applicable carbon price by its share of emissions – as shown by the black dots and line in Figure 3.1. Huge exemptions for major emitting sectors mean that, in effect, even the countries that have high carbon prices don't really apply these high prices to all emissions. Indeed, they typically exempt or rebate some sectors – in particular, highly trade-sensitive sectors. This logic applies equally to carbon markets and carbon taxes (both policy instruments are included in the figure) because the underlying political and administrative logic that leads

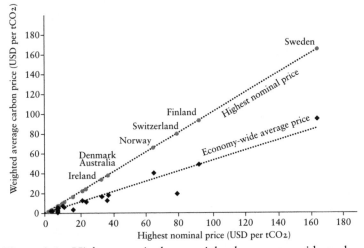

Figure 3.1 Highest nominal vs. weighted economy-wide carbon prices

Source: Based on data for carbon prices in 2014. Sector-specific data were provided by Geoffroy Dolphin and weighted average prices are published in Geoffroy Dolphin, Michael G. Pollitt, and David M. Newbery, "The political economy of carbon pricing: a panel analysis," *Oxford Economics Papers* 72(2) (2020): 472–500. For more information, see *http:// geoffroydolphin.eu/carbon-prices-data/*.

some sectors to exemption operates independently of the
instrument involved. Trade-sensitive sectors know what they
want, and they are organized politically to get it.

The second perspective on coverage comes from looking in
a granular way at exactly which sectors are included in cap
and trade systems, as summarized in Table 3.1 for the major
carbon markets around the world.

Notably, every single program includes the electricity sector
because it is the most inward-looking, the least trade-sensitive,
and the most manageable through existing regulatory structures. (Perhaps not coincidentally, the electricity sector is
also where the most promising low-carbon technologies are
already commercialized – recall Figure 1.2 – and the most
ambitious regulatory policies can be found as well.) Including
utilities in cap-and-trade programs has the added advantage

Table 3.1 Sectoral coverage of major carbon markets

	Electricity	Industry	Transport	Forestry / Agriculture
Regional Greenhouse Gas Initiative (RGGI)	X			
European Union Emissions Trading System (EU ETS)	X	X		
Western Climate Initiative (WCI) (California, Québec)	X	X	X	
South Korea	X	X	X	
New Zealand	X	X	X	X
China (National)	X			
China (Subnational)	All	All	Beijing and Shenzhen only	

Source: Authors' summary based on International Carbon Action
Partnership, Emissions Trading Worldwide: Status Report 2019.

of allowing a cap-and-trade program to expand its coverage to areas of the local economy, including residential and commercial buildings, where direct regulation of emissions is all but impossible as a practical matter: no realistic policy could impose direct obligations on every single home, office building, and community center, but requiring the utilities that serve all of these customers to manage their customers' climate pollution is eminently more tractable.

In contrast, the industrial sector presents greater challenges. Not only do firms in this sector generally face significant trade exposure that can lead to competitiveness problems and leakage of emissions, investment, and jobs, but policymakers generally have fewer tools available to accommodate affected industries. They primarily rely on free allowance allocation, as discussed below. For these reasons, fewer cap-and-trade programs include industrial emitters.

The transport sector presents multiple political challenges. For one, the political visibility of transportation fuel price impacts is an acute concern for elected officials. Worse still, the cost of major shifts in vehicle or fuel technologies is often much higher than decarbonization programs in other sectors, like electricity, where clean technologies are more advanced. That's why Potemkin markets never generate many emission reductions in the transportation sector. Getting serious in this sector requires higher prices, but many of the stakeholder firms are highly trade-sensitive because they make refined products that are traded commodities. Voters are also disproportionately sensitive to what they pay. Because regulators have few tools for managing transportation price impacts, only a few markets include transportation fuels.

Finally, the forestry and agriculture sectors are almost always excluded from programs. These sectors are highly exposed to competitive pressures, highly organized to oppose regulation of all kinds, and difficult to managing owing to the diffuse and scientifically challenging problems associated with monitoring emissions from land-use-related activities. Rather than end up covered under mandatory cap-and-trade programs, these politically powerful sectors are usually engaged exclusively via voluntary carbon offset incentives – an issue we return to in chapter 5.[4]

Why sectors are treated differently

The fundamental political challenge with a multi-sector cap-and-trade program is the law of one price. Once a sector is included in the program, the market equilibrates on a single price that applies to all sectors. For theorists, this phenomenon embodies the beauty of the market: it is how market forces find least-cost solutions across multiple sectors. For politicians, however, the law of one price can be a nightmare. Governments need to be politically responsive to the politically organized concerns of each sector – each with its own distinctive concerns, yet each now facing the same price on emissions. In a single-sector market, the law of one price presents fewer political challenges because the whole scheme can be adjusted to address the organized political pressures of the sector. But when a trading system covers multiple sectors – or multiple different industries, as is the case when the expansive "industrial sector" is included – then the political challenges multiply.

The key to understanding why sectors are treated differently in cap-and-trade systems lies with understanding the interaction between key stakeholders' demand for accommodations, as discussed above, and the tools available to policymakers to satisfy those demands. We characterize the demand for a policy response and the tools available to policymakers by sector in Figure 3.2 (see p. 64 below).

The full toolkit of mechanisms available to policymakers that want to be politically responsive is complex. In the broadest sense, however, it includes two main elements that are already familiar from the earlier discussion. One element is direct regulation in the sector – so that politically important impacts from carbon prices can be compensated in other ways. The other element is free allowance allocations, which compensate firms that are worried about economic harms from the market's cap on pollution. The suite of available tools helps explain why sectors are treated differently from theory and from one another.

For purists, these kinds of political needs are orthogonal to the beauty of the market concept – indeed, most pure visions for emissions trading simply ignore these kinds of sectoral details. For practical analysts, however, they present a necessary condition for markets' enactment and political durability. The question for practical people is not whether politically organized groups will demand compensation. Rather, the question is whether government can deliver that compensation efficiently with minimal distortion to the rest of the economy and the environmental goals of the policy. If compensation is laser-guided, then the real-world operation of pollution markets can be a lot more effective at achieving environmental goals while remaining politically viable. But if compensation is clumsily excessive, firms will receive excessive rents.

The waste of public resources is concerning enough, but what is most problematic about inefficient accommodations is that it signals to exposed industries that the terms of market design are up for constant political renegotiation. If some firms succeed in capturing greater accommodations than they need, then all firms might draw the lesson that the best reaction to inconvenient market conditions in the future should be in the form of political lobbying for their own fresh accommodations, not cost-effective compliance.

The industrial sector is most complex, so we start there. Industry is largely rooted in free enterprise in most western countries, where, to date, there has been the most robust experience with efforts to create emissions trading systems. The industrial sector is still subject to regulatory requirements, to be sure, but most major investment decisions are based on market forces. The ability of government to intervene without consequence is limited. Moreover, a growing share of industry is exposed to international competition, which makes such firms highly sensitive to the cost of key inputs like energy. If political leaders want to include the industrial sectors in emissions trading schemes, they must be ready to address the reality that these sectors will have acute exposure to program costs and thus will demand political responses. And in most of industry – at least outside the electric power sector – the only element of the toolkit available is the free allocation of emission credits. For sectors whose industrial organization is largely around free enterprise, direct regulation isn't available as a powerful and reliable element of the toolkit.

If free allocation is the main instrument that industry requires, we must look closely at how government makes decisions about how many free allocations to offer. An extensive academic literature has developed to suggest that these kinds of political responses don't need to undermine the market price's fundamental incentive to reduce emissions. According to this logic, the "opportunity cost" of freely allocated allowances means that even companies receiving complete free allocation nonetheless have an incentive to reduce their own emissions if the cost of any such reduction is less than the prevailing price for allowances – just as they would if they had to purchase allowances from the government at auction. The reasoning goes that if a company receives some or all of the allowances it needs for compliance purposes yet could reduce emissions at the cost of $10/tCO_2e$ when the allowance price is $15/tCO_2e$, then it would make a profit of $5 for every ton it reduces – and therefore it should do so, whether or not it receives some or all of those allowances for free.

One clever concept designed to harness the option value of allowances to protect firms against leakage while retaining a meaningful policy incentive to reduce emissions is called "output-based allocation" – in essence, a formula that determines the number of free allowances a firm receives based on the levels of its actual production and typically scaled by its emissions intensity relative to industry-wide benchmarks.[5] Firms that consider the opportunity cost of free allowances they receive under output-based allocation methods should face a similar economic incentive compared to firms that buy all of their allowances at auction. (Nevertheless, all of these approaches shift wealth from the public – as reflected in the value of the emission allowances that governments might otherwise auction – into private hands.)

The academic logic behind free allocation strategies is impeccable under idealized conditions, but like almost everything we discuss in this book what really matters is how decisions are made and markets operate under real-world conditions. In the real world, allocations of free credits – and the corresponding transfer of wealth from public to private – reflect powerful political and organizational forces that distort policy outcomes in ways that undermine the efficacy of market-based strategies. Most important is that the interest groups that demand political responses have no incentive to limit their demands.[6] Instead, extensive lobbying efforts make it difficult for policymakers to implement complex allocation formulas on the basis of actual leakage risks. Affected groups are powerful politically, and policymakers are contemplating allocation formulas under conditions of high uncertainty. Nobody really knows the exact level of compensation needed, and empirical evidence about the impacts of emissions trading systems is hard to come by.[7] Under those conditions, technocratic methods are imprecise and it is easier for politically organized groups to demand more as a hedge against uncertainty. The most prominent example of this behavior recently occurred in California's cap-and-trade program, which was scheduled, pursuant to extensive regulatory analysis and outside academic research, to significantly reduce free allowance allocation over time.[8] However, a political negotiation in 2017 required regulators to abandon those efforts and return to a more generous allocation formula that primarily benefits the state's highly organized oil and gas industry.[9]

The uncomfortable truth about free allowance allocation is that its primary motivation – legitimate political and economic concerns about carbon markets' impacts on competitiveness – makes it hard for policymakers to provide free allocations that are laser-guided in precision. Firms that are highly organized press for free allowances, but have no incentive to ask only for what they need. Once they get a handout, they have no incentive not to ask again. For some companies, especially those operating in razor-thin global commodity markets, the question of free allocation is a matter of economic life and death; uncertainties in what they actually need can cut both ways, which amplifies their demand for generous free allocations lest they be crushed by overseas competitors that do not face those costs. For others, free allocation is a question of how much compliance is going to cost when business isn't going to change that much; what these firms want is a transfer of wealth, not a lifeline – and the bigger, the better. The challenge facing policymakers is how to tell the difference between the needy and the greedy – a huge challenge in public administration when it is impossible to observe true need accurately.

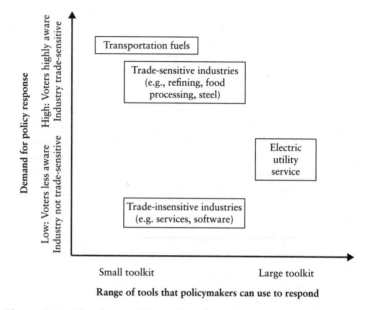

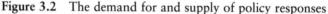

Figure 3.2 The demand for and supply of policy responses

Figure 3.2 thus outlines the pressures on politicians to be responsive to political interests arising in sectors that may be included in a cap-and-trade system and the tools that are available to offer that response. It suggests two interlocking implications for how variations in political responses will affect the operation of cap-and-trade systems in practice. First, politicians will understand that it is just too complex to include many sectors under real-world conditions – where those sectors demand politically responsive treatment but the tools available are too limited. That's a chief reason why so many cap-and-trade systems have a narrow scope. Second, because the decisions to provide free allocations are political, they are also, with some institutional constraints, always in play. In the idealized vision of market systems, rules are fixed and it doesn't matter much what messy deals are needed to get the program going. But if firms know that there will be ongoing political negotiations, then the rules of the market no longer deliver incentives at the margin for firms to cut emissions. Instead, the rules become endogenous to the interests of organized political groups.

In the real world, these insights explain why markets' coverage is limited and why covered sectors are subject to different political and economic incentives.

Many hope that politicians could broaden sectoral coverage of markets if they expanded their toolkit. The most-discussed option is called a border carbon adjustment. Rather than subsidize a trade-exposed firm with free allowances to keep it competitive in global markets, simply adjusting the price on carbon emissions at the border would have the same effect. This policy would level the playing field by imposing a carbon price on imports (with the level of the fee set according to the emissions associated with the imported product) and a corresponding rebate when domestic firms export. A border carbon adjustment would create fairer market competition and obviate the need for free allowance allocation, allowing policymakers to auction valuable allowances and raise more carbon revenue for public purposes.

Border carbon adjustments are another area where beautiful theory has collided with practical political and administrative realities. One challenge has been simply calculating the level of border adjustment needed – especially for complex commodities where it is all but impossible to observe the level of emissions overseas that arise during production processes. Several methods have been proposed, but these remain mainly prototype activities that have not been seriously tested in the face of real-world incentives for firms and governments to hide critical information.[10] These challenges are hard enough to manage when energy and emission prices are transparent, but when the costs of production arise through a blend of markets and regulation, then estimating the implicit carbon prices – which is what local firms seeking policy adjustment ultimately care about – is even harder.

In addition to difficult administrative challenges, important legal and political barriers must be cleared. For one thing, border adjustments could raise issues under international trade law, including the World Trade Organization (WTO) – a challenge that could be surmountable with careful design, but the fragile state of the WTO may make more governments wary of policies that create new, challenging tests for that organization.[11] Subnational governments may face additional legal challenges, including legal challenges to their ability to affect national or international commerce.[12] Even with border adjustments available, in principle, industries receiving generous free allocations might be unwilling to make the leap and will fight any attempt to claw back their free allowances.

It's no wonder, then, that few examples of border carbon adjustments exist. A recent study of global efforts to implement border carbon adjustments finds that administrative, legal, and political barriers, including opposition from incumbent free allocation recipients, have frustrated even the most promising opportunities to implement this concept.[13] Later in this book, when we turn to reforms in chapters 7 and 8, we will examine ways to implement border adjustments as part of a larger strategy for international cooperation. But realism is needed about how quickly this can be done. Success will hinge less on comprehensive efforts to harmonize the explicit and implicit costs for all traded products across the whole economy, and more on focused programs targeting individual industries and commodity markets where it is easiest to administer the necessary calculations and interventions. For example, it is possible that industry-specific tariffs and other trade policies could develop in Europe around key industries, such as steel or cement, where European policymakers are investing in deep decarbonization and it is relatively easy to measure the embodied greenhouse gas emissions associated with traded products. These actions can be tailored to address the vagaries of a particular industry even as it proves harder to adopt border adjustments that apply comprehensively to all goods. Under a best-case scenario in which a handful of targeted border carbon adjustments emerge, free allocation is here to stay.

In contrast to trade-sensitive industrial firms, less sensitive sectors like electricity are capable of sustaining minimal free allocation. Freed from that need to be politically responsive by awarding free allowances, these sectors more commonly rely instead on allowance auctions that raise state revenues. The wealth created by the program stays in public hands. (Whether and how that money is spent well, however, is a subject we address in the next chapter.) For example, the

RGGI program auctions the dominant majority of allowances in its electricity-only program; most states that participate in RGGI choose to use these funds to pursue energy efficiency and other clean energy programs.[14] Similarly, after a controversial initial experience involving generous free allocation to power plants, the European Union has also moved to reduce most free allocation and switch to an auction-based approach in the electricity sector.[15]

Other arrangements that recycle revenues are also possible in the electricity sector. California, for example, has pursued a hybrid outcome in this sector that illustrates how the organization of business and consumer interests affects allocation policies. Electric utilities have long been supporters of the state's cap-and-trade program, in part because they received extremely generous free allocation schedules. In the case of private utilities, these allowances must be consigned and sold at auction, with the proceeds used to benefit ratepayers. Although not a direct subsidy to firms' owners, this approach helps cross-subsidize the electricity sector as a whole to achieve lower rates, a matter of concern to utility customer advocates and utility regulators who organized to advocate for these outcomes. Publicly owned utilities receive similarly generous allocations, but are allowed to use free allowances however they like. Thus, the California example shows how the electricity industry's support for carbon pricing is connected to generous free allocation, but the value of that transfer of wealth is diverted in large part to utility customers (in the case of privately owned utilities) and to local governments (in the case of publicly owned utilities).[16] The share of the transfer made to ratepayers is a reflection of a pre-existing regulatory structure that allows utilities to rebate funds to each customer. And because those rebates are not tied to the price of electricity, they maintain the carbon market's incentive to reduce emissions.[17]

The transportation sector presents particularly acute challenges because "transportation" spans two very different categories of actors in Figure 3.2. Two elements of transportation are industrial – crude oil production and refining – and the logic is exactly the same as that which we discussed above for trade-sensitive industries. But these industrial processes, while important, account for only a portion of total emissions that are linked to using oil-based products. The majority of emissions occur outside the fencelines of industrial facilities themselves and arise as a vast number of customers burn refined transportation fuels.

In contrast, transportation fuel markets are distinct from both industrial facilities and electric utilities. For fuels, what customers see is the net price of the fuel on a per gallon or per liter basis, inclusive of taxes and other policy costs. For electric utility service, however, the price customers face is a lot more complex. Electric service ratemaking allows regulators to pass the cost of consuming polluting electricity to the consumer on a volumetric basis – think cost per kilowatt-hour – while nevertheless enabling rebates at the individual customer level. As a result, rebates can keep customer bills from rising too much while nevertheless preserving the incentive to reduce consumption. Those arrangements simply are not administratively possible in existing transportation fuel markets.

When governments have few tools to address the consumer-facing impacts from including transportation fuels in carbon markets, the pressure on political leaders to allocate allowances generously in the sector and to keep prices low is magnified. For example, oil and gas firms in California receive free allocations to cover a large share of their own emissions, but consumers still pay fully for the marginal cost of emissions. Because industry firms are well organized from the start and consumers are politically powerful if prices get too high, overallocation prevails. As a result, California's market is stuck with lower prices that affect not just the transportation sector but also every other sector in its market.[18]

Conclusion

The economic benefits of carbon pricing derive from a uniform price signal that applies across all sectors of the economy – a feature that also presents a major political liability for policymakers. As a result, program coverage in practice is rarely universal and often only applies to a handful of economic sectors. Two factors help explain what sectors are included: key stakeholders' sensitivity to price impacts (based on the visibility of price impacts to consumers, and firms' trade sensitivity), and the government's institutional capacity to respond to these stakeholder demands. Industrial emitters that are subject to competitive pressures in global commodity markets are hard to include in a market; those that are highly regulated and inwardly focused, like electric utilities, are much easier to include. The transportation sector is difficult to include because it is the most politically sensitive for consumers and lacks any obvious means to mitigate highly visible cost impacts.

The uneven treatment of sectors tells us three things about cap-and-trade systems that will be important as the rest of the book unfolds. First, trading systems will have much more modest leverage on emissions than originally expected because only a small share of total emissions is typically included. With improved administrative capacity and better toolkits – something evident, notably, in the EU today – coverage could expand, but the conditions that make that feasible are politically demanding. Second, where policy-makers do expand coverage prematurely, their programs could end up stuck in Potemkin conditions if they are unable to respond to stakeholders' demands for policy accommodations – just as California relies on allowance overallocation to maintain low prices and preserve the market's political acceptability in the face of concern over gasoline price impacts. Third, because each political jurisdiction will make decisions about coverage and treatment that are bespoke to local conditions, it is likely that there will be variations – possibly large variations – in the practical implementation of trading systems across countries. Simply linking together these highly dissimilar systems will not be practical as a means to facilitate international climate policy cooperation.

Each of these topics we now take up in more detail – starting with the implications of emissions trading systems that are Potemkin-like in design, thin in coverage, and plagued by low prices.

4

Revenue and spending

"Follow the money," as the old adage goes.

Cap-and-trade programs create valuable new property rights in the form of pollution allowances that can be distributed to emitting firms for free or auctioned by the government to raise funds. Many industries demand free allocations, as discussed in chapter 3, but in most emissions trading systems governments rely, at least partially, on auctions. Moreover, the fraction of allowances auctioned generally tends to rise as governments reduce – or at least aim to reduce – the extent of free allowance allocations. Over time, revenues grow.

How societies spend the money raised through these sales is vital to understanding the politics of emissions trading.

Technical studies of cap-and-trade programs generally treat auction revenues as a secondary consideration. What really matters is environmental effectiveness, and what creates effectiveness is broad coverage and sufficient program ambition: that is, tight and declining program caps that require serious emission reductions. Together, the theory goes, these factors will send a signal to firms that they must shift toward a low-carbon trajectory. Insofar as there has been much thinking about what happens to the revenues that are raised along the way, economists have urged that they be spent on reducing other distortions in the economy, such as taxes on labor or capital. This is why, ironically, some studies of carbon markets have shown that these policies may actually expand economic output even as they reduce the costly externality of global warming emissions. Indeed, the field of green tax and fiscal reform is inspired by this kind of logic.[1]

In the idealized view of emissions trading systems, all allowances are auctioned and emission limits are strict. These conditions lead to large and growing public revenues as carbon prices rise. Those massive revenues, in turn, create massive opportunities for broader tax reform. Center-right political interest groups in the United States have recently called for a gradually rising carbon tax to replace direct federal regulation of greenhouse gases, with carbon tax revenues returned to US citizens as flat, per capita dividends.[2] Many others on the left and center-left have made similar cases for taxing carbon (without rolling back other regulations) and spending the potentially huge revenues in various ways, including dividends.[3] Over the last fifteen years, many market-based proposals have been introduced in the US Congress.[4] None has yet become law, but the proposals reflect the view, among elite experts, that large carbon revenues could reduce federal budget deficits or a wide variety of corporate, payroll, and personal income taxes.

Our view is different. We appreciate the appeal of broad-based markets that primarily recycle revenues in economically efficient or socially attractive ways. That logic, however, is not particularly relevant to the real world of policy design for two reasons. One is that the revenues from cap-and-trade auctions and carbon taxes are much smaller than theorists imagine for the reasons outlined in chapters 2 and 3. (Tax systems tend to generate much more predictable revenues, so outcomes tend to match expectations for these instruments.) The other is that in a world of small revenues the political groups that tend to organize around how revenues are spent push for outcomes that are radically different from those predicted by analysts who imagine that a flood of revenues will inspire broader tax reform.

Revenues from carbon markets have been small because these schemes follow the logic of Potemkin markets. Prices are low because far more ambitious controls are imposed on firms through direct regulation, sectoral coverage is often narrow, and many industries are able to secure extensive free allowance allocations from climate policymakers. Those are the messages from chapters 2 and 3. Moreover, as we show next in chapter 5, firms can often rely heavily on carbon offsets, which depresses prices further and reduces the volume of money that can be raised through auctions. As a result, real-world implementation of emissions trading schemes yields low carbon prices and modest program revenues, at least initially.

To give a numerical example, consider the European Union over the three-year period 2013 through 2015, a representative time for which there is full and reliable reporting. If one were to apply the social cost of carbon – a US-based metric that attempts to calculate the global costs of climate pollution, which was estimated at about $36 (€32) per ton of CO_2-equivalent in 2015[5] – then the potential revenues from a comprehensive carbon pricing program would be massive. Over that three-year time period, the EU emitted about 13.5 billion tons of CO_2-equivalent,[6] which would be worth about $542 (€453) billion at the then-applicable social cost of carbon. But the actual revenue raised by the EU ETS carbon market was only $14.3 (€11.8) billion over this period, or about 2.6% of the potential.[7] This forty-fold difference between potential and actual revenue is rooted in three explanations – all political. First, actual carbon prices in the EU ETS were much lower than the social cost of carbon, ranging from about €3–7 per ton over this period in history, rather than €32.[8] Second, the EU ETS only covered about 41% of total EU-wide emissions, spanning the electricity and industrial sectors, where it was easier for EU regulators to manage the politics and also easier to monitor and administer emission sources. And, third, many emitters received free allowances and thus didn't have to buy them from the government at auction; indeed, over this period only about half of allowances were sold at auction.[9] (As an even more extreme example, the South Korean market has freely allocated more than 97% of its allowance budgets through 2020.[10])

Without massive revenues, there are no massive political forces organized to shunt the money into sundry worthy social purposes. Instead, small revenue streams attract only the attention of more specialized interest groups that are able to operate without much notice or any meaningful political competition. For the most part, those groups are the same ones that are already organized to push climate policy – green groups and their allies – and they have specific ideas about how the money should be spent. What these groups want is "green spending," and how they achieve that goal is central to the topic of this chapter: how revenues get spent.

How the money is spent matters enormously for the long-term impacts of carbon markets. If well managed, this approach can fund programs that lower emissions – in effect, compensating for the fact that the market itself has a narrow scope, low prices, or usually both.[11] Spending also matters because there are other market failures that can't be solved with efficient markets: for example, market prices aren't a substitute for R&D and deployment programs that allow testing of radical new technologies that will be required for truly transformative technological change. These radical new ideas are public goods; markets, even with an ambitious price on carbon, won't adequately supply them.[12]

The logic for why good spending strategies are important is clear enough. The problem is that the politics, at present, mostly don't reinforce good spending practices. Interest groups that line up for funds want money that supports their own near-term agendas, whereas the firms that would benefit most from transformative investments either do not exist or are relatively powerless in their economic youth. That is the perennial problem of politics when transformation is the goal, as must be the case with climate change. Politics is the domain of the incumbents, for the most part, and transformation is a threat. This challenge is particularly acute when it comes to spending the funds raised by market-based instruments, because those revenues are precious and, handled well, could facilitate the needed transformation toward deep decarbonization.[13]

The problem of bad spending – in the case of climate change, not allocating funds to the most efficient investments for cutting emissions over the long term – is a familiar problem in public finance and is often called "pork." Politically powerful groups channel funds to their interest groups at the expense of the broader public good. The challenge for any climate policy is that there are two flavors of pork – one a lot more rancid than the other. Constructive pork is the normal stuff in any policy that raises revenue, with some revenues channeled to specific beneficiaries to get the policy enacted and sustained. It is fun to dream about perfect policy, but in politics deals must be made. More pernicious is what we will call "green pork" – funds spent on programs that pretend to advance environmental goals, but do so inefficiently. Political forces favor green spending, which could be a boon for the environment, but they also favor green pork.

This chapter will explain the two key steps in this logic: first, why green spending programs are so important to the politics of emissions trading; and, second, why the political forces that shape these programs also turn them into inefficient green pork. We see the former argument as immutable – it is intrinsic to the politics of emissions trading. But the latter is not, and thus one key to making emissions trading work better is rewiring the politics to favor greater environmental impact and economic efficiency in how the revenues are spent.

Why politics favor green spending

In an imaginary world where carbon revenues are huge, policymakers could use market instruments not just to help cut pollution, but also to catalyze broader fiscal reforms: for example, direct payments to voters to buy their support and redistribute wealth, or reductions on income or corporate taxes. In theory, these reforms would make it possible to engineer the political, social, and economic outcomes of market-based schemes to build broader and more durable political support. In the United States, where political polarization on climate is extreme, some dream of grand political bargains to couple environmental action to tax reforms that magnify political support among conservatives, who have consistently been less supportive of mandatory climate policy but have strongly favored tax cuts.

In the real world, where revenues are modest, the politics are quite different. The revenues raised are significant for climate policy, but they aren't large enough to motivate broad fiscal reforms or attract the kind of attention that large-scale tax and fiscal policy processes usually do in their respective jurisdictions.

Climate insiders are all too familiar with the problems of Potemkin markets and free allocation compromises, which come as no surprise to those working on these policy systems in practice. Many key stakeholders – including both government policymakers and their NGO allies – tend to prioritize carbon markets' limited revenues as a mechanism to make up for lost environmental ambition from low prices. These groups typically organize around a green spending model that channels revenues toward additional emission reductions.

What is remarkable given the importance of how revenues are spent is how little research has tried to explain these patterns.[14] To get started, in Figure 4.1 we show the shares of green spending observed in cap-and-trade and carbon tax systems around the world, compiled by the World Bank and based on an insightful dataset from researchers at the Institute for Climate Economics in Paris. While this figure shows detail on all the major programs, Figure 4.2 zooms out and looks at the broad trends. Across all forms of market instrument, green spending is the largest single mode of expenditure, accounting for about $25 billion of the total $46 billion raised by carbon pricing policies in 2018. Substantial resources are also raised, especially with carbon taxes, for general revenue – a reminder that governments are always on the prowl for funds. A serious industrial policy program, as we will outline in chapter 8, will magnify those needs.

As with any political process, however, the details vary a lot because the politics are complex. For example, an important share of California's allowance budget goes to private, investor-owned utilities for free. Utilities then consign these allowance to auction for sale and are required to use the proceeds for the benefit of ratepayers. The result: a twice-a-year climate credit on residential ratepayers' bills. This outcome reflects the multitude of other political forces needed for ongoing support of the program: consumer advocates who need to secure lower customer bills; utility companies that

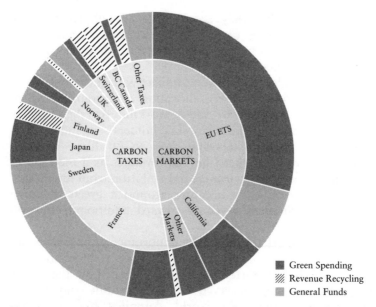

Figure 4.1 Global revenue use patterns for carbon taxes (left) and markets (right) in 2018

Source: World Bank, "Using Carbon Revenues," Partnership for Market Readiness Technical Note 16 (Aug. 2019).

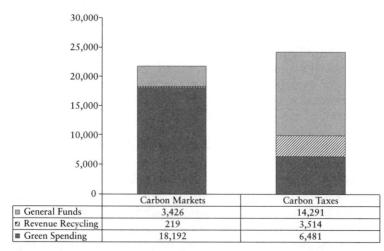

	Carbon Markets	Carbon Taxes
General Funds	3,426	14,291
Revenue Recycling	219	3,514
Green Spending	18,192	6,481

Figure 4.2 Revenue uses by policy instrument (million USD in 2018)

Source: World Bank, "Using Carbon Revenues," Partnership for Market Readiness Technical Note 16 (Aug. 2019).

don't want climate policy costs to crowd out their ability to propose profit-making (and rate-increasing) investments; and policymakers who need to demonstrate that cherished policies don't cause a visible cost for residential customers, a huge voting bloc. Notably, policy proponents were able to lock this system into place via requirements that apply outside of an annual government appropriations process – and because these funds are never appropriated by governments, they do not show up in any of the data behind Figures 4.1 and 4.2.

In other contexts, the politics are different. Under the RGGI program, the details vary by state since each controls its own revenue spending (Figure 4.3). Most states devote most of the resources to green spending, with the majority of funds flowing to state energy efficiency and clean energy programs. A few states – such as Maryland and New Hampshire – use a portion of their proceeds for revenue recycling purposes. As policymakers try to have a bigger impact on the status quo, they will be forced to find the revenues they will need to compensate more groups that are disrupted – which, over

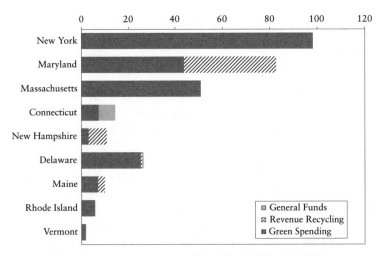

Figure 4.3 Revenue uses in RGGI (million USD in 2017)

Source: RGGI, "The Investment of RGGI Proceeds in 2017" (Oct. 2019), *https://www.rggi.org/investments/proceeds-investments.* We include reported spending on energy efficiency, clean energy, and climate mitigation in our "green spending" category.

time, may raise the use of revenue recycling and targeting to specific groups. However, at least in the early stages of implementation – when prices are low, revenues are small, and special interests are highly organized to capture them for green investments – the data show that revenue recycling plays only a minor player overall.

The RGGI program also reveals some of the political dynamics that can emerge when political leaders decide to re-purpose funds. The Governors of New York and New Jersey have both diverted RGGI revenues to the state's general fund at points in the program's history, raising concern from environmental NGOs and others who have supported a green spending agenda.[15] Similarly, California's Governor borrowed $500 million from California's green fund for the state's general budget fund in 2016.[16] That these experiences were noticed and generated some pushback suggests organized political support for green spending is resilient.

So far, so good. Revenues from market-based systems are smaller than might be imagined. And while the details differ from market to market, at least the political forces seem to favor greenery.

Why green spending becomes green pork

Unfortunately, the political and institutional forces that yield green spending have not generated the same scrutiny of whether green spending is actually producing much greenery. Instead, what has happened to these programs is pork. In politics, pork is an expenditure that is designed to disproportionately benefit other a special interest rather than the broader public good. This could be, for example, a prominent employer or campaign donor in the district of a politician who is concerned about the impact of carbon prices on his or her constituents; or it could be the pet project of an NGO that reliably promotes the climate policymaker's excellence with the general public. In the world of spending, green pork is the result when expenditures are cloaked in the green rhetoric of climate benefits, but motivated primarily by other political objectives.

Some politically oriented spending may well be necessary, so we don't mean to suggest that all pork is bad. What's so problematic about green pork is its tendency to produce spending that is politically inefficient: that is, money that is essentially diverted away from the most effective means of purchasing political support for more ambitious carbon pricing, or delivering true public goods in the form of environmentally effective investments. Because recipients of wasteful green pork spending become entrenched and organize to retain their funding, politically suboptimal commitments can get locked into place.

The central reason why green spending becomes pork is institutional. Where financial spending mechanisms are disconnected from the rigorous systems of accountability typical of public finance, it is easy for special interest groups to channel resources to favored causes without normal scrutiny. Most cap-and-trade spending programs have minimal transparency and oversight of carbon revenue expenditures; when spending decisions are made by entities outside of the central budgeting process, there are fewer public interest stakeholders and there is less sunlight shining on the process. All these attributes make it harder for political constituencies that favor more diligent spending to organize and be effective. Because the funds are small, at least at the outset, the potential benefit from such political mobilization is small and elusive. Without political allies to support better choices, green spending tends to become green pork.

What's particularly interesting is that two different kinds of pork operate under the same banner of greenery. One is traditional pork that re-brands as green: some interest groups that are pursuing self-interested goals that are largely unrelated to climate can plausibly assert minimal climate co-benefits, and therefore make a claim of being green. (The possibilities here are enormous because practically everything is linked to climate change one way or another.) This kind of pork, if essential to holding political support and narrowly targeted, is often critically important in the messy world of politics.

The second kind of green pork is more pernicious: spending motivated to address the climate problem but not scrutinized for real impact. This is money that green groups – usually the ones that are already organized to support carbon markets and thus best positioned to understand and manipulate how the funds are allocated – want spent on their theory of greenery. There are many worthy causes when it comes to climate change, such as funding for land conservation, environmentally friendly agricultural practices, and a variety of applications that are not unrelated to climate pollution. Because this mix of goals is complex – and because proponents can purposely hide behind the lack of clear missions or metrics in unsupervised green spending programs – it is hard to smell the pork, let alone redirect the funds in ways that more directly contribute to the long-term challenges of decarbonization. Public interest finance watchdogs that do such a good job in this role in other areas of public finance tend to focus on other topics where the money is bigger and the waste more apparent. Despite the prominence of green spending in nearly every market-based approach to climate pollution, however, there is almost no independent research that scrutinizes the effectiveness of carbon revenue spending portfolios.

Not only do special interests have an outsized influence in generating porky outcomes, but policymakers themselves have a strong tendency to use carbon revenues to pursue politically motivated goals rather than real greenery. Over time, policymakers may come to look at special green funds as tempting targets. That role can lead to mission creep as funds are diverted toward non-climate ends, including spending earmarked for political leaders' self-interest.

Fortuitously, it is now possible to measure (often imperfectly) the efficacy of these expenditure programs. And the results reveal how variation in institutional discipline – one of the key explanatory factors we identified in chapter 1 – explains variations in the quality of green spending. We begin with California because the data are increasingly clear and the state's spending strategy is seen as a model for emulation. Unfortunately, California's experience with carbon revenue spending illustrates how even the most celebrated spending programs face major challenges to the effective use of scarce public funding. Funds collected from carbon market auctions go to the state's Greenhouse Gas Reduction Fund, from which most funds are appropriated in support of a portfolio of expenditures called the California Climate Investments

(CCI). State law requires that all of these funds go to support climate mitigation activities, at least in theory; but policymakers have, over time, increasingly diverted these funds to activities that have little to do with climate mitigation.[17]

By March 2020, California's cap-and-trade auctions had collected $12.5 billion, of which $5.3 billion had been fully appropriated and implemented by specific CCI projects.[18] (The bulk of the remainder has been appropriated to specific government agencies and programs, but not yet fully implemented.) Periodic metrics purport to align self-reported costs and projected emission benefits of these projects, although the agency process that generates those data does not undergo independent analysis or external review. Notably, the reporting metrics calculate the cost-effectiveness on a dollar-per-ton basis using each project's total expected climate benefits, but only the portion of the project funding that is attributable to auction revenues.[19] This dramatically overstates the cost-effectiveness of funded projects because on average these projects receive about $3 in non-climate funds for every $1 in carbon revenues. Thus, the climate regulator's self-reported cost-effectiveness averages $99 per ton CO_2-equivalent across its portfolio of green spending as of March 2020;[20] but once that number is recalculated by looking at total project costs and total project benefits, it clocks in at $478 per ton CO_2-equivalent (see Figure 4.4). For comparison, state carbon prices have remained below $18 per ton CO_2-equivalent through 2019 and the state's climate regulator projects that even the most ambitious regulatory policies planned for the state's 2030 climate limits will cost no more than $200 per ton CO_2-equivalent.

Even if all of the self-reported costs and benefits are perfectly accurate, California's climate spending is not a particularly cost-effective way to appropriate limited public funds in the service of climate solutions. While some of the state's spending might be targeting transformative investments – and a great deal is surely going to projects that predominantly benefit local air pollution and economic development, rather than global climate change – the governance and oversight regimes are not designed to put a priority on spending that maximizes climate benefits. It remains extremely difficult to discern the transformative from the

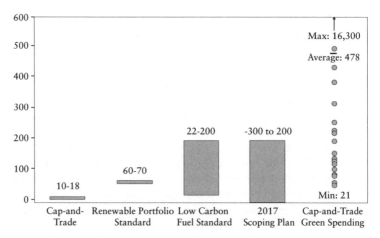

Figure 4.4   California climate policies and their equivalent carbon prices (USD per tCO$_2$-equivalent)

Source: Danny Cullenward, "Testimony before the California Senate Budget and Fiscal Committee" (Feb. 18, 2020), *https://www.ghgpolicy. org/law-and-policy/climate-budget-2020-2021.* Individual data citations available in testimony; green spending costs updated based on California Air Resources Board, "California Climate Investments: 2020 Annual Report" (Mar. 2020), *http://www.caclimateinvestments.ca.gov/annual-report.*

transactional – an opacity that survives because it serves interests that benefit most when the system is opaque.

The RGGI program provides a useful counterpoint, as the organizations that spend RGGI funds are better designed to provide more discipline and accountability on how those funds are spent. Because RGGI states use the vast majority of their funds to support utility energy efficiency programs or reduce customer bills, both of which are typically overseen by state utility regulators that have more robust systems of accountability anchored in public finance – the temptation is reduced for a climate policymaker to become political kingmaker or for a broad array of special interest groups to make the case for healthy forests, climate-resilient soils, or whatever green-flavored spin on their self-interest resonates at the moment. State clean energy programs are not without their complications and potential shortcomings, but a robust ecosystem of analysis has developed and is situated in a well-established regulatory context in which consumer, environmental, and utility advocates can also express their views.[21] Similarly, California's climate dividend program to provide rebates to utility customers is overseen by the state utility regulator in a public process that is highly accountable. The contrast with green spending programs' near-total lack of independent oversight is notable.

Finally, we note that the largest source of carbon revenues on the planet is also the least transparent in terms of how those funds are spent. Following the EU's successful reforms to increase EU ETS program ambitions, prices rose and revenues skyrocketed to €14 billion in 2018 (Figure 4.5). The volume of those funds is clear, but their ultimate use remains opaque and understudied.[22] As far as we can tell, member countries self-report only the aggregate funds spent on climate-related purposes. What counts, and how that definition varies by country, remains a mystery.

Nevertheless, an interesting pattern emerges when comparing outcomes across the core fifteen EU member

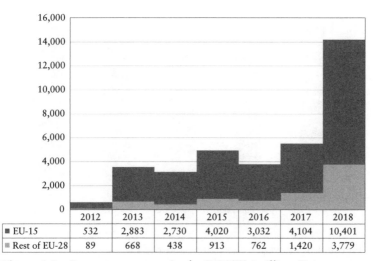

	2012	2013	2014	2015	2016	2017	2018
■ EU-15	532	2,883	2,730	4,020	3,032	4,104	10,401
■ Rest of EU-28	89	668	438	913	762	1,420	3,779

Figure 4.5 Program revenues in the EU ETS (million €)

Source: European Commission, "Report from the Commission to the European Parliament and the Council, Report on the Functioning of the European Carbon Market," COM/2019/557 final/2 (Jan. 16, 2020), *https://eur-lex.europa.eu/legal-content/EN/TXT/?uri=CELEX:52019DC 0557R(01).*

states (including the United Kingdom) with those that subsequently joined to form the EU-28 (see Figure 4.6). The EU-15 member states dominate the GDP statistics for the EU as a whole, but receive a smaller proportion of program revenues – reflecting the fact that many of the non-core members, like Poland, have more carbon-intensive economies. These different groups also make different spending choices. The EU-15 member states report that 88% of their revenues are dedicated to green spending, accounting for 83% of the total EU ETS funds going toward those purposes. In contrast, the broader EU-28 membership reports spending just 54% of their revenues on green spending outcomes, delivering only 17% of the total funds EU ETS dedicated toward those ends. In short, the wealthy European nations dominate the green spending agenda for the EU ETS as a whole, allowing the EU's newer (and often less wealthy and less politically green) members to spend funds on a broader array of politically motivated outcomes.

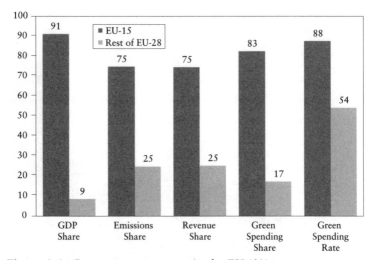

Figure 4.6   Revenue use patterns in the EU (%)

Source: European Commission, Commission Staff Working Document, Technical Information, "Report from the European Commission to the European Parliament and the Council EU and the Paris Climate Agreement: Taking Stock of Progress at Katowice COP," SWD(2018) 453 final, document 52018SC0453, *https://eur-lex.europa.eu/legal-content/EN/ALL/?uri=SWD:2018:453:FIN.*

Conclusion

Low market prices, limited sectoral coverage, and extensive free allowance allocation significantly reduce the amount of revenue that climate policymakers collect from real-world markets. With smaller revenues, special interests are better able to organize to capture funds, especially when revenues are appropriated outside the normal institutional processes for public finance. All the talk about market-based strategies for controlling pollution has led to extensive analysis of options for recycling the vast revenues that might come from these systems. But a much smaller and different model – green spending – has dominated in practice.

Subjecting green spending to fiscal discipline has proven difficult, however, so much of the money has gone instead to pork. Not all pork is bad; some amount of politically efficient pork can generate coalitions in support of higher prices and therefore greater revenues. But if large portions of climate funds are handed out too liberally for green pork, then the opportunity to use revenues to advance the goals of deep decarbonization will be lost. Where we can measure that opportunity, such as in California, there is a massive disconnect between how the society is actually spending precious revenues and the real opportunities for cost-effective deep decarbonization. The lack of independent oversight and accountability allows special interests to capture limited public funds and operate as insiders. Program administrators that control funds become powerful political players themselves, capable of funding NGO and academic allies to increase their own power and retain control in the policymaking arena.

In the next chapter, we follow the same trail of special interests aided by opaque procedures, insider status, and the lack of sufficiently powerful independent oversight to look at another pernicious element of cap-and-trade programs: carbon offsets. Carbon offsets reduce public revenues because they enable polluters to skip paying the government for allowances and instead offer firms an alternative form of cap-and-trade program compliance – with the flow of funds directed by climate policymakers and allied environmental NGOs, all outside of the normal channels of public finance. With minimal oversight, powerful incumbents push for quantity, not quality; as a result, offsets end up enriching a small number of special interests at the expense of climate policy ambition.

5
Offsets

The previous three chapters have addressed the internal design and implementation of market programs. Now we turn to the relationship between those markets and the outside world. Those outside relationships are an essential part of the story if markets are to proliferate from their geographically disparate origins to cover, eventually, the whole planet. Greenhouse gases warm the climate regardless of wherever they are emitted geographically; emission reductions, therefore, are valuable to the climate wherever they are physically realized.[1] In this chapter we look at one type of outside relationship, called offsets, and in chapter 6 we look at another, formal links between markets.

"Offsets" are emission credits that are earned one-off: a firm that wants to earn a credit identifies an emission-reducing project – potentially anywhere in the world, if the rules that govern offsets allow. The project developer estimates the level of credit they should earn from the project, and then files an application with the market administrator to gain credit.[2] Offset credits are valuable when cap-and-trade program regulations allow covered emitters to use offsets to cover a portion of their compliance obligations, effectively increasing emissions within capped sectors on the theory that offsets recognize a corresponding amount of emission reductions outside of capped sectors. In other words, offsets are designed to change *where* reductions occur, but not the total amount.[3]

If this sounds complex, that's because it is. Offsets' complexity is why most theoretical studies of emissions trading schemes favor direct links between cap-and-trade programs – direct links don't require the resource-intensive project-by-project or sector-by-sector approach used to award offset credits. Because offset programs impose significant transaction costs and focus on relatively narrow applications, the standard theoretical view is that direct market links offer a superior mechanism for cooperation. What we observe in the real world, however, is the opposite. Offsets are the main mechanism for cross-border cooperation. But the quality of those offsets is particularly low – so low, in fact, that we will argue that essentially all offsets should be prohibited.

According to the standard theory of emission market design, offsets are important for two reasons. First, carbon offsets lower polluters' compliance costs, and therefore their opposition to climate policy. Second, carbon offsets extend the incentives of carbon pricing to sectors and jurisdictions that lack their own pollution markets. Some even believe that by exporting voluntary climate policy incentives, carbon offsets also encourage the expansion of legally binding climate policies – potentially even new markets that link together – as policymakers learn about new sectors and new sectors become comfortable with market-based regulations.

This chapter shows why the practical experience is completely different. Offset programs are plagued by environmental quality problems because they create rents and special interest groups that entrench low-quality programs, rather than expanding the opportunity for real emission cuts. This dark outcome reflects the politics of markets, which tilt carbon offset rules heavily in favor of regulated emitters' interests.

Incumbent firms are highly motivated to increase the volume of compliance instruments, and generally indifferent about whether offsets preserve environmental integrity. They seek quantity, not quality. The stewards of quality – such as environmental groups and regulatory staff – tend to be focused on other missions, under-resourced, and unwilling to self-criticize. Some are unaware that the systems for administering offsets are systematically biased in favor of low-quality projects, perhaps in part because the more robust project assessments that reveal this fact are mind-numbingly complex. Others are better informed, but nevertheless accept – or even promote – dubious offset schemes because they imagine that other benefits, such as engaging industry or generating revenues for prized purposes, are worth the cost. They imagine that funds attracted can be used for worthy purposes – for example, conservation and other forms of payment-based "ecosystem services" – but do not recognize that scaling up a funding system anchored on low-quality projects is bound to crash.

Complex arguments about why the quality of offsets can and will improve are proffered, but – once the complexity is stripped away and the evidence comes into focus – it is hard to escape the conclusion that offsets have allowed higher volumes of emission credits and lower compliance costs primarily by eroding environmental quality. Better outcomes are possible in theory, but there is no potent constituency that favors the reforms needed. For the most part, offset programs offer a stealthy strategy for emitters to water down program ambitions.

Not only do the politics of offsets explain why low-quality programs become entrenched, but they also help explain the geography of the offset projects that policymakers approve. Textbook theory suggests that offset policies should be designed to encourage firms and investors to shop the world to find the cheapest projects, wherever they might be located. The biggest opportunities are typically overseas – in places where poor administration leads to inefficient behavior that causes high emissions. Many offset programs are designed with this logic – allowing, in principle, geographically diverse efforts to reduce emissions that support policymakers' claims that market systems will deliver benefits both at home and around the world. Politically, however, global interests are rarely as well organized or politically influential in local markets as local interests. Thus, the logic of "shop the world" gives way, at least in part, to "buy local." Industry may love all varieties of offset credits equally, but there is not much political support for far-flung offset projects.

In contrast, local offset projects – whether high quality or not – create relevant political constituencies in the form of domestic investment and, potentially, co-benefits to environmental concerns like local air or water quality.

The political logic we outline in this chapter explains why offsets always fall short of their promise. The most important reason is that incumbent emitters care primarily about compliance costs, and therefore seek quantity over quality. That interest leads them to seek generous offset rules, including rules that allow them to "shop the world." Far-flung emission credits satisfy industry's demands, but have no constituency of their own. When scandalous evidence of poorly administered offsets emerges, reform follows a predictable logic. Well-organized political groups all get their say; offset rules are pared back and re-focused locally, where they have stronger supporters who are politically powerful in the local jurisdiction where offset rules are set. Despite all these reforms, the problem of assuring quality remains – a problem so serious that we think it can't be solved.

This political logic also explains why offsets can create perverse incentives for groups to resist mandatory emission reductions. Offset credits are issued only when a regulator deems the emission-reducing activity to be additional; if that reduction is separately required by law, then it is no longer additional. Thus, rather than expand the reach of climate policy through voluntary initiatives, offsets end up creating strong incentives for emitters to entrench and oppose the expansion of legally binding policy regimes.

Why quality lacks a constituency

The fundamental challenge of carbon offsets arises from the fact that credits are awarded on the basis of purported climate benefits that can only be estimated, never observed. In order to generate real emission reductions, offset projects must be "additional": that is, they must reflect efforts that would not happen in the absence of the extra value provided by the offset credit. The additionality standard is extremely difficult to operationalize because the only thing policymakers can observe is the conditions that occur after a project is pursued, not what conditions would have been if an offset project were not funded. Offset credits must be based on the difference between these scenarios: what happened with the offset investment, and what would have happened counterfactually without it. Although the necessary calculations might be tractable with enough effort, political forces put a heavy thumb on the scale.

The concept of additionality can be vexing to those encountering it for the first time. Readers with a legal background may recognize it as essentially the same as the concept of "proximate cause" in torts law: an offset project that is additional is a "but-for" cause of the emission reductions it credits as well as the causal force most responsible for explaining avoided or reduced emissions. Put simply, an offset project claims that bad things will happen unless it receives a valuable offset credit to do better.

Additionality can be framed in a positive or a negative light. The offsets industry chooses the positive framing, of course. In the case of a forest carbon offset, for example, a project proponent would say: "If climate regulators see fit to award us offset credits, we can leverage sustainable finance to deliver climate benefits and healthy forests. This creates a win-win outcome that won't happen on its own, but can be achieved with your permission to earn offset credits and our triple-bottom-line investment strategy." A more direct argument lays bare the incentives: "Give us an offset credit or we'll cut down these trees." The key insight is that the project proponent claims emissions will be relatively higher without offset credits, and that solely as the result of a regulator issuing offset credits, emissions will go down by a corresponding amount.

Although offsets are generally portrayed as environmentally friendly, the logic of additionality is actually quite sinister. Additionality is critical because regulated firms can use offset credits to comply with cap-and-trade program limits, so every offset credit that is issued enables higher pollution within the cap-and-trade program. Offsets will do no harm if and only if every credit reflects a real emission reduction to account for the higher emissions allowed within the closely administered core cap-and-trade system – if quality is assured, there is no net change in climate pollution. Perfection is required because anything less undermines climate progress.[4] Yet perfection is a hard standard to meet, especially when there are political and administrative forces arrayed against the public interest.

Not only do offsets require counterfactual estimates about the offset project itself, but they also require detailed counterfactual knowledge about competing projects and market conditions. For example, if a forest carbon offset project causes a certain forest parcel owner to adopt sustainable management practices that increase forest carbon stocks, what effect does this have on neighboring forest parcel owners or on substitute commodity markets? We know that drivers of deforestation, for example, don't disappear simply because certain landowners protect their holdings; even if they were prepared to clear-cut their land prior to earning an offset credit, but now are prepared to manage the land wisely with credits in hand, that doesn't eliminate demand for the forest products that created the incentive to clear-cut in the first place. Some of the avoided harvest will be displaced to other lands, causing emission leakage. Estimating emission leakage for issues like forest protections is an incredibly difficult task because, just as with additionality, it can't be observed directly but can only be estimated as a counterfactual. Few credible estimates exist for important sectors that receive offset credits (such as forestry), and therefore offset policies often lack a scientific basis for key parameters like leakage factors that set the number of credits that are awarded to participating projects.

Climate policymakers have approached the offsets debate as though these technical issues can be resolved with sufficient engagement from non-profit, scientific, and other concerned stakeholders. Their mindset is that, with a sufficiently large phalanx of government staff and outside partners, the scientific and social complexity of additionality, leakage, and other technical problems could be managed to perfection. In practice, however, the deck is stacked against exactly these outcomes because the most powerful stakeholders – regulated industries – care first and foremost about lowering overall compliance costs. That is, they demand high volumes of low-cost offsets to keep carbon prices low. Policymakers tend to deliver these outcomes, especially when prominent environmental groups and scientists provide public cover for their actions.

In contrast, the forces that seek high-quality offsets are politically weaker and relatively disorganized. Environmental justice organizations strongly oppose offsets because large stationary-source emitters whose facilities are located in low-income communities of color rely on offsets to maintain business-as-usual while claiming someone else has reduced emissions.[5] But these groups generally lack influence with market administrators, in no small part because they tend to oppose all cap-and-trade programs, which they see as mechanisms to perpetuate inequitable pollution outcomes under the guise of economic efficiency. Thus, even the environmental justice community's most organized efforts to point out the flaws of offset policies are generally not welcomed by policymakers. Beyond environmental justice criticisms, few other environmental NGOs have carefully studied offset risks and are willing to invest resources in the maddening effort to require quality in a field where quality can only be estimated, not observed. Regulators, too, lack the capacity to manage these issues with the care that would be needed to do the job well. For example, California has only eight staff members working on its carbon offsets team.[6] It is a questionable assertion that eight staff members could monitor seven offset protocols that purport to estimate what is almost but not quite feasible under fast-evolving market conditions in sectors as wide-ranging as North American forests, tropical forests, methane capture at coal and trona mines, methane capture at dairies, and rice production.[7] It is likely that most of the California regulators' staff time goes into managing paperwork and compliance requirements for an industry that is worth more than $1 billion to date. The volume and complexity of the offsets market are simply overwhelming for a small staff.

Why knife-edge incentives encourage low quality

Beyond the structural imbalance between pro-quality and pro-quantity constituencies, the economics of additionality leads to a pernicious problem we call knife-edge incentives. In order to deliver cost containment, regulated industries and policymakers seek high volumes of offsets at the lowest cost. Ironically, the economics of this goal dramatically increases the risks that offset projects will be awarded credits even when the projects don't achieve all (or any) of the additional emission reductions claimed.

In order to meet the additionality standard, an offset project must claim that its emission-reducing activity is economically infeasible in isolation – otherwise, the project could be financed on its own without an offset credit. But a low-cost offset project is also claiming to be *just barely infeasible*: that is, the project almost makes sense on its own, but purportedly doesn't unless climate regulators award it an offset credit. Infeasibility is a binary condition, but the real-world circumstances that define what is feasible rarely sit neatly inside or outside the feasibility box. Small changes in commodity prices, technology, and market conditions could easily swing a project into economic feasibility in the absence of offset credit incentives – many of those changes are hard for regulators to observe. Similarly, if project proponents put their thumb on the scale – even just a little – they may be able to show how a project that would be pursued on its own merits looks to be just barely infeasible in the context of an offset additionality claim. A project claiming low costs stands on a knife's edge: a small change in project costs in one direction makes it truly additional, and a small change in the other direction makes it totally non-additional. Under these technical conditions, a completely one-side political economy takes effect with predictable results.

An extreme example shows how knife-edge incentives penalize activities that would be truly additional. Consider direct air capture (DAC) technologies that remove low-concentration CO_2 out of the ambient air for geologic sequestration or industrial application. These technologies could conceivably play an important role in cleaning up excess pollution, especially as society gets much more concerned about rapid warming. But they are prohibitively expensive today. Some three startup companies are developing pilot projects with costs estimated at up to $600/tCO_2 or more: that is, one to two orders of magnitude more expensive than explicit carbon prices observed in the real world.[8] Unlike a low-cost offset project, one can be extremely confident that a DAC project will deliver truly additional credits – there is no knife-edge concern because the economics of DAC are so unattractive with today's emission credit prices. In contrast, incumbents seeking to maximize offset credits will avoid things that are hard and costly and seek, instead, projects as close to the knife's edge as possible.

Offsets consistently end up with low quality in the real world because the forces that prefer quantity dominate those that prefer quality and because low-price offsets that satisfy emitters' demand for quantity are the most likely to be non-additional in the first place. A brief review of the major programs confirms these observations.

The first major offset program was called the Clean Development Mechanism (CDM), a voluntary international structure under the 1997 Kyoto Protocol that allowed wealthy countries that pledged legally binding emission cuts to earn credit for low-carbon investments in developing countries that did not. The experience with the CDM was, in short, a disaster. Project-level additionality assessments encouraged developers to fudge their numbers and even deploy capital to create more pollution they would then destroy in return for more offset credits.[9] Similar games were observed in the Joint Implementation (JI) program, a comparable structure for voluntary trading with former Soviet Union countries under the Kyoto Protocol.[10] Most of the CDM credits were purchased for use in the EU's carbon market, although others were used by Japan and other countries to comply with their Kyoto pledges. All told, more than a billion CDM and JI credits were used in the EU ETS.[11] But as concerns grew about the quality of CDM credits, the EU moved to restrict CDM eligibility, banning the use of the most problematic projects going forward and limiting the total number of credits that could be used. Ultimately, a comprehensive study commissioned by the European Commission found that 73% of potential total CDM offset supplies have a low likelihood of producing real emission reductions that satisfy the additionality standard, with only 7% of potential total supplies delivering a high likelihood of the same.[12] As of this writing, the EU has indicated that it does not intend to use any international offsets in its carbon market going forward[13] – but the EU ETS is still recovering from a market-wide supply–demand imbalance caused, in part, by the use of more than a billion questionable offset credits.

The other major carbon offset program is found in California; the northeastern states' market, RGGI, does allow but hasn't relied on any significant number of offsets, perhaps because the carbon price is too low for offsets to make much of a difference to polluters' bottom lines.[14] California has promoted its approach to offsets as learning from the lessons of the CDM, but in practice it faces the same technical challenges surrounding the calculation of additionality, leakage, and other critical factors that proved problematic in that program.[15] As of May 2020, California had issued just over 174 million offset credits, with about 80% of these credits coming from projects that claimed to reduce or avoid emissions from forests.[16] A significant and ongoing controversy is brewing over the environmental integrity of the state's forest offset protocol, with recent research arguing that the protocol's treatment of leakage leads to 82% of its credits likely not representing real emission reductions.[17] This work led a group of state legislators to raise concerns with the program administrator, which dismissed all criticisms and promised further but unspecified review of the forest offset protocol.[18] Time will tell how policymakers and the research community respond, but for all the back-and-forth between the program's critics and defenders, it is undisputed that there is no specific evidence or study underlying the regulator's choice of leakage factors.[19]

Time and time again offset programs become large, cheap, and low quality. An enormous volume of pro-offsets material is put out by program beneficiaries, allied environmental groups that seek funding for conservation finance, and researchers who share donors and policy goals with their

environmental NGO allies. Much of this effort is put forward
in good faith: there can be no escaping the fact that progress
in sectors that tend to benefit from offsets, like forests and
agriculture, will be an essential part of an effective global
climate response. But offset project developers, financiers,
and traders all make their money on the basis of the regulations the government develops, often with these same players'
involvement. In turn, this constituency has a powerful and
concentrated interest in defending the regulatory system in
which it operates.

Conflicts of interest run rife in the offsets world. Many
non-profit and for-profit firms have become so closely
involved in the operation of carbon offset programs that it
is hard to tell the difference between the interests of these
groups and the offset program itself. One large environmental NGO recently told a court that it "helped develop
and implement California's cap-and-trade program, particularly its offsets program," and "is intimately familiar with
its history and technical aspects" as a result.[20] Conflicts are
arguably even greater among for-profit enterprises, which
play a large role in the implementation and verification of
carbon offset regimes.[21] As leading climate strategist Hal
Harvey recently noted, the firms that verify offset projects'
purported emission reductions are nearly always paid by the
project developers themselves.[22] The same firms often help
write the regulations they help offset developers implement.
A prominent consulting firm even advertises on its website
that it helped write the standards for earning offset credits
in a specific application for which it also collects the data
that the US government uses for its official emissions
inventory.[23] Offsets were intended to align market forces
with environmental protection, but have not.

Once one cuts through all the noise, it is hard to avoid
the conclusion that real-world offset programs are set up in
ways that stealthily weaken the ambition of carbon pricing
programs. The problems with offsets are structural, not
experiential, and therefore offsets have limited potential for
reform. On promise that the science and economics will be
perfect – and despite the opacity, minimal administrative
oversight, and heavy greenwashing observed in practice –
offsets allow incumbent emitters to buy their way, cheaply,

out of the obligation to reduce capped emissions from the
conventional fossil fuel energy system.

Why political forces favor local offsets

Carbon offset programs were initially set up under a theory
of change that sought to tap emission reductions wherever in
the world they can be found cheaply. For example, the CDM
program was developed so that wealthier countries that took
legally binding pledges under the Kyoto Protocol would
be able to invest in emission-reducing projects that would
aid sustainable development in developing countries that
didn't face any mandatory cuts in emissions. California has
also promoted a variety of offset-related activities abroad,
most notably in the form of its Tropical Forest Standard, an
international forest crediting program the state approved for
others' use in September 2019;[24] for years, the California Air
Resources Board advocated the use of international forest
offsets in its cap-and-trade program, mirroring the basic
approach to global affairs seen in the CDM.[25]

The problem with a global approach to emission reductions is that it isn't well aligned with the politics back at
home. The story with local offsets is different precisely
because local offset projects create tangible political benefits.
Investing in local offsets – whether high quality or not
– supports jobs, economic development, and local environmental benefits. These outcomes seed political support in
constituencies that matter to those operating cap-and-trade
programs. For example, a significant number of forest carbon
offsets in California come from lands managed by the Yurok
tribe, a Native American people who live in the far northern
part of the state. Although the use of carbon offsets is controversial within the Yurok tribe – some members of which
outright oppose the use of offsets as a form of environmental
injustice, for example, or as a neocolonial exploitation of
the natural world – it has become a significant share of
the tribe's discretionary income and a visible force in state
politics, from Yurok ancestral lands on the Klamath River
in Del Norte County to the halls of the state capitol building

in Sacramento.[26] Although some of these same issues are surely present in other forests participating in California's offset program, the fact is that they don't matter as much to California politicians when they arise in Alaska.

A dynamic theory of offset politics helps explain how general concern about the quality of offsets leads policymakers, first, to impose restrictions on far-flung offsets before they reduce investment in local projects. The first major example of this phenomenon occurred in California, which not only reduced offset usage in a 2017 bill, but also limited far-flung offsets to no more than half of total usage limits.[27] Similar restrictions have since emerged in a number of US jurisdictions considering or adopting carbon pricing policies. Oregon, for example, considered cap-and-trade legislation that fell short in 2019, but which included similar limits on far-flung offsets;[28] Washington State is discussing the same concept as of this writing.[29] New York made news in 2019 for adopting a comprehensive state-wide climate law that establishes a state-wide carbon neutrality standard with minimal offsetting. Not only would offsets be restricted to just 15% of state-wide baseline emissions, but all offset projects are required to be located within 25 miles of the emissions source using its credits "to the extent practicable."[30] Europe, too, exemplifies a similar type of restriction – as mentioned above, the EU intends to prohibit all international offset credits in its post-2020 carbon market.[31]

Thus, when push comes to shove, the market philosophy of "shop the world" gives way to "buy local." Carbon offsets have greater political support when they create local benefits, no matter the quality or price of those offset projects. Even though the supply of local offsets is likely to be much smaller and more expensive than a geographically broader search would obtain, restricting far-flung offsets faces fewer political barriers than would limits that restrain domestic offset beneficiaries.

Why offsets entrench rather than expand markets

Finally, we address why, contrary to many hopes and bold policy claims, carbon offsets do not provide an initial entry point for market-based incentives to expand into new sectors and jurisdictions. Rather than encourage a proliferation of effective market-based policies abroad, the fact that offset schemes concentrate on low-quality credits helps explain why these schemes entrench and reduce the environmental integrity of their associated carbon markets. In theory, these schemes can lead to expansion; in reality, they yield the opposite.

The most important reason why offsets have not led to greater use of market-based policies is that the beneficiaries of offsets receive financial income that would be lost if emission reductions became mandatory. The additionality standard requires that credited emission-reducing activities are not required by law, which is necessary to make sure offsets compensate for the higher emissions they enable inside program caps. If the activities an offset protocol supports were to become mandatory – whether through direct regulation or the expansion of cap-and-trade to the sector hosting offsets projects – emission reduction projects would lose their opportunity to generate offsets. Instead, they would face the need to pay for mandated emission reductions instead. It's no wonder, then, that there aren't any examples of successful carbon offset programs that have evolved into mandatory reductions: every offset project creates a direct financial incentive to oppose that evolution.

In fact, there is even some evidence to suggest that offsets may perversely delay or prevent regulation. During the early years of the CDM, for example, some Latin American governments appear to have refrained from adopting mandatory clean energy policies because to do so would deprive projects of the potential to earn CDM credits.[32] More recently, representatives of the US federal government under the Obama Administration acknowledged considering how lost carbon revenues from California's coal mine methane capture protocol would affect coal mines when considering whether to regulate methane emissions from the same sources.[33] These examples illustrate how offsets create perverse incentives to avoid, rather than proliferate, mandatory climate policy in the sectors and jurisdictions that host offset projects.

Not all the evidence points in this pernicious direction. Some analysts have suggested that China's experience dominating the CDM market may have created a constituency of carbon trading experts, policymakers, and businesses that benefited from this process and therefore sought future opportunities to support the regional pilot markets or planned national market currently under development in China's power sector.[34] While it may be true that China's early experience with CDM offsets created a network of pro-market advocates that participated in the development of country's nascent climate policies, it would be a stretch to suggest these network effects were the primary drivers of Beijing's decision to promote climate policy in the run-up to the 2015 Paris Agreement and the subsequent decision to develop a national cap-and-trade program in the electricity sector.[35] China's domestic incentives to tackle local air pollution and enhance its global credibility as an emerging global power, for example, are surely far more significant considerations. There may well be effects from the exposure of individuals, firms, and governments to offsets, but these are likely to remain far less important than core political economy drivers of climate policy.[36]

Conclusion

Offset credits allow polluters to emit more within cap-and-trade programs in exchange for estimated emission reductions outside the program's boundaries. Program oversight is hard enough under idealized circumstances because estimated emission reductions turn on a counterfactual scenario that is never observed. Under real-world conditions, where political forces put heavy thumbs on the scales, accurate estimation becomes all but impossible. Regulated industries demand high volumes of low-cost offset credits in order to limit market-wide carbon prices. In contrast, groups that advocate for offset quality are weaker politically, less well organized, and less informed about the critical minute details of offset protocols. Worse, all these forces – which are aligned to create generous supplies of low-cost offsets – concentrate investment into projects that just barely meet knife-edge additionality criteria. The simplest and least costly projects that generate readily the largest volumes of credits crowd out more worthy, complex, and costly ventures.

Encouraged by non-profit organizations with conservation and other global missions, policymakers initially "shop the world" to find emission reductions wherever they are cheapest or most closely aligned with related policy goals. But overseas activities don't have much of a constituency in the local politics where offsets rules are created. Thus, as political opposition to offsets grows – as it does inevitably when more people probe the quality of such schemes – policymakers tend to first restrict the eligibility of distant projects. They prefer projects that deliver local economic, environmental, and political benefits at home.

And if all that isn't bad enough, offsets create perverse incentives. Rather than offer an initial step on the road to new markets and deeper market links, offsets become an entrenched source of cheap but low-quality compliance. They water down the ambition of cap-and-trade programs, and they create strong incentives to avoid further regulation because any legal requirement to reduce emissions would cut off the flow of funds from offset credits.

6

Market links

We now turn to a second type of interaction between local carbon markets and the outside world. The previous chapter showed why the practice of carbon offsetting has led to outcomes that diverge starkly from expectations. In this chapter, we do the same for direct, formal links between carbon markets.

In theory, direct linkage is the best way for carbon markets to expand their geographical coverage. And the best linkages will connect many markets of very different types such that programs with high compliance costs can benefit from access to programs where costs are much lower. Connecting markets that have large differences offers the opportunity to maximize the gains from trade. While that logic is impeccable, what we observe in the real world is the exact opposite pattern. Linkages between markets are rare and fleeting, and when they happen they occur between similar markets, where gains from trade are small.

The enthusiasm for market linkages has emerged because decades of climate diplomacy have failed to create a single global carbon market.[1] Instead, lots of different national and subnational policy strategies are bubbling "bottom-up." One of the many fears about pure bottom-upism is the lack of economic coherence that could arise if countries pursue climate policy at different paces. Market linkages would dampen these concerns by propagating the law of one price: linkages would create gains from trade and expand the geographical scope of market-based policies.[2] As market links proliferate, a broader international (eventually global) program might emerge – resulting in "one price to rule them all," as the cynical reference to J.R.R. Tolkien's *Lord of the Rings* trilogy goes – and begin to fill the gap left by the international community's inability to agree on a comprehensive, integrated global climate policy.

The practical experience with market links looks very different. Most markets feature low prices and limited ambition, reducing the potential for gains from cross-border trade. As we explained in chapter 2, Potemkin-market outcomes are not an accident but occur by design: climate policymakers enjoy greater control and face less political opposition when carbon prices are low and regulations are strong. Because only low-priced markets have been created, all one can observe so far are attempts to forge links between low-price systems. But deeper market links between differently priced systems are unlikely to ever be common, owing to political and institutional factors.

In this chapter, we explain this huge divergence between ideal theory – featuring lots of formalk, direct links between diverse systems and huge gains from trade – and the reality that links are rare and generate few gains from connection.

We do this in two steps. A first step explains why political leaders are wary of direct links. Those leaders are accountable to local interests, and they must focus on the complex task of responding to politically organized interest groups. In that context, direct links between markets are a political nightmare: they reduce the ability of political interventions to address local political concerns. They diminish control and also, when markets equilibrate, have the risk of generating capital outflows and other politically disadvantageous outcomes.

In fact, existing links involve not just similar market designs, but nearly identical ones. The dozen or so examples of market links can be grouped into three multilateral systems: the Western Climate Initiative (comprised of California and Québec), the Regional Greenhouse Gas Initiative (comprised of ten northeastern US states as of this writing, and likely to include more soon), and the European Union's Emissions Trading System (comprised of the core EU-27 nations, plus Iceland, Liechtenstein, Norway, and Switzerland, with the United Kingdom potentially linked in ways yet to be determined after Brexit).[3] There are no links between these three systems, nor any between them and any other country's program. Meanwhile, the links within each of these systems involve programs that are nearly identical in terms of their policy ambition, sectoral coverage, and use of free allowance allocation or auctioning.

Second, we explore why it has been easy for jurisdictions to announce that markets would be linked only to discover that the institutional capabilities on both sides of the linkage do not allow that outcome. The political benefits of announcing linkages are large and proximate, and the reckoning with the difficulties is easily pushed into the future. That reckoning, we show, hinges on the capabilities of political institutions to compensate domestic constituents whose political support is essential while preserving the integrity of the linked market system. We see little evidence that this capacity already exists – except perhaps in the European Union, where member states that see losses from climate policy have multiple institutional opportunities to negotiate for compensation and gains in other areas, including trade policy and intra-EU fiscal decisions.

A clear-eyed examination of the practical experience with market links is essential because the success of substantial linking within Europe must be understood for what it is: an aberration built on the unusual conditions of strong, shared governing institutions and systems for accountability that were built over more than five decades as Europe (mostly) coalesced into a common economic and political system. Outside of Europe, there is no evidence that market links themselves have encouraged the expansion of cap-and-trade programs to new jurisdictions. Because market links tend to create more political problems than they solve, it may well be that the pattern of market linking today represents something close to the upper bound on what is possible with bottom-up carbon market cooperation, rather than a stepping stone on the road to a global carbon market.

Why links are rare, thin, and between similar systems

What is a market link? Mechanically speaking, linked markets feature the mutual recognition of allowances and offsets, such that compliance instruments from one jurisdiction are valid for compliance purposes in the other(s). The building block of market links is the unilateral recognition that one jurisdiction makes with respect to another's compliance instruments. When two jurisdictions execute unilateral links with one another, they form a bilateral link; when multiple jurisdictions execute reciprocal links, they form a multilateral link.[4] The economic effect of market links, in turn, reflects the fungibility of each type of compliance instrument in each market. Whereas before a link each market's compliance instruments would trade on separate terms, such that California's allowances might cost one price and Québec's allowances another, the cross-fungibility of these instruments following a market link causes their prices to converge. From the standpoint of the instruments' ultimate buyers – that is, polluters who face compliance obligations under domestic program rules – each type of compliance instrument in a linked market is as good as the next.[5]

Diplomats wired the core logic of market links into the 1992 United Nations Framework Convention on Climate Change, which envisioned that countries would begin to reduce their emissions and would use efficient market instruments where possible to achieve that outcome. Even more explicitly, the 1997 Kyoto Protocol formally outlined a plan for industrialized and developing countries to participate in a global trade of emission credits. Efforts undertaken by wealthier nations, which faced binding limits on emissions under the Kyoto agreement, would be combined with offsets sourced voluntarily from developing economies. Countries that took binding targets could trade amongst one another to achieve their shared goals at lower overall costs.[6] Some governments acted on this theory, taking initial steps to harness the power of markets to reduce emissions. And that momentum continued, at least on paper, with Article 6 of the 2015 Paris Agreement, which contemplates international trading of countries' emission reduction pledges.[7]

Despite decades of advocacy and efforts to include formal market links in the framework treaties and agreements underlying international climate change policy, there are few examples of such links. Those that exist today are between programs with similar prices and nearly identical program designs, featuring either a shared market design or minor variations on the approach taken by linked programs covering the same sectors with similar levels of ambition.

Given the potential gains from trade, what explains the limited extent of market links, their relative thinness, and why they occur between similar programs rather than markets with divergent prices where joint gains would be larger?

The simple answer is that market links introduce profound new political challenges. Deep market links between programs with divergent prices or distinct market designs will lead to capital outflows, as market forces, not policymakers, dictate where investments, emission reductions, and a variety of co-benefits arise. By definition, a link producing significant gains from trade will rearrange where those outcomes occur. The greater the difference in the programs' pre-existing prices, the larger the potential for capital outflows; and the greater the difference in program designs, the bigger the challenge of managing the consequences of any such capital outflows on business and labour interests. Yet as we showed in chapters 2 and 3, real-world policymakers prefer to rely more heavily on regulations than markets in the first place; and when they use markets, they accommodate sensitive consumer and business interests with sector-specific strategies that involve significant government intervention and generous allowance allocations. No wonder governments are reluctant to forge deep market links.

Gains from trade could be realized if relatively high- and low-priced systems were to link together and converge on an intermediate price. Under these conditions, the formerly high-priced jurisdiction would benefit from lower costs, but largely via capital outflows to the formerly low-priced jurisdiction, which would see the prices its industries pay rise as a result. These challenges can be mitigated, and perhaps some of the benefits of trade can be realized, if sufficiently robust

government institutions are in place to manage the consequences of capital outflows and compensate well-organized
interest groups that are negatively affected on both sides of
a market link. But the fundamental consequence of a deep
market link would be to destabilize the domestic accommodations policymakers had initially developed with respect
to ambition and variation in sectoral treatment in the design
of their initial programs. If the individual program administrators are not already capable of managing the political
consequences of a significant shift in market prices prior
to a market link, there is little reason to think a market
link between high- and low-price systems will be politically
sustainable.

The institutional challenges of managing cross-border
market governance are particularly acute for subnational
governments. Of the three multilateral systems in existence,
two are led by subnational governments in North America:
the WCI and RGGI programs. Subnational governments
are more aggressive on climate change than their respective
national governments. The political forces that generate these
outcomes are unlikely to change, but, as discussed in chapter
2, subnational governments lack the legal authority to sign
treaties. The agreements they produce are voluntary, and
therefore the market links they support are fragile and thin.

Critically, subnational governments are unable to sign
legally binding treaties or otherwise effect mandatory cooperation agreements with foreign governments.[8] Indeed, even
the non-binding agreement governing the WCI program[9]
– signed by California, Québec, and Ontario – has recently
come under legal attack from the Trump Administration,
which challenged the constitutionality of California's actions
just a few days before formally notifying the United Nations
Framework Convention on Climate Change of the United
States' intention to withdraw from the Paris Agreement. Many
arguments will be made to support the view that California
is exercising its proper authority in executing non-binding
intergovernmental agreements and recognizing the validity of
foreign compliance instruments in its domestic regulations,[10]
but the fact remains that subnational governments lack the
capacity to make legally binding commitments with foreign
governments. That's precisely why Ontario ignored the WCI

linking agreement's non-binding provisions and unilaterally withdrew when the politics of carbon markets fell apart in Ontario with the election of conservative Premier Doug Ford in 2018.[11] Although the ensuing de-linking process prompted regulators in California to make an unprecedented intervention to suspend cross-border trading with Ontario-registered entities[12] and took more than a year to make market corrections designed to remedy these impacts,[13] the long-term effect on the market's supply–demand balance was minimal precisely because Ontario's program was quite similar to the rest of the WCI. Market participants knew that political change in Ontario could lead to de-linking, but didn't have to worry about long-term price effects of linking and de-linking because each program was designed to the same level of overall program ambition.

RGGI faces similar institutional constraints and is even more decentralized than the WCI program, owing to its broader membership with more diverse state interests. As a legal matter, RGGI is largely a series of state-specific statutes and regulations that duplicate, with some unique state-specific accommodations, a model rule developed and periodically updated by participating jurisdictions. A 2005 Memorandum of Understanding and its subsequent amendments provide some specific provisions for the shared operation of the market and allow for states to withdraw on thirty days' notice, but since then many of the program design details have been managed through the development and updating of the RGGI Model Rule.[14] There is no real pretense of control beyond what participating states agree to do together. When New Jersey's Republican Governor Chris Christie decided to withdraw from the program, for example, a state court found that legal challengers could not compel the state to retain its cap-and-trade regulations following withdrawal.[15]

Critically, what holds this system together is not law and the creation of robust, tradeable property rights, but rather a shared vision of parallel efforts at low levels of ambition. Design decisions are made according to the evolving political views of current and prospective participants. And because RGGI features so many parties – none of which hegemonically dominates the group's overall agenda – the program

Table 6.1 Direct market links and offsets

Category	System 1	System 2	Type of link	Effective date
European Union and periphery	28 EU ETS member states		Multilateral	2005
	Norway	EU ETS	Multilateral	2008
	Iceland	EU ETS	Multilateral	2008
	Lichtenstein	EU ETS	Multilateral	2008
	Switzerland	EU ETS	Multilateral	2020
	United Kingdom (Brexit transition)	EU ETS	Multilateral	Proposed
Regional Greenhouse Gas Initiative	10 US states (RGGI)		Multilateral	2005
	New Jersey	RGGI	De-linking	2011
	New Jersey	RGGI	Re-linking	2020
	Pennsylvania	RGGI	Multilateral	Pending
	Virginia	RGGI	Multilateral	Pending
Western Climate Initiative	California	Québec	Bilateral	2013
	Ontario	WCI	Multilateral	2018
	Ontario	WCI	De-linking	2018

Category	System 1	System 2	Type of link	Effective date
Links to carbon offset programs and Kyoto-era credit systems	EU ETS	CDM, JI	Unilateral	2004
	EU ETS	CDM, JI	De-linking	Pending (2021)
	Switzerland	CDM	Unilateral	1999
	New Zealand	CDM, JI, RMU	Unilateral	2008
	New Zealand	CDM, JI, RMU	De-linking	2015
	Australia	CDM, JI	Unilateral	2012
	Australia	CDM, JI	De-linking	2014
	California	Acre, Chiapas	Unilateral	Proposed
	Québec	Acre, Chiapas	Unilateral	Proposed
	South Korea	CDM	Unilateral	2015
	Tokyo ETS	CDM	Unilateral	2010

Source: Updated from Matthew Ranson and Robert N. Stavins, "Linkage of greenhouse gas emissions trading systems: learning from experience," *Climate Policy* 16(3) (2016): 284–300.

must be transparent and predictable. (Indeed, as we will discuss in the next chapter, RGGI may have a modest level of ambition and low carbon prices, but its market design anticipates and resolves many of the political challenges with allowance oversupply that hobble the WCI system.) The largely egalitarian cooperation of RGGI states works because it is anchored in stability-oriented market design features that make market behavior more predictable and risk management more tractable.

Given subnational governments' limited institutional capacities and legal authorities, it's no wonder that both the WCI and RGGI programs feature links between programs that are almost identical at the individual level. Each system features identical sectoral coverage: RGGI applies to the electricity sector in each of its members; WCI applies to the electricity, industrial, and transportation fuels sectors in each member. Similarly, each system applies the same system-level architecture for auctioning or freely allocating allowances: RGGI relies primarily on allowance auctioning, whereas the WCI system relies heavily on free allowance allocation in the industrial sector.

The primary variation in program designs within RGGI and WCI markets reflects the use of revenues – the one major area of market design where it is not necessary for each member of a linked market to follow similar procedures. Individual RGGI states choose how to spend the funds raised at auction, with most electing to fund clean energy programs overseen by state utility regulators and a handful including some element of customer rebating or even diversion of carbon revenues to the state's general fund.[16] The WCI program also displays substantial variations. California pursues a hybrid revenue recycling structure for its electricity sector; no such accommodation is needed in Québec, where low-carbon hydropower dominates and therefore carbon pricing has minimal impacts on customers' bills. Similarly, the two WCI governments retain unilateral control over their respective revenues and prioritize different "green spending" outcomes.

Even the EU ETS features nearly identical market designs across its linked partners. The coverage, allocation rule processes, and program caps are now determined by the

European Commission's Directorate-General for Climate Action, rather than the individual member states. Although the EU ETS had considered linking with a short-lived program in Australia and has reportedly evaluated potential links with the nascent market being developed in China, all of its existing market links are between countries that either are or have been core members of the European Union itself (including the immediate post-Brexit United Kingdom); periphery countries that are part of the European Economic Area (Norway, Iceland, and Lichtenstein); or Switzerland, which has bilateral agreements that resemble the economic integration of formal EEA members.

Some advocates of market linking like to point to the large number of individual market links, but counting individual market links belies the fact that there are only three multilateral programs in existence – along with a set of less meaningful links between individual markets and Kyoto-era carbon offset programs. Table 6.1 (*supra* pp. 110–11) collects these links into four categories: members of the EU ETS and its peripheral linked partners, members of the northeastern US states' RGGI program, members of the North American WCI program, and a series of carbon offset links to individual markets.

Why political actors overpromise the value of market links

The case for linking markets has been made for decades on the view that trading between programs will lower the total cost of achieving climate goals via gains from trade. We don't dispute that potential – the opportunities for cost-effective climate mitigation really do vary widely by sector and geography.[17] Nevertheless, this framing reverses what matters in practice. Carbon offsets have indeed achieved cost reductions, but, as discussed in the previous chapter, they do so largely on the basis of false environmental benefits that weaken climate policy goals. Formal market links, meanwhile, have not delivered many significant economic benefits, as where they exist at all they are usually shallow.

That's because deep market links that deliver gains from trade are possible if and only if there are substantial government capacities available to mitigate the consequences of capital outflows and other disruptions to the domestic accommodations made in every local market that links.

Climate policy insiders know this. Rather than address these challenges head on, however, many policymakers tend to focus on the short-term reputational gains from announcing new market links. Nothing excites their NGO allies, philanthropic foundations, and the press like the prospect of another government joining forces with those bold leaders who dare to act when others shirk a global environmental crisis. These pressures are particularly acute for subnational governments whose national counterparts oppose climate policies. Subnational efforts in the RGGI and WCI programs were born under the Bush Administration in the United States and the Harper Administration in Canada, both of which opposed the international Kyoto Protocol and domestic climate policies alike. In the United States, Democratic governors announce that "we are still in" the Paris Agreement in response to the Trump Administration's planned withdrawal, and stalwart supporters of clean energy leadership like California and New York trumpet their efforts to fight federal environmental rollbacks in court.

California's situation exemplifies the problem of focusing on political optics ahead of practical realities. At the behest of industry, state policymakers have maintained a large and growing bank of allowances that help keep market prices low.[18] Notwithstanding Ontario's unfortunate departure in 2018, many in the western United States hoped that California would welcome Oregon as a new entrant to the WCI program in 2019.[19] California policymakers advertised their oversupply conditions as an enticement to others, like Oregon, who might want to set up their own markets to link with the WCI system – mostly in private, but occasionally in public, too.[20] By relying on a large number of surplus allowances in California, other programs, like Oregon's planned market, could announce bold long-term goals supported by markets without worrying as much about near-term price impacts. But given that the California rules feature maximum prices that could range as high as $65 per ton in the near term, and over $100 by 2030 – far above historical prices in the $15–18 per ton range – the political consequences of actually getting rid of excess allowance supplies are significant. These challenges remain unaddressed in current program rules, even if overallocation conditions in the WCI program show no signs of going away anytime soon. Time will tell whether Oregon, Washington, or other jurisdictions emerge with proposals to copy the market design seen in California and link to the WCI program. Meanwhile, not having enough linked partners to absorb some of that oversupply raises fundamental questions about the WCI program's ability to achieve its existing participants' climate policy goals.[21] By putting public relations ahead of robust institutional designs, Californian policymakers are avoiding the more important conversation: whether it makes political sense to rely principally on markets to cut emissions.

In contrast, RGGI is better positioned to accommodate new entrants without risking the stability of its program. As discussed later in chapter 7, its market is designed with a number of price containment mechanisms to ensure prices are neither too low nor too high, at least as far as the politics are concerned. As a result, new entrants and the firms in their electricity sectors have significantly more confidence about likely market prices than those considering membership in the WCI program. By developing stable market expectations through transparent, adaptive market rules, RGGI is able to expand the reach of its carbon price, providing a turnkey solution to periphery states whose political leadership decides to prioritize climate policy – however modestly. Because RGGI has proven highly adept at expanding (and occasionally contracting), it continues to attract new members.

The focus on potential gains from trade and a superficial emphasis on the public relations benefits of collecting external partners obscure what we believe to be the single most important yet least emphasized market link. The link between Germany and Poland – both of which are subject to the EU ETS – is far and away the greatest accomplishment in the history of multilateral cap-and-trade programs. What makes this link so remarkable is the difference in national priorities. Germany is among the world's most ambitious climate policy advocates, but Poland literally promoted an exhibition booth filled with local coal samples when it hosted the 2018 United Nations climate meeting in Katowice.[22] Yet both face the same carbon price determined by the EU ETS.

How did two diametrically opposed polities come to be subject to the same carbon market? The answer, in short, is that the institutional rules of the European Union enabled its many members who are climate leaders to require all EU members to adopt more ambitious climate policies. By no means was the initial EU-wide market easy to create, nor was it simple to strengthen the program over time.[23] The fact remains, however, that the EU ETS is the only multilateral market in existence that features a polity whose leaders have consistently opposed climate mitigation policy. What made this possible is the ability of pro-climate EU nations to build a European coalition that included compensation for opposing members, notably Poland. Decisions that were favorable to Polish interests on allocation of program revenue helped, as did repeated policy engagements on other issues like trade. All these outcomes were then made legally binding within European law so they would not come unglued easily when political winds shifted. These institutional capacities are rooted in many years of effort and evolution that have taken place across a broad set of policy issues – which are all part and parcel of the expansion of Europe – not the product of flashy climate summits that aim to create deep climate cooperation out of whole cloth.[24]

Because governments' institutional capacity is the critical constraint on links between systems with different prices or different market designs, a lot of talk about deeper integration of markets is just that – talk. Australia and the EU made the most progress in negotiating what would have been the first link between systems with different origins and different market designs, with sophisticated considerations about cross-border governance on both sides. But those discussions fell apart when the political coalition supporting climate policy frayed under Australian PM Tony Abbot's conservative government in 2014.[25] Others consider the prospect of linking the RGGI and WCI programs into a bicoastal North American regime,[26] but any such link would have to contend with cultural clashes between RGGI's transparency-oriented, consensus-building process and California's tendency to prefer hegemonic leadership. Consideration of a RGGI–WCI link would require navigating differences in sectoral coverage and would also highlight the contrasting ways the two programs manage prices, with RGGI employing explicit market design elements to guide prices within a modest range of acceptable outcomes, and California relying on excess allowances to keep prices from reaching the politically unacceptable maximums its market technically allows. These differences in philosophy and market design only heighten the challenge of developing shared institutional capacities to manage market links across subnational governments.[27]

Conclusion

For nearly thirty years, market links and international burden-sharing have been promoted as a means to reduce the costs of countries' climate goals, on the theory that greater economic efficiency frees up the potential for bolder overall policy ambition. By enabling governments that seek strong climate policy to pursue cheaper reductions abroad, direct market links offer the promise of significant economic gains from trade and a path toward global integration. In the real world, however, market links that are more than superficial risk destabilizing the sector- and jurisdiction-specific accommodations policymakers develop to manage the politics of climate policy at home. Deep market links between programs with different prices, sectoral coverage, and other elements of design would put the market, not policymakers, in charge of where emission reductions take place, at what cost, and with what co-benefits. Furthermore, two of the world's three multilateral markets are subnational in nature – a special challenge since those governments can't create legally enforceable agreements with their linked partners. Policymakers, NGO advocates, and market participants know this, which is why market links are rare, thin, and between similar systems. Rather than seek to build institutional capacities to manage the consequences of deeper cross-border links, however, policymakers and their NGO allies tend to focus on promoting market links for the public relations benefits they generate. Those reputational benefits may be significant, but if the promoted links are brittle or their underlying market designs are unprepared to deal with the political consequences of linked markets, then precious political effort will be wasted. The only market to illustrate the capacity to manage cross-border links is the one that is rarely celebrated for that achievement – Europe's – because a successful multilateral program looks, in all meaningful respects, like a single market operated by a single regulator.

7

Getting the most out of markets

The previous five chapters have explained how, in practice, political forces relegate carbon markets to supporting roles, where they deliver only a mere fraction of their promised potential. In some respects, this is a pessimistic story. It is also a realistic one.

This chapter provides a set of recommendations designed to redirect political forces in ways that help make markets more effective in serving the public interest. It draws on our theory of politics to show how policy reforms designed around these insights can improve the performance of both new and existing markets.

Nevertheless, our vision for politically viable reforms does not change the most important, central argument of this book: policymakers and policy advocates have relied and are relying too heavily on market forces. Market-based climate policies are doing very little today to reduce emissions. With careful reforms, they can be made to do more. Even then, the dominant – if not overwhelming – majority of emission reductions are likely to come from smart industrial policy strategies, not carbon prices. We offer suggestions for reform in the spirit of pragmatism and because we are mindful that others may see a greater role for markets than we do. For them, this chapter offers a vision for how to make their favored strategies more effective. That task requires confronting the political barriers that have undermined markets' performance to date, instead of wishing them away or blaming weak outcomes on a lack of political will.[1] Bemoaning a lack of political support for serious climate policy is no excuse for doubling down on policy strategies that make poor use of scarce political capital. Yet that is exactly what the standard playbook for markets does today.

Our reform strategy is about "rightsizing" markets. It begins with the recognition that the climate policy playbook overemphasizes the role of markets in driving change – particularly in the early stages of climate policy development – and develops a set of reforms that can harness the political forces identified in chapter 1 in ways that make markets more effective while also navigating around political barriers to efficacy. Rightsized markets, if designed well, can encourage static economic efficiency in tailored applications where technologies are mature and economic risks are well known. They can also generate modest but important revenues to support climate goals.

We offer three sets of recommendations to help markets scale in line with political demand for effective climate policy.

The first topic is how to increase policy ambition, drawing on insights from chapters 2 and 3. We focus on the need to tackle the problem of allowance oversupply conditions in order to evolve markets away from Potemkin designs. Getting rid of excess allowances will be easier when accompanied by reforms designed to raise carbon prices on a predictable schedule and with limited price volatility. In essence, markets must be made to operate more like taxes, which are strictly superior to cap-and-trade in practice. Successful regulations depress the demand for emission allowances in cap-and-trade systems, and because regulations are politically easier to strengthen and more resilient in the face of opposition, markets frequently end up with low prices and few climate benefits.[2] Taxes and tax-like markets with minimum and maximum prices don't have this problem because the tax rate (or minimum market price) applies regardless of the strength of regulatory policies. Predictable prices from taxes and tax-like markets also reduce volatility and uncertainty, which helps mitigate political opposition while making it less risky for firms and governments to invest in decarbonization technologies for the long haul. We also strongly recommend limiting markets' scope to individual economic sectors, rather than seeking broad coverage that promises economic efficiency but more frequently delivers a race to the bottom in terms of policy ambition.

A second area of reform concerns the institutional design for spending carbon market revenues. Today most programs pursue green spending models that, as discussed in chapter 4, tend to become porky and wasteful in practice. Reforms are needed to root out and isolate the waste. Policymakers should segregate program spending that is fundamentally political in nature from spending designed to achieve measurable environmental goals. While political spending is by nature opaque and is intrinsically inefficient as a means of achieving environmental goals, it is often politically essential. By contrast, successful environmental spending programs must be isolated from that pork and subjected to serious independent oversight and assessment using standard tools of accountability in public finance. We suggest ways that the institutional design of program spending can be set up to improve outcomes over time, while still preserving policymakers' flexibility to adapt to changing political circumstances and to deploy revenues strategically to build political coalitions in support of higher carbon prices.

Finally, the third set of reforms addresses the outward engagement of cap-and-trade programs, both through offsets and through direct, formal market links. In chapters 5 and 6, we argued that these two types of outward links have performed especially poorly in the real world.

We see carbon offsets as fundamentally counterproductive because they create structural incentives to reduce program ambition, require government oversight capabilities that few governments (if any) are likely to have or build, and deliver economically and politically inefficient benefits. Every one of the legitimate goals of offsets can be accommodated more readily through other policy means. Offsets' role in containing the cost of cap-and-trade schemes should be addressed through explicit price controls, as discussed above. Their role in directing incentives to outside parties should be addressed through competitive spending programs focused on places where there are big opportunities to cut or avoid emissions, such as forests or short-lived climate pollutants. We expect a limited future for external market links. Links make sense, but only when they build on, rather than pre-date, competent government institutions that are needed to administer a high-quality market program. In fact, linking markets that aren't ready can propagate bad market designs and undermine the essential incentive to build institutions capable of governing complex climate policy systems. Rather than pursue market links designed to promote the public appearance of political followership, we encourage policymakers to focus first on building the institutional capacity needed to sustain high prices at home, and then link outward only when prospective partners demonstrate comparable institutional capacity to manage the impacts that would result from deep links between serious programs. Leaders can encourage followership through linkage by making transparent the quality standards that must be achieved before linkage – an action that can help guide institutional reforms in emerging markets that are keen to link when possible. Demonstrating a successful high-priced market at home is more important than linking multiple partners under a single low-priced program – precisely because this can influence the rules other set for themselves.

How to increase program ambition

The central problem with nearly all real-world market instruments for cutting carbon is that they lack ambition: that is, the carbon prices and emission reductions they produce are far smaller than what societies are willing to pursue via regulatory strategies. The compromises policymakers frequently make to accommodate the interests of emitting sectors end up producing markets that reflect the lowest ambition of all covered sectors. Worse, these markets are brittle and unable to respond when conditions change. When prices are low – as they are almost everywhere – these flaws aren't particularly visible or problematic. They become an additional barrier to change, however, because any proposal to tighten markets leads to two outcomes that undermine political support. One is prices that drift too far from what societies are willing to pay to tackle the global climate problem. The other is price volatility that could ensue if markets are reformed to do more without setting up price guardrails first.

Making it feasible for markets to deliver more ambition requires a three-fold strategy. First is a set of reforms designed to avoid or mitigate oversupply conditions. Second, reformers should shift to market designs that reduce price volatility and create predictability, such as price collars or well-administered reserve schemes. Following these first two suggestions will bring the supply of emission allowances in cap-and-trade systems more in line with demand and will cause these programs to operate more like price-based instruments. Third, we argue that reformers should keep sectoral coverage of markets narrow and avoid, especially, linking sectors where political sensitivity to rising prices is high to those where higher prices for pollution externalities are easier to manage.

The primary technical barrier to increased program ambition is market oversupply: the condition in which allowance and offset supplies persistently exceed emissions covered by cap-and-trade programs. This condition enables market participants to build up surplus compliance instruments they can bank and rely on later to maintain their emission levels in the presence of declining program caps. The result: low market prices and minimal emission reductions, a problem that has plagued practically every carbon market to date. To address it, policymakers must measure its incidence and design rule-based adjustments to the volume of allowance supplies. It is tempting to focus on technical solutions because oversupply is the main technical barrier limiting markets' potential, but the reason oversupply persists is political. That's why fixing the problem requires a combination of technical and political responses.

The good news is that two of the world's three major cap-and-trade programs have demonstrated the capacity to acknowledge and address oversupply conditions, albeit with different levels of program ambition. Most notably, policymakers and researchers in the European Union have spent years debating the causes of and remedies for the EU ETS's significant oversupply condition.[3] Reforms now underway show how the job can be done. The northeastern United States' RGGI program has also made similar adjustments, although with far lower levels of intended program ambition – RGGI illustrates the kinds of reforms that work, but, like a concept car at a trade show, the program hasn't really been put to use. Unfortunately, California and the Western Climate Initiative lag farther behind, illustrating how difficult politics can increase program opacity instead of creating clear expectations behind a workable policy agenda.[4]

We begin with the EU ETS. Europe created not only the first major carbon market, but also the first carbon market to suffer a major oversupply problem. A combination of strong EU member state renewable energy mandates and a massive number of low-quality international carbon offsets exogenously lowered demand for allowances. These forces – both products of the fundamental political economy of climate policy that produces Potemkin markets – combined with lower-than-anticipated economic growth following the global recession in the early 2010s to create a large bank of surplus EU allowances and therefore low carbon prices.[5] In 2015, Europe decided to track excess compliance instrument supplies and created the initial EU ETS Market Stability Reserve.[6] The EU ETS first responded to market oversupply by temporarily deferring the auction of 900 million EU allowances – an approach called "backloading," which was criticized for its anticipated ineffectiveness.[7] Markets yawned; prices stayed low. Eventually, however, the European Commission decided to remove these allowances from the normal auction supply and sent them instead to the Market Stability Reserve, creating a more permanent and effective solution to oversupply.[8]

The Market Stability Reserve's reform in 2019 has caused EU ETS prices to recover from their anemic levels such that they now constitute, based on the volume of emissions they affect, the most important carbon pricing signal on the planet. It works as follows. The European Commission measures the number of surplus allowances in circulation based on an objective formula. If that number is less than 400 million, the Market Stability Reserve injects an additional 100 million allowances into circulation. If the number exceeds 833 million, the Market Stability Reserve absorbs up to 24% of the total by deducting this amount from future years' auction budgets.[9] If the number is in between 400 and 833 million, no action is taken.

The practical effect of the Market Stability Reserve is to clear a significant excess buildup of allowances in the EU ETS. When the EU began its reporting, the number of surplus allowances in the program has hovered in the range of 1.6 to 1.7 billion, close to a full year's worth of covered emissions (see Table 7.1). As of the 2019 program year – the most recent available as of this writing – an additional 994 million allowances have been transferred or scheduled for transfer to the Reserve, on top of the original 900 million removed under the initial "backloading" initiative. More will soon follow.

In essence, the Market Stability Reserve provides a kind of central banking function that aims to stabilize prices by

Table 7.1 EU ETS emissions, allowances, and Market Stability Reserve adjustments

	2016	2017	2018	2019
EU ETS verified emissions (million tCO$_2$e)	1,750.5	1,754.6	1,682.0	1,527
Total number of allowances in circulation (millions)	1,694.0	1,654.6	1,654.9	1,385.5
Allowances scheduled for the Market Stability Reserve (millions)	0	264.7	397.2	332.5

Source: Emissions data from European Environmental Agency, EU Emissions Trading (ETS) data viewer (July 4, 2019), https://www.eea.europa.eu/data-and-maps/dashboards/emissions-trading-viewer-1; European Commission, Emissions trading: greenhouse gas emissions reduced by 8.7% in 2019, https://ec.europa.eu/clima/news/emissions-trading-greenhouse-gas-emissions-reduced-87-2019_en; allowance data from European Commission Communications C(2017) 3228 (12 May 2017), C(2018) 2801 (May 15, 2018), C(2019) 3288 (May 14, 2019), and C(2020) 2835 (May 8, 2020), https://ec.europa.eu/clima/policies/ets/reform_en#tab-0-1.

altering the supply of money – a Goldilocks strategy for managing allowance supplies. If the EU market has too many allowances, prices will fall to unacceptably low levels; to prevent that outcome, the Reserve absorbs excess allowances to nudge prices back up. If the market is too tight, then prices could rise to unacceptable levels; in this case, the Reserve injects new allowance supplies to moderate prices. If the market's supply–demand balance remains within a desired range, then all is well and the market is left alone to do its work.

Notably, the triggering mechanism is a quantity of surplus allowances, even though the impact on prices is arguably the primary rationale for this policy intervention. As with Europe's adoption of a cap-and-trade program rather than a carbon tax in the first place, a quantity-based trigger reflects institutional constraints on what the European Commission can do on the basis of simple majority votes – price-based triggers could raise legal questions about the market regulator's ability to implement reforms.[10] A quantity-based intervention like the Market Stability Reserve can effectively manage program prices if it is carefully modeled, transparently monitored, and updated in light of any new information that comes to light about the possible price trajectories implied by its dynamic supply adjustments. It transforms a quantity-based system in which prices could fluctuate widely, as they had in the past, into one with a soft collar – more like a tax, even though legally it isn't a tax.

The northeastern United States' RGGI program takes a similar approach through a pair of one-time cap adjustments, as well as a dynamic intervention that resembles the Market Stability Reserve. Like the EU ETS, RGGI experienced market oversupply conditions and very low prices in the 2010s. The situation with RGGI was more extreme, however, because this cap-and-trade program only applies to the electricity sector and the United States' electricity sector began a profound transformation alongside (but not because of) RGGI. Not only did many of its participating states implement aggressive renewable energy and energy efficiency regulations, but also the rise of cheap natural gas from fracking dramatically accelerated the replacement of high-emitting coal-fired electricity with relatively clean natural gas and zero-carbon renewables. Emissions have been falling steadily, despite – not because of – anemic RGGI prices. As emissions fell owing to exogenous forces, the market became oversupplied. In response, RGGI's two cap adjustments removed almost 140 million allowances – about two years' worth of total emissions – from the supply of allowance budgets through program year 2020.[11]

In addition to these one-time adjustments, RGGI also developed a dynamic mechanism to alter the supply of allowances.[12] This additional market feature is triggered by observed market prices, rather than the EU ETS Market Stability Reserve's measurement of excess allowance supplies. Like the EU ETS Reserve, RGGI's approach is two-fold: RGGI features a Cost Containment Reserve that releases 10% of the program-wide allowance budget into the market if prices reach $13 per allowance in 2021; and if prices fall below $6 per allowance in 2021, an Emissions Containment Reserve will absorb 10% of the program's annual allowance budget and remove these allowances from circulation. When the market remains in between the two triggering prices, allowances supplies are fixed – just as in the EU ETS, where supplies are fixed so long as the total number of surplus allowances stays within a specified range. (Both triggering prices increase at 7% per year to increase ambition over time, but not even the high-end prices are significant when compared to the policy incentives supporting renewable or nuclear energy in participating RGGI states.)[13]

The RGGI and EU ETS market designs illustrate how dynamic, rule-based adjustments to allowance supplies can help policymakers push their markets to achieve greater emission reductions. There are important technical nuances between price- and quantity-triggered interventions, to be sure, but each approach provides its market regulator with the capacity to set clear expectations in the market and automatically adjust program rules to achieve those outcomes. In turn, careful modeling of the desired market outcomes enables regulators to set and update their desired triggering conditions and automatic program adjustments that follow. At the same time, the level and type of organized political pressure nevertheless affect policy ambition: RGGI is intentionally designed to be a low-priced market in a fast-evolving sector driven primarily by regulation and technological change, not carbon prices, whereas Europe is increasingly leaning on the EU ETS to deliver a substantial component of its EU-wide climate commitments – even though many EU member states continue to push on clean energy mandates at home.

In contrast to the experience in RGGI and the EU ETS, California – the anchor jurisdiction in the Western Climate Initiative – denies that its market is in a state of oversupply.[14] California's approach is notable because it officially intends for its cap-and-trade program to deliver nearly half of the reductions required to achieve its legally binding emissions limit for 2030 – a further 40% cut from 2020 levels, comparable to the ambition of the European Union's own 2030 climate goals.[15] The promised contribution of cap-and-trade in the state's 2030 climate strategy is a dramatic departure from its 2020 strategy, for which cap-and-trade played only a minor supporting role.[16] While the state's official new climate strategy relies on cap-and-trade to drive progress to 2030, policymakers have consistently rebuffed criticism about its performance from academics, government analysts, journalists, and – during Ontario's brief participation in the WCI – even the Ontario Government's independent environmental watchdog agency.[17]

Not only does the California regulator deny that its market has too many allowances, but it has also so far resisted multiple calls for an objective set of metrics to track these outcomes, as is done in the RGGI and EU ETS programs.[18] This posture is all the more remarkable because the market regulator's own public reporting data contradict its statements about the number of excess allowances expected in the years ahead.[19] Meanwhile, academic modeling shows that oversupply conditions are likely to continue, with the number of excess allowances accumulated in market participants' accounts sufficient to comply with program rules even while enabling emissions that significantly exceed state policy goals.[20] Despite promises to the contrary, the program is not designed to guarantee California hits its 2030 emissions limit.

Having a strategy for containing oversupply is essential because these dynamics can easily emerge in light of macroeconomic uncertainty, strong overlapping regulatory policies, heavy reliance on carbon offsets, or technological change.

But getting a handle on oversupply creates a second set of problems – problems that lie at the heart of California's challenge and will face any other market that aims for more than Potemkin outcomes.

Carbon prices will increase once oversupply is addressed and market ambition is ratcheted up – but the rate and magnitude of the price increase will be uncertain. This creates problems for affected industries and thus political problems for leaders, who must stay attuned to their base of political support. If visible prices rise too high relative to what society is willing to pay, policymakers risk political backlash. In addition, prices may become highly volatile owing to the interaction between relatively thin markets and strong regulations. Uncertainty about the magnitude of price increases and the volatility that might follow are serious political problems that must be addressed in parallel with reforms to address oversupply concerns.

Uncertainty and volatility are particularly challenging problems. Economists Severin Borenstein, James Bushnell, Frank Wolak, and Matthew Zaragoza-Watkins have analyzed how deep uncertainty over future emissions in the WCI program leads to outcomes in which market prices likely equilibrate at the program's minimum floor or maximum ceiling price, but only infrequently in between.[21] Macroeconomic uncertainty means that baseline emissions could be high or low, leading to correspondingly higher or lower levels of effort needed from climate policy. That uncertainty is further exacerbated by the fact that ambitious regulations are anticipated to drive emission reductions in the near term, reducing the share of additional emission reductions required by the market. If strong regulation continues and economic growth is relatively low, regulations could get California most if not all of the way toward its 2030 emissions limit without asking much of the market. But if growth is high or if regulations are unsuccessful, then the market will tighten and prices could soar. Together these forces produce a bimodal distribution of expected price outcomes, clustering at the market's minimum and maximum prices, with relatively few scenarios equilibrating in between these two levels.[22] Uncertainty on this scale creates problems for policymakers and regulated firms alike.

Implementing a carbon market in the face of this uncertainty wouldn't necessarily be so challenging if regulators had selected a price ceiling that represents costs California is willing to pay. With a realistic price ceiling, the market could absorb and manage this uncertainty. The worst-case outcome would be a politically tolerable price level – albeit one in which emissions may exceed program goals if the going gets tough. In California, however, the price ceiling that regulators selected is not politically tolerable today. The program's price ceiling begins at $65 in 2021 – almost four times current market prices – and escalates from there at 5% per year plus inflation, clearing $90 by 2030.[23] Market regulators have taken great pains to publicly signal that the program will never achieve these levels, describing high prices as a sign of failure rather than climate policy success.[24] Relying on market oversupply ensures their goals, at least for the time being, but puts the regulator in a bind: reforms to increase program ambition by paring back oversupply necessarily destabilize the very market design feature that keeps prices in a politically acceptable range. And the more regulators signal that they don't believe in their own price ceiling, the less anyone else will, either. What is missing is a connection between official expectations and political reality; deepening those connections is necessary to show all parties that the market system is credible and politically durable. Meanwhile, any errors in market administration create impacts on prices and liquidity that, when they deviate from what is expected and tolerable to politically organized groups, can generate significant political liabilities.

The solution to these problems is to implement a market design that limits volatility and guides prices from low to high levels on a predictable schedule. In a price-oriented reform regime, such as the RGGI program, this can be done through mechanisms that automatically release or remove allowances in response to actual market prices. In a quantity-based reform regime, such as the EU ETS, this can be done through central-banking-like supply controls signaled far in advance of actual reforms taking place. In either system, explicit price or quantity guardrails must be based on politically realistic objectives that are informed by careful technical modeling exercises. Both can and should be combined with a minimum price floor and maximum price ceiling that rise together from relatively low origins, with only a modest spread between the two price extremes. Decisions about where to set price or quantity guardrails should be revisited on a planned schedule to account for improved understanding of market conditions or to take advantage of new political opportunities to increase program ambition – after all, what seems implausible today may look different in a rapidly warming world.

Tight and well-administered price collars (or central-banking rules, as in the EU) reduce price volatility and opposition to increasing program ambitions, but they don't eliminate political resistance to higher prices. Unfortunately, those challenges grow bigger the broader the market's sectoral coverage, precisely because in linked markets the system overall is only as viable as the viability in the sector where political sensitivity to prices is the greatest. Thus, our final recommendation on how to design markets capable of supporting greater ambition is to limit their scope to sectors that share similar organizational attributes.

Markets with narrow sectoral coverage can help policymakers keep political challenges more manageable. The fact is that some sectors will be quite difficult to decarbonize. Others will be relatively easy. Some may be particularly trade-sensitive and therefore will demand significant accommodations through generous allowance allocations or trade policy protections. Lumping all of these problems together in a single market design forces the accommodations made for the most well-connected or trade-sensitive parties to affect the price and pace of mitigation expected from all others. Policymakers should avoid this quandary by including only similarly situated industries in a single market, and developing multiple, separate markets if they wish to address dissimilar industries with market-based policies.

The idea of limiting sectoral coverage runs contrary to the standard economic prescription, but it follows directly from the political structures discussed throughout this book. Broad coverage is of course what economic theory recommends because the more sectors and territories that are subject to a market, the greater the opportunities for cost-effective reductions and therefore the greater the economic efficiency of achieving the program's goals. From a political perspective, however, broad coverage itself is a barrier to increasing ambition. Every participating sector faces the same price signal under a carbon market – owing to the law of one price – and therefore any change to the stringency of the overall program affects every participating industry and consumer segment. What results is typically the lowest common denominator for program-wide ambition, rather than a dynamic policy instrument that responds to changing political and technological opportunity. In contrast, if policy-makers reach an accord with major emitters in a narrow program – or if political support for forcing change in that industry is sufficient – they can proceed with targeted reforms without generating consensus across all major industries in the economy.

Our recommendation to narrow sectoral coverage likely matters most for those setting up new programs. Dis-aggregating existing multi-sector programs would likely face stiff opposition from market participants who benefit from lowest-common-denominator outcomes and might organize to block disaggregating reforms. However, in places where existing markets suffer from the politics of broad coverage – for example, in California – policymakers may want to explore options for disaggregation because that strategy might liberate market instruments to be used in more effective ways. Policymakers managing existing markets would also do well to avoid the temptation to expand their markets further to include new price-sensitive sectors.

How to make spending more effective

Most cap-and-trade programs operate under green spending paradigms where revenues are spent on initiatives to further reduce emissions. As described in chapter 4, however, political forces tend to make green spending programs wasteful and inefficient.

Carbon market administrators need to make the most of limited program revenues, harnessing them to deliver the most important public goods in pursuit of climate solutions. Their task is made more difficult by a wide variety of interest groups – including NGOs, incumbent emitters, and politicians themselves – that seek to capture program revenues for private gain or pet theories of change. A certain amount of spending on politically essential ends may be necessary to sustain and increase policy efforts over time, but these spending choices are in tension with those that aim to deliver cost-effective and transformative change on the climate front. Figuring out how to accommodate the political without overwhelming the publicly beneficial is the central challenge in reforming green spending paradigms. In every system there is some level of pork that must be delivered for political viability, but the mechanisms that allocate that pork must not be allowed to dominate the mechanisms by which a growing share of revenues is spent on well-targeted green investments. Put simply, pork and green are different political processes and must therefore be managed in different ways.

In practice, most institutional processes for appropriating carbon revenues do not distinguish between political and environmental goals, nor do they incorporate mechanisms designed to increase their respective efficiencies. Thus, by design, these institutions don't help policymakers tackle this central political challenge. The result, through co-mingling of funds and wooly oversight, is that vaguely defined pork crowds out good green investments. Both elements – pork and green – must be reformed to unlock the greatest potential for environmental gain.

The solution to ineffective program spending lies in the architecture of public finance. The central problem is that political support for global public goods – for example, investment in potentially transformative low-carbon technology – is weak, whereas concentrated political demands for pork are strong. When relatively modest carbon revenues are appropriated in an omnibus process with limited oversight, this imbalance is magnified and pork tends to edge out public goods. To rebalance the playing field, policymakers need to alter institutional rules so that they strengthen the ability of political forces to identify and mobilize around the best uses of the funds. As the role of green spending rises, the institutional environment must make it easier for powerful political constituencies to form around the efficient deployment of public funds towards climate solutions.

The first step in this type of institutional reform requires separating incoming carbon revenues across three independent accounts – with each account serving a distinct purpose with distinct rules and accountability. One fund would be designated for political expenditures; the second for climate pollution mitigation programs, focusing separately on transformative investments in one portfolio and low-cost mitigation investments in another; and an optional third for revenue recycling (see Figure 7.1). There should be complete transparency around the shares of total program revenues allocated across the three funds, but very different requirements for program oversight in each. We are under no illusion about the difficulty of reforming these kinds of institutions – especially when reforms threaten to redirect revenues away from well-connected interests – which is why we see the first step in reforms as the simpler move to transparency about the size of funds in each bucket.

The climate mitigation fund should be heavily scrutinized with independent expert review because it can be assessed against the clearest objective functions: climate benefits. It should contain two portfolios, each with distinct performance metrics and oversight goals.

The first mitigation portfolio is the most important and would target what we call transformative investments.[25] These expenditures are likely to be more expensive than the

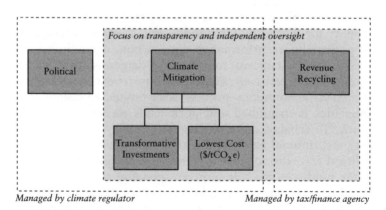

Figure 7.1   Fund structure

least-cost mitigation options on a dollar-per-tCO_2e basis. They must, therefore, hold the potential to create major reductions in the future cost of climate mitigation – including, if desired, in sectors that lie outside the market's coverage. In effect, this portfolio would be placing bets on transformation that could unlock lower-cost pathways for emission reductions in tough sectors, such as zero-carbon liquid fuels that could be used in the transportation or aviation sectors.[26] It could also include investments to deploy or evaluate novel technologies, like the direct capture of CO_2 from ambient air or soil management techniques that sequester significant volumes of CO_2. Program oversight would be more holistic, with program administrators articulating theories of change to achieve transformative outcomes and independent oversight scrutinizing whether those particular theories of change hold promise. Although less objective, the evaluation of these system-level concepts is not new. In many respects, it resembles the challenge facing the United States' Advanced Research Projects Agency-Energy (ARPA-E), an energy innovation funding agency tasked with supporting transformative research. A growing literature and practitioner base provides lessons for how these kinds of programs can be operated and overseen.[27]

The second mitigation portfolio should target the maximum emission reductions at the lowest possible costs. Its purpose would be to advance the ambition of climate policy that can't be achieved directly because there are so many political limits on high emission prices. Expenditures in this portfolio should be evaluated on the basis of their marginal cost (cost per ton of CO_2e abated), with program administration and independent oversight focused on minimizing – and publicizing – revealed marginal costs. This portfolio would therefore concentrate its investments on known, scalable technologies.

The political fund would be designed differently because it would aim to achieve different outcomes. There would be no restriction on the activities these funds support, and there would be modest transparency and oversight requirements. Critics readily bemoan the role of politics and politically oriented spending, but the fact is that wise political spending can be an effective mechanism for developing and maintaining a supportive coalition for higher carbon prices and the greater use of market-based policies. When political spending is wasteful, however, no one benefits – other than special interests, of course. Segregating political spending into a separate account without imposing additional transparency requirements preserves the opacity required for effective political accommodations. Yet it also signals how much of program revenue is being diverted to these ends and therefore creates an incentive for policymakers to maximize the political benefits of these revenues – as well as for stakeholders to push for reallocation of funds if the balance between spending on political and climate mitigation ends isn't delivering.

Finally, the third fund would be for any revenue recycling used in the program. It should be subject to strict oversight and managed not by the environmental regulator, but by the implementing jurisdiction's tax or fiscal department. Revenue recycling strategies – whether tax swaps, with carbon revenues replacing personal or income tax receipts, or direct rebates, with funds directed at broad segments of the public – rely on the distinct administrative capabilities that tax and fiscal agencies already possess. Consistent with tax and fiscal policy, transparency and oversight are both needed and relatively straightforward. Those tasks are easier to manage when integrated with the rest of a polity's fiscal framework and the standard rules and disciplines of public finance.

An example may help illustrate how this institutional structure helps to generate more effective outcomes. Consider a proposal to invest public funds in forest management practices that are intended to increase the amount of carbon stored in healthy forests. Is this proposal primarily an environmental or a political affair? The advantage of the segregated fund structure is that we don't need to know the answer to this question – the proponents of the project can make their claims and be evaluated according to the logic of each potential rationale. If the investment is primarily about reducing climate pollution, it can compete on one of two dimensions: either on the basis of low marginal costs or on its potentially transformative effects. Transparent metrics and independent review will help focus and evaluate these claims. If the project isn't competitive – that is, if policymakers have alternatives that deliver climate benefits at lower costs and if the project's long-term benefits are deemed to be less than transformative – then it won't get resources from the climate mitigation fund. Perhaps the intended beneficiary is politically influential, however, and may be willing to support higher carbon prices in the future. In that case, the project could seek support from the political fund. If policymakers judge the project to be politically valuable – not on the basis of marginal costs, but on the basis of relative political appeal – the project will secure funds; and if other, more compelling expenditures are available, then it won't. By forcing potential public spending projects to compete either on a political basis or under a rigorous review of their environmental performance, the segregated fund structure seeks efficiency in both dimensions.

Changing the architecture of program spending to this tripartite approach opens up opportunities to improve the operation of spending over time. Because the allocation of money across the three funds would be transparent, policymakers and stakeholders would be able to advocate for a rebalancing when conditions warrant. In turn, this would create strong incentives for program administrators to increase the efficiency of their investments within each fund in order to remain competitive.

Beyond helping to optimize each of these three distinct funds at any given moment, this institutional approach should also generate useful information about program outcomes. Such information can help improve responsiveness to changing political conditions – especially new waves of political support for increasing program ambitions. For example, oversight data from the climate mitigation fund would generate useful information about the sufficiency of program ambition and the reliance on near- versus long-term mitigation investments. Estimated marginal costs for climate mitigation expenditures would allow policymakers to compare the benefits of their investments against the stringency of the carbon market, and transparency would help raise the odds that policymakers would be held accountable against those metrics. If the marginal cost of well-administered climate investments significantly exceeds actual market prices, that would be a signal that the carbon market is not as ambitious as is needed to achieve policymakers' goals.[28] Similarly, policymakers and independent experts would be able to monitor the two portfolios of climate-related expenditures targeted at near-term emission reductions versus investment in opportunities to unlock transformative change in the years ahead. That monitoring could help improve program administration while also offering the information needed to build political coalitions for bigger spending programs.

Although most carbon markets lean heavily on green spending paradigms, rather than broad-based tax reform or direct consumer rebates, revenue recycling could become an increasingly important consideration when carbon prices – and therefore cost impacts – grow to significant levels. As discussed in chapter 4, the academic literature is replete with arguments about the superiority of revenue recycling approaches; some advocacy groups on the left and the right advocate for recycling-dominated expenditure plans. One of us (Cullenward) even helped draft legislation in California that would have shifted the state's green spending model into a program where the bulk of the revenues would go to per-capita rebates to state residents.[29] Despite the appeal of revenue recycling to budget-conscious conservatives or equity-minded progressives, we worry that the political efficiency of broad-based recycling strategies is weaker than many appreciate. That is, the political support purchased with a dollar of broad-based revenue recycling may be less than what one can achieve through carefully targeted political programs or well-administered environmental investments. That may well be true when market prices are low, as they are today. As coalitions emerge to enable higher market prices, the political and normative value of revenue recycling may grow over time. A dynamic fund structure anticipates this potential and creates a path forward for these kinds of reforms over time as the political demand for equity protections grows.

Meanwhile, green spending prevails. By segregating expenditures across three funds, strengthening oversight for environmental effectiveness, and providing an institutional mechanism to reallocate revenues across political, climate mitigation, and revenue-recycling purposes, our reforms create an institutional setting that can nimbly respond to growing demands for more ambitious climate policy.

How to make external relations work

A third set of reforms addresses the interaction between individual cap-and-trade programs and the outside world. Those links have happened in two ways: through carbon offsets and the direct integration of markets. Today, as we discussed in chapters 5 and 6, neither offsets nor linking markets is working well. Carbon offsets dilute markets' environmental integrity because industries push for quantity over quality, with strong support from NGOs that are steeped in the business of offsets. Opposition to these problematic programs tends to be weak and comes, if at all, from under-resourced public interest voices and administrators.

Most of the dominant paradigm for markets focuses on the potential for leading climate jurisdictions to focus outward, promoting their efforts that engage other jurisdictions as the best possible sign of policy success. We would reverse that framing. The most important thing climate leaders can do is demonstrate what successful carbon pricing looks like at home. Policymakers will retain greater control over the quality of their home market if they channel resources through competitive spending initiatives to invest in outside programs, rather than offset schemes that undermine the home market. (When quality problems manifest, spending programs are more readily corrected because changes don't impose higher costs on domestic polluters – unlike offset reforms). Instead of focusing on accumulating market links, policymakers should look to develop simple, streamlined programs that are easily adopted or emulated – with inter-governmental cooperation typically taking a more indirect, but ultimately more effective, form.

This is not to say that climate leaders shouldn't think about how to influence neighbors, trading partners, and other foreign governments. Quite the opposite: global climate change policy is, at heart, a question of foreign relations, not just domestic policy. But the conventional focus on offsets and market links risks creating low-quality inter-governmental relations, not a stepping stone to serious cross-border policy cooperation. Offsets present an essentially insurmountable administrative problem and offer no benefits that cannot be achieved through smart foreign relations and strategic spending. In turn, the conditions under which formal interactions between cap-and-trade programs can sustain high-quality outcomes are much more limited than most proponents acknowledge.

Our recommendation on offsets is simple: get rid of them. All of the legitimate motivations for offsets can be better accommodated through a combination of price containment features in the home market design and competitive spending programs in other jurisdictions.

The effective regulatory oversight of carbon offsets requires an army of talented civil servants charged with evaluating counterfactual scenarios across multiple industries, many of which lie outside the core expertise of their host agencies. Those sectors typically experience significant technological change and shifting market dynamics – all in the face of well-organized lobbying pressure to increase credit volumes from offset-project owners, self-interested intermediaries, and regulated industries. The task of delivering high-quality, low-cost offsets under these conditions is enormous, if not impossible. It is also unnecessary. Every motivation for carbon offsets – whether the goal is to reduce compliance costs for industry, pursuing local environmental co-benefits, sending revenues to politically favored actors, or spreading the reach of carbon pricing incentives – can and should be accomplished through other mechanisms.

From a political perspective, the dominant reason for offsets has been to accommodate industry's demand for low prices. A large volume of offsets keeps program costs low and enables incumbent firms to continue business-as-usual emissions, while paying modest fees to third parties that secure offset credits under the less-than-watchful eyes of market administrators. The right way to deal with industry pressure to reduce costs is to manage market prices directly, rather than indirectly through the flow of dubious offset credits. Policymakers should employ tight price collars and other price- or quantity-triggered, rule-based policy interventions designed to keep market prices within a politically tolerable zone. Offsets purport to achieve these goals without sacrificing program ambition, but time and time again, offset programs end up producing low-quality environmental outcomes that obviate this claim. It is far better to have a program with lower explicit price ambitions than one that claims to deliver the moon, but mostly delivers low-quality offsets instead.

A second rationale for offsets is that they can generate important environmental co-benefits, such as to species or land conservation.[30] These policy goals can be more readily achieved in other ways, including competition among programs on an even playing field with other claims for direct public funding. This approach would require project proponents to make their case in competition against other potential expenditures on cost-effectiveness criteria. Competition will help increase environmental and economic co-benefits and also create transparency (and political support) for the most effective programs. As an added benefit, the consequences of imperfect implementation are significantly lower in the context of expenditures than in the context of offsets. Getting offset calculations wrong – on additionality, leakage, or any of the other host of unverifiable and technically maddening concepts – ends up generating a net increase in climate emissions because regulated emitters can increase their capped emissions for every offset credit in circulation. In contrast, a less-than-perfect expenditure may exhibit room for improvement, but the perfect need not be the enemy of the good – an imperfect spending program still reduces emissions. That is, when public funds are spent to reduce emissions but only achieve 75% of their intended effects, the outcome is still a net win: the policy delivered 75% of its benefits, instead of increasing net emissions by 25%.

Offsets are also promoted for a third set of reasons: their ability to channel funds to target sectors. Perhaps their intended beneficiaries are politically influential, or perhaps policymakers wish to ramp up investment in uncapped sectors where mitigation is especially difficult. Whatever the case, these rationales are better accommodated through spending approaches instead. To attract funds, the purported benefit of a project would have to survive competition with like projects – whether in terms of political or climate benefits – creating incentives to identify only those investments with the greatest expected benefits. Serious projects will survive, and the wheat will be separated from the chaff.

When offset programs go wrong, they create difficult and lasting challenges that slow down the pace of climate policy. Policymakers have given too little thought about what to do when large offset programs fall short. It's easier to change spending priorities than it is to remedy the structural consequences of low-quality offsets, which have been vexing in practice. Consider the canonical example of Europe's reliance on international Clean Development Mechanism offsets in its early carbon market. As public awareness about the low quality of CDM credits grew, pressure mounted to reform the use of offsets in the EU ETS program. Ultimately, the European Commission decided to ban the use of the most problematic CDM offsets and significantly limit total CDM usage beginning in 2013, the start of the third phase of the EU ETS.[31] But by the end of the second phase – when lax limits still applied – regulated emitters used more than 1 billion CDM offset and Joint Implementation credits in the EU ETS.[32] While not the only cause of low market prices in the years that followed, emitters' ability to rely heavily on offsets in the second phase of the EU ETS allowed them to bank a large number of EU allowances for use in the third phase, contributed to market oversupply conditions that have only just begun to diminish in light of recent, hard-fought reforms. This story matters because quality control problems with the EU's reliance on international offset credits created a political problem that took years to resolve. Emitters that held offsets or expected to use them opposed reforms, which meant that the only realistic path forward was to enable emitters to spike their use of offsets in phase 2 of the EU ETS and, as a result, to carry forward a large bank of allowances into phase 3. As Table 7.1 indicates, the Market Stability Reserve's dynamic rules have finally removed about as many allowances from the program as the use of international offsets freed up in phase 2.

Another example illustrates how policymakers have greater options when they pursue environmental programs through expenditures instead of offsets. Consider the case of deforestation in the Brazilian Amazon, a hotly contested issue.

For many years, the governments of Norway and Germany have invested heavily in payment-based systems called REDD+ programs, where funds flow to parties that purport to protect intact tropical forests. Norway, in particular, has invested about $1 billion in the Brazilian Amazon.[33] Under Brazilian President Bolsonaro, however, deforestation rates have skyrocketed as his administration dismantles the environmental governance regimes developed over years to manage its tropical forests. President Bolsonaro's radical agenda met with widespread international condemnation in 2019, with Norway and Germany withdrawing their forest funds, multinational companies threatening to divest from Brazilian products in their supply chains, and a number of European countries discussing whether to take punitive measures against Brazil in trade policy.[34]

Time will tell how effective these punishments are in forcing a hostile administration to reverse course on its domestic policy, but contrast this situation with what would have happened had international aid to Brazil come in the form of carbon offsets. For years the California government has been promoting an international offsets program called the Tropical Forest Standard (see chapter 5), eyeing the Brazilian state of Acre as its first prospective partner.[35] If California emitters had been buying offsets from Acre in the years running up to President Bolsonaro's election, the sudden spike in deforestation rates would have completely overwhelmed the offset protocol's meager 10% buffer pool[36] and led to massive non-additional crediting inside California. What could state policymakers have done in response? Addressing the damage to the carbon market's environmental integrity would have required them to impose punitive costs not on the Brazilian regime, but on their own domestic industries, which would presumably point out they were just following the state government's own rules and fight any reform affecting the credits they had already purchased. An outcome like that of Europe's response to the crisis with CDM offset credits would be the most likely outcome: controls phasing in over time, but with whack-a-mole problems following as a cut in offsets leads to a glut of bankable allowances, which in turn need to be balanced after the fact. In contrast, payment-based systems can just as easily blow up – but managing the consequences that follow only requires political leaders to stand up for international norms and environmental values, not impose major costs on their own people.

Any proposal to get rid of offsets will kick the hornet's nest of offset developers, whose entire business model depends on preserving the status quo – not to mention their environmental NGO allies. Policymakers considering such a proposal should expect concentrated resistance from these quarters, but may find success if they coordinate their reforms with comprehensive strategies designed to accommodate industry interests and retain sufficient funding to support politically connected projects. Getting rid of offsets also brings benefits that could increase the size or strength of the pro-climate coalition. Most notably, offsets deprive the state of revenues raised at auction because offset programs depress market prices in proportion to their size. Forcing companies to buy more allowances from the state – possibly at higher prices – will raise additional revenues that can be deployed to build interest in reform. Thus, by pursuing offset reforms alongside inward-facing reforms to market designs that raise political support for higher prices, policymakers may be able to wrest control over the funds offsets inefficiently divert to third parties.

Our final recommendation with regard to external relations concerns direct links between markets. The standard market playbook emphasizes the benefits of linking together markets from the "bottom up" – possibly offering a way around the failure to implement international markets from the "top down." This advice has reality backwards. Successful market links require sophisticated institutional capacity in every single partner jurisdiction. Pursuing links before those institutions are ready creates multilateral markets that are thin and fragile.

We see a limited role for external market links going forward. Instead of aiming to maximize market links, policymakers should instead focus on proving the effectiveness of their policy models for export and emulation, rather than formal linking.

When it comes to external market links, what matters most is institutional capacity. Analysts have focused, wrongly, on potential gains from trade owing to differences in marginal prices across prospective market links; and policymakers have focused, unwisely, on promoting the number of governments participating in a linked system as a kind of validation of their own wisdom or a sign of growing climate policy ambition. Both groups have it wrong. The debate over market links needs to focus first and foremost on the institutional conditions necessary to sustain strong programs, otherwise market links will remain thin and brittle – or, worse, the links may create new structural barriers to growing ambition within a linked system over time, as the ambition of one jurisdiction crashes head-first into the weaker effort of its linked partner.

Practically speaking, the potential for external market links that meet the conditions for effective integration is likely to be small. This reflects, in part, the limits facing subnational governments, many of which are leading the charge on climate policy. California may be the fifth largest economy in the world by GDP, but it lacks a dedicated civil service focused on foreign affairs and is prohibited by the US Constitution from signing legally binding treaties.[37] As a result, the Western Climate Initiative – featuring California, Québec, and, temporarily in 2018, Ontario – is thinner than it might appear. Legally, market links take the form of domestic rules that recognize the compliance instruments of foreign partners as equal to the value of their domestic equivalents – essentially, a fixed exchange rate between foreign currencies.[38] As discussed in chapter 6, however, agreements between subnational governments are unenforceable as a legal matter.

It bears repeating that the standard playbook on market links reverses the order of operations that is required to achieve deep and substantial cross-border cooperation. Oversupplied markets with low prices make the most attractive linking partners. Forging new links with such a low-cost market allows policymakers to show that they are acting on climate without imposing the costs needed to actually deliver the goods. For these reasons, some policymakers actually suggest that oversupply is a desirable incentive to expand markets' reach through linking.[39] Put in simpler terms, when one market has too many allowances to achieve its goals, it can sell those to others, essentially infecting the new entrant's program with the oversupply virus. If the end goal is to link markets, there is no question this tactic has merits – after all, nothing makes the politics of markets easier than strategies that trade environmental effectiveness for low costs. But this approach gets the logic backwards. Serious market-based policies require the institutional capacity to manage cross-border economic impacts from rising prices, not short-term solutions designed to create the appearance of cost-effective environmental success while kicking the can of institutional reform down the road. Those approaches defer the investments in the institutional capacities to support cross-border cooperation and replace them with liabilities that are harder to manage in a multilateral context.

Rather than focus on thin market links, policymakers would be wise to consider other forms of policy leadership. Chief among them should be the concept of identifying and demonstrating model market designs and institutions that others can emulate – particularly those with smaller or less sophisticated governments. The learning that follows would be no less important and arguably far more useful than what actually happens in the context of thin market links.

With careful and comprehensive reform (see Table 7.2), markets should be able to contribute significantly more to climate policy. And if large nation-states like the United States or China commit the necessary resources and political capital to implementing well-designed home markets, there may be some potential for deep cross-market links in the future. But even in the best-case scenario, markets are unlikely to come close to displacing regulation-dominated climate strategies. The primary value of well-run markets will instead be to improve the static economic efficiency of a climate policy portfolio in sectors where the costs and opportunities for achieving deep reductions become clear, and the institutional capacity to compensate policy losers is sufficient. As explained further in the next chapter, regulations and industrial policy are here to stay. They need to be managed wisely to address the shortcomings of real-world markets, whether Potemkin or reformed.

Table 7.2 Summary of market reform recommendations

Issue	Do:	Do not:
Program ambition and coverage	Measure oversupply transparently and reduce oversupply using rule-based program reforms	Ignore evidence and history
	Manage market prices via a price collar and/or through central-banking-like supply management	Rely on oversupply to contain program costs
	Narrow program coverage to one or at most two sectors; implement multiple programs, rather than one	Pursue economy-wide programs that create multiple veto points for regulated industries
Revenue use	Set up separate funds with each dedicated to a distinct purpose	Lump expenditures together in an omnibus appropriations process
	Impose oversight on environmental and revenue recycling programs	Co-mingle political and environmental expenditures
	Require transparency in how much money is spent on political projects	Impose additional oversight on political expenditures
	Separate low-cost and transformative environmental investments and use metrics to evaluate program effectiveness	Co-mingle high-cost and low-cost environmental spending programs
	Fund near-term deployment and long-term R&D	Fund long-lived capital-intensive infrastructure projects
External relations	Eliminate offsets; replace them with price collars and program spending	Rely heavily on offsets or allow any low-cost offsets
	Focus inward to develop politically stable coalitions before linking	Focus outward on superficial market links before program ambition
	Focus on institutional capacity to manage market links before linking	Focus on potential gains from trade or public relations opportunities
	Promote successful internal policy models for export or emulation	Fetishize market links as a means of substantiating climate leadership

8

Rightsizing markets and industrial policy

Most of this book is about setting the right expectations for market-based policies. Its core assertion is that advocates for market-based strategies have overplayed what market-based policy instruments can deliver in the real world where economies must be put on a trajectory for deep decarbonization. A growing number of policymakers, firms, and lobby groups have joined in the chorus advocating market-based strategies for various reasons: some because market forces sound powerful and modern, some because they hope that market-based strategies will appeal to a broad political spectrum needed for politically sustainable climate policy, and others for an array of well-intentioned yet cynical logics. This increasingly powerful coalition is screaming "markets" when the data, for the most part, show that market-based strategies have failed to have much impact on climate pollution and on the development of innovative technologies for deep decarbonization.

Fixing what ails market-based approaches to pollution control isn't simply a matter of tweaking policy variables here and there. Rather, the problems are built into the structure of politics and the capabilities of governments to adopt and manage market-based policy instruments. There are no magic wands that change those constraints. Carbon markets, except in a handful of societies that are unified on the need for action and also have highly capable systems of market administration, have failed to generate the price levels and confidence needed to encourage much change because they end up as Potemkin markets. After more than a decade of reform efforts, only the EU ETS has emerged as a notable exception to this sobering fact. Emission taxes have performed better, but only for a tiny portion of global emissions and in a handful of trade-insulated sectors; they are unlikely to scale any faster than markets because their acute political visibility makes them even more difficult to enact in the first place. Even where cap-and-trade and emission tax systems have performed the best, most of the real work for developing new technologies and cutting emissions has been accomplished through other policy instruments.

Fixing what ails market-based approaches is also not merely a matter of building more political support for effective climate policy. To be sure, more powerful political support in more countries is essential to taking the climate problem seriously. But political motivation, alone, will not overcome the structural failures of market-based strategies. Recognizing these limits is an invitation to rethink how market-based policy instruments could be deployed as part of a larger and more effective strategy for achieving deep decarbonization.

The first step in developing that larger strategy involves rightsizing markets – understanding that the roles for market-based policies are much narrower than originally thought. These approaches must be designed principally to work within countries where it is possible to administer them reliably. They must be designed for a Potemkin world – where markets operate alongside regulation, which is and will remain the policy instrument of choice in most countries. They should be targeted to sectors where it is easier to manage the politics of highly visible market signals and where the process of decarbonization involves firms and consumers choosing from among mature technologies with known properties and investment risks. That role has been observed, so far, mainly in the power sector, where market signals, such as in the United Kingdom, have played a big role in favoring zero-emission renewables and relatively low-emission gas over coal. Indeed, the earliest and most highly effective market-based strategies, such as for cutting lead from gasoline, worked in settings where technology performance was largely known – where market signals offered a powerful and flexible incentive for firms to cut pollution in optimal ways within a single, well-defined sector with a well-defined suite of technological responses.[1]

A sector-by-sector approach for carbon pricing should recognize that the rule of one price, which is so attractive to the theory of market-based pollution control, is a political millstone when applied across the economy as a whole. The politics of decarbonization vary by sector, as do the tasks of industrial transformation. In most sectors, deep decarbonization requires support for fledgling technologies and new markets. In some sectors, interest groups are highly sensitive to visible changes in price – a sensitivity that, if accommodated through markets that span multiple sectors, leads to low prices and ineffective market systems in every sector they touch. Coupling diverse sectors into a single market that operates under a single price dilutes the entire, broader effort. The benefit of multi-sectoral coupling through common markets is flexibility of effort, but the cost is much greater and pernicious: locking markets into low ambition.

The logic of rightsizing will be a bitter pill to swallow for those who advocate heavy reliance upon markets. It is a pill that must be swallowed, however, if societies are to focus on strategies that have the potential to work.

In this chapter, we look at what is left after the pill is swallowed. If the role of market policies is highly constrained, what can be done to bend down emission curves and achieve deep decarbonization? Many studies have outlined trajectories for deep decarbonization without much attention to the policies that will be needed to achieve that outcome.[2] A growing number of studies have also articulated collections of policies and other interventions to reduce emissions.[3] And some scholarship has focused on the styles of policymaking and administration needed to steer these kinds of deep transformations.[4] A few studies look, as well, at the politics of industrial transformation.[5] These are big questions with complex answers. Here we sketch out what else is needed, after expectations and designs for markets are rightsized.

Effective climate policy requires two main elements. The first is industrial policy: that is, direct intervention into key sectors of the economy to support fledgling technologies and build new systems for industrial production. The standard view that market-based strategies would be more efficient than direct government action – that is, "command and control" regulation, as it was known pejoratively – was formulated at a time when regulation often performed poorly. Regulators directly selected technology, often with little knowledge of whether their choices were best, and had no system in place to learn quickly; they created rigidities in the economy that drove up costs. Government R&D programs poured money into incumbent technologies – a pork barrel rather than a wellspring of innovation.[6] When market-based strategies were compared against old-school regulatory interventions, the former looked much superior.[7] But those comparisons are misleading from today's vantage point. Managed well, today's regulatory systems are much more adaptive, flexible, and responsive to new information.[8] When applied to the challenge of warming emissions, direct regulation and complementary industrial policies are well suited to the task of creating the conditions for deep trans-formation in technology systems and then identifying the technology pathways that are viable. For some policy analysts and advocates, our support for regulation may be seen as throwing down a gauntlet in favor of "the state" over "the market." We see this differently: as a blend of efforts where the role of the state must be large because market forces, even when well designed to the limit of what is politically feasible, can only do so much – especially at the early stages of developing, testing, and deploying new decarbonization technologies and infrastructures. Indeed, the best studies of pollution markets have usually found that the market and the state work in tandem.[9]

Our thinking about smart industrial policy draws heavily on the concepts of "experimentalist governance" (XG). It is about creating the incentives for firms and governments to test new ideas, learn quickly what works, and then adjust goals and directions in light of that learned experience. It requires highly motivated and capable governments and industries; fortuitously, those conditions exist across many of the jurisdictions that are poised to lead on climate policy.[10] One of the most important insights from XG scholarship, pioneered by Charles Sabel and Jonathan Zeitlin, concerns incentives. Firms and governments invest in the search for radical solutions – such as industrial transformations that yield deep decarbonization – not because they face small changes in the relative prices of production factors such as the cost of natural gas or coal. Rather, they are motivated by big hammers that create existential threats to their industry and political support.[11] Radical change is risky, and the key players won't grapple with the need to take those risks if policy is merely designed to internalize externalities through modest market signals.

The second essential element of effective climate policy is international strategy. The standard view is that cooperation is important because the problem of climate change is global. Our view is that cooperation is required because success in achieving deep transformation requires industrial strategies that test new ideas across many circumstances: that is, collections of experiments and joint learning rather than just singleton settings. Chapters 5 and 6 explained why markets won't become a major mechanism for achieving deep international cooperation; recognizing that reality requires looking for different approaches instead. Direct market linkages between cap-and-trade systems are thin and few; international offsets, for the most part, have been used to dilute the power of market forces rather than expand them effectively to new jurisdictions. By contrast, industrial policy is much easier to coordinate across borders. Acting alone, neither government nor business has the scope and authority needed to achieve deep decarbonization across multiple markets where technology, ideas, and capital are fungible. Working together will make that possible, but it will require rethinking many accepted wisdoms. For example, the Paris Agreement has a role to play in supporting climate policy deepening, but at best it will only be an umbrella under which more focused joint action by business and government can flourish. In terms of membership, Paris is too big and too unwieldy because it involves nearly every nation on the planet and operates by consensus rule. It is also too focused on governments because serious problem-solving will require other actors as well. Working in small public–private clubs of cooperating nations and industries will make it possible to achieve cooperation far beyond what Paris, alone, can achieve.[12]

A system of coordinated industrial policy is well suited to the early stage of technological development in most of the industries that will be pivotal to deep decarbonization. The places in the world where there is large and growing public support for climate policy are creating strong incentives – big hammers – that are motivating firms and governments to invest in new technologies and to build new industrial policies. These politically motivated industrial policies have taken on many different names, such as the "green new deal" or the "new carbon economy." Existing firms that are incumbents in those markets – and fear losing their license to operate – have similarly powerful incentives to invest in a decarbonized future. Successful industrial policies will also create incentives for new firms to emerge – as those new entrants grow in market share, they will gain political power, a process that is evident today with the rising political influence of Tesla, BYD, and other new entrants into clean personal vehicle and bus markets.

The right balance of incumbent and new firms is one of the great unknowns in this process. Attention to that question must lie at the center of industrial decarbonization strategy. Incumbent firms with new missions may be part of the solution to the climate problem – something that is visible today with global electric power incumbents that have taken on the mission of deploying renewables; global incumbents who build nuclear plants, such as the South Korean-designed plant beginning operations in Abu Dhabi; and a few established auto makers that are making big bets on electric vehicles, such as Volkswagen. Or incumbents might remain a core part of the problem as blockers of radical transformation. That danger that may be emerging among the aircraft industry (and its regulators), which is focused more on using offsets to cut emissions than on radical technological innovation. Smart industrial policy, coordinated across a critical mass of leader jurisdictions, must mobilize both incumbents and new entrants. The incumbents offer the advantage of scale and alignment with existing infrastructure, which can speed the process of technological transformation, but the disadvantage of deep investment in old orders. The new entrants offer the advantage of fresh thinking (and easy failure), but the disadvantages from a lack of heft and political power.

A smart international strategy must look far beyond the jurisdictions that are motivated to be climate leaders. At best, today, governments within the nations and subnational units that are willing to be climate leaders account for about one-fifth of global emissions. Their leadership is essential to framing the options for deep decarbonization and proving new technological concepts, but leaders have limited direct leverage on global climate politics because they constitute a small and shrinking share of global emissions (see Figure 8.1). In 1990, the jurisdictions that would become reliable climate leaders – all of the European core, plus about half the United States and other parts of the advanced industrialized economy – accounted for about one-third of global emissions. Today their share is much smaller. Indeed, it is now on par with the countries that have been reliable blockers of climate policy efforts, such as Russia, key OPEC members, and other big carbon exporters.

Leaders, we argue, must rethink how they invest in leadership. They must shift away from measures that look good at home but don't scale: for example, purchasing offsets so that firms or governments can pretend they are carbon neutral, or cutting emissions through technological measures that are so expensive that they are unlikely to be adopted widely. Instead, every action by leaders must be evaluated through the lens of followership: does the early investment that befits leadership raise the odds of pervasive followership? Strategic leadership requires active, coordinated industrial policies to explore the range of technologies needed for deep decarbonization and to learn quickly what works through the logic of XG. It also requires active promotion of followership, so that the politics and markets in leader jurisdictions become more actively connected to those in the rest of the world. Globalization of ideas, political movements, and technologies is potentially a boon for rapid, deep decarbonization and is a force that must be mobilized to that end.

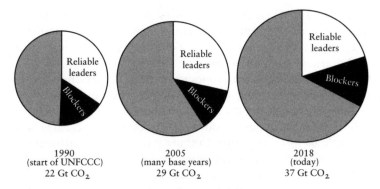

Figure 8.1 Climate policy leaders and followers

Chart shows fraction of global CO_2 from fossil energy use in 1990, 2005, and 2018 from countries and jurisdictions that are reliable leaders on climate change, along with big carbon exporters that have reliably tried to block effective global policy. The size of the pies is proportional to total global emissions.

Source: Computed from the EDGAR energy-related CO_2 emissions data set, using the logic of "leadership" and "followership" outlined in David G. Victor, "We have climate leaders. Now we need followers," *The New York Times* (Dec. 13, 2019); Monica Crippa et al., "Fossil CO_2 and GHG Emissions of All World Countries – 2019 Report" (2019), *https://edgar.jrc. ec.europa.eu/overview.php?v=booklet2019.*

This approach – decarbonization through industrial policy and strategic internationalization – is designed to realign the political forces we identified in chapter 1. The incumbency of big carbon is firmly established almost everywhere in the world, and that incumbency helps explain why so many market-based systems (especially cap-and-trade) end up as Potemkin markets. Active industrial policy must be designed to redirect and rattle that incumbency and create new political forces – a blend of incumbents that have rethought their strategy, along with organized new firms that have a stake in successful decarbonization. Success will see the status quo reconfigured around the logic of deep decarbonization. That process of industrial and political co-evolution is easier to organize when focused sector by sector, because the politics (and the roles of incumbents and new entrants) vary by sector. Indeed, the world's most successful examples of active industrial policy around clean energy reveal exactly those kinds of political processes at work, such as the emergence of politically powerful renewable energy policies in Germany or the emergence of electric vehicle industries in lead markets such as Norway, California, and now China.[13] While most analysts tend to focus on deep decarbonization as a process of identifying and following technological pathways to low emissions, in the real world success in this venture will require a dynamic political process that creates and strengthens interest groups that are paving those pathways to a low-carbon future. Technology and investment, marshalled strategically, create new politics as organized groups that favor deep decarbonization command greater market shares, deeper alliances, and a louder political voice.

Toward a new industrial policy

Deep decarbonization is a complex process that is fraught with political and administrative challenges. At its core it requires doing three things. The first is encouraging the emergence of radical new technologies and business practices. The second involves diffusing those technologies into more widespread service so that innovators can gain experience and improve their technology through learning and scaling. And the third involves pervasive – in the case of climate pollution, global – reconfiguration of markets so that essentially all firms and households shift to low- and zero-emission technologies.[14]

Market incentives can be particularly effective during the diffusion and reconfiguration stages of technology development, when the best approaches are generally known but many firms and households need encouragement to adopt them. But unless prices are extremely high, market strategies don't have much impact on emergence. And even where new technologies are emerging, firms won't bear the risk and cost of developing completely new production methods in the face of only marginal – and highly unstable – incentives for change.

Today, as we argued in chapter 1, the process of deep decarbonization is at the early, emergence stages for new technology in nearly every major emitting sector. New business practices and technologies have been imagined and a few tested – for example, advanced methods for making green steel and plastics, or advanced power plants that capture all their pollution or even have negative emissions – but the overall state of development is still fledgling. This insight helps to reveal why the promise and reality of markets have been so different. Not only are there major structural barriers to making market instruments work effectively, but the market instrument itself is not well suited, on its own, to the very stage of technological and business development the world is in today with regard to deep decarbonization.[15]

Fixing this problem requires much more active intervention in the places where new technologies must emerge. The good news is that over the last few decades scholars and policymakers have learned a lot about how to organize that intervention, so that government works closely with industry to gather and test information about which technology pathways are most promising, to learn quickly from mistakes, and to adapt to changing conditions. These insights have traveled under different names, such as "adaptive management" – a popular idea developed, in part, by thinking about the policy process as an ecosystem of ideas and technologies that must constantly adjust to new information.[16] The place where such ideas have been applied most extensively is Europe, which is hardly surprising since state intervention in Europe is generally greater than in the United States and because the rise of the EU has required building a sophisticated administrative system that can respond not only to shifts in technology but also to the diversity of business and political settings across the many different EU member states.[17]

Scholars who have looked closely at how the EU has used XG approaches to tackle problems have found that its patterns of state–firm interactions are very similar to those in jurisdictions that want to be climate leaders. There is powerful and growing pressure to invest in transformative solutions, but the best routes forward are unknown. Experimentalism is designed for these settings – where uncertainty is high, as are risks for early investors, because new technologies and business practices are taking shape. Only with government and business working together is it possible to narrow uncertainties – a process that requires information from field trials that reveal practical insights about what works and scales. Traditional self-regulation by firms acting on their own behalf does not work because they have neither sufficient incentive for action nor enough control over their broader environment to solve problems on their own. And traditional regulation where government does all the work also fails, but for different reasons: because state policymakers do not have sufficient information about new technologies to avoid making egregious and expensive errors. What's new about XG is that it explains why these actors are motivated to work together to narrow uncertainties and transform markets.

The best research on XG has identified four main elements of effective systems.[18]

The first is that big problems are broken down into smaller and more tractable units. Applied to climate change, this logic requires breaking down the big challenge of deep decarbonization into smaller units – most likely industrial sectors, as well as cross-cutting applications such as energy carriers (e.g., hydrogen) and fundamental services (e.g., mobility). Within each unit, overall provisional goals can be set – just as, for example, today many policy efforts are benchmarked against consistency with the goal of stopping warming at 2 or 1.5 degrees above pre-industrial levels. Nobody really knows if those goals are achievable, but they are a corrigible first draft. Breaking down big problems into smaller ones makes it possible to focus resources and incentives on the nub of each problem – to tailor incentives and actions to the particulars of decarbonizing electric power, which is distinct from decarbonizing cement, different yet again from steel, and such.[19]

The second element is an incentive for change. Unlike market-based incentives – which work at the margin and are generally small – the incentives that cause the biggest changes are known as "penalty defaults." They are big hammers. Examples include loss of reputation and access to whole markets from failure to respond to a pressing problem – extreme outcomes that motivate firms to search for profound solutions. Unlike compliance penalties – where there are agreed-upon standards for performance and firms know what it costs to fail – penalty defaults are both more draconian and more ambiguous. They could be catastrophic to firms that fail to respond, but they are provisional – if good efforts are made and solutions prove more difficult to find, then penalties are delayed and additional rounds of problem-solving follow. For example, when palm oil traders organized themselves to create a large supply of sustainable palm oil – indeed, a supply that is so large that today it outstrips demand – they did so because they feared exclusion from the European market. European policymakers (and political parties) were increasingly aware of the consequences of destruction of rain forests, notably in Indonesia, owing to palm oil expansion, and were looking for draconian solutions. Airlines find themselves in a similar situation, where draconian threats in Europe have motivated a search for solutions. So does the gas and oil industry, where many firms (starting with those headquartered in Europe) are now actively hunting for solutions to deep decarbonization in ways they didn't before policy threats became existential for the industry. The intensity of harmful consequences motivates action. These penalties, although severe, are not automatic; they are applied only when firms fail to make an effort, which creates an incentive for them to reveal information about what they are trying and about the real pace of progress.

The third step in XG is experimentation. Firms and governments that face penalty defaults have strong incentives to make good-faith efforts to find solutions. Those solutions include testing of new technologies, learning what works, and creating the conditions – with public finance, with assured markets (such as the public procurement of green products), and other measures – to allow still further experimentation at scale. All of XG pivots around this stage in development, where hypothetical ideas are put to the test.

Fourth is learning and adjustment. Because government and business work together in testing, they are also well positioned to learn what works and adjust accordingly. And because they operate under the shadow of penalty defaults, the adjustment process is guided by the compass of performance – seeking options that will scale and address the conditions that created an incentive for transformation in the first place. Working in small niches – in particular sectors on particular problems – makes it easier to strip away uncertainties and focus on problem-solving. Lessons learned in each sector and each problem make it possible to adjust original goals – to accelerate timetables if technologies and new businesses prove easier to create than expect, or slow down and readjust if problem-solving is trickier.

XG sounds like an alien and fragile species that requires special skills from government. What has emerged from the study of regulation, however, is the realization that these kinds of systems are commonplace; they just have not been comprehensively understood – which the lens of XG aims to remedy. Within Europe, XG-like processes explain how governments have successfully managed some of the region's most complex water pollution problems: namely, from highly decentralized and complex sources such as fertilizer residues on farms that run off into rivers.[20] In California, the Air Resources Board engaged in a form of XG when it tried, in the 1990s, to transform automobiles into electric vehicles. It set ambitious goals (10% of new car sales as electric) that motivated at least a segment of the industry to run experiments and learn what was feasible – which turned out to include a large deployment of hybrid electric cars. And then it constantly redirected and reframed those goals as government and industry, together, discovered that electrification wasn't immediately practical, although there were other technological pathways to deep reductions in emissions. (Today's electric vehicle revolution seems to have more sticking power – in large part because battery storage has improved so much since the 1990s.[21]) The Montreal Protocol worked in much the same way: breaking down a big problem (ozone-depleting substances) into categories where action to find substitutes could be focused, with goals ratcheted as lessons were learned and firms were motivated by fear of being unable to keep up with change.[22]

Applying this logic to climate change can inspire and organize an industrial decarbonization strategy. Industrial policy has become a bogeyman in some countries – such as the United States, where much of the political elite abhors the idea – because it conjures images of a Leviathan state that dictates change through faceless bureaucrats who are far removed from reality. The reality is that industrial policy, done properly, is highly adaptive to frontier conditions – about technological and market opportunity and industrial organization. This is how the Chinese government, among many other examples, learned to spend resources efficiently – much more efficiently than in earlier forms of industrial policy – to advance key technologies such as electric buses, advanced nuclear reactors, and wind power.[23] And this phenomenon is hardly unique to state-dominated societies. In the United States, when firms want to take big risks on advanced technology – for example, building the next generation of nuclear plants (as Southern Company is struggling to do, albeit with no small degree of challenges) or the first offshore wind generators on the Atlantic coast – they turn to a blend of private capital and ingenuity alongside state support such as direct grants and loan guarantees. What matters is not whether the state is involved; it nearly always is when it comes to large, risky changes in technology and market. Instead, the important questions revolve around *how* the state and private industry work together. And the best answers lie with XG.

Getting serious about climate change requires applying the XG logic to every major emitting sector. In nearly every case, transformation in the sector will require radical technological changes that involve big risks for first movers. In the steel industry, for example, it requires new methods for producing steel that capture CO_2 that is intrinsically released during the process – which means new configurations for furnaces and combining technological insights for which the steel industry is expert, along with technologies and infrastructures far beyond traditional expertise, such as carbon capture and storage (CCS). It may also require rethinking the role of blast furnaces altogether – and reducing iron ore to steel directly by using hydrogen, which can be produced in a variety of methods to reduce climate emissions. That requires combining the steel industry with the fledgling hydrogen industry, along with methods for investing in hydrogen production and transmission industries. There are many routes to green steel – all expensive and risky from today's vantage point – and at these early stages it is critical to map out the full range of options (which has been done) and to run experiments (which are just beginning).[24]

For those who think that industry, on its own, will do this best if it just faces high enough carbon prices and is left to its own ingenuity, it is instructive to look at the emergence of the example of CCS technologies and efforts to decarbonize clusters of industries. Consider the Northern Lights project being crafted by Norway's oil and gas company, Equinor, along with Shell and Total. (Equinor is partially state-owned but operates like a private company – one of the world's best-performing petroleum firms.) The project will gather CO_2 from many different sources and aggregate it into large volumes, which Equinor will then pump under the North Sea – a technical area in which the company has world-leading experience. Despite the fact that Norway and surrounding states (which will also supply CO_2) have some of the world's most aggressive carbon reduction policies and highest carbon taxes, the firm on its own can't justify the risk of investing in the needed infrastructure on the basis of market-based policies. It must rely directly on government – first in Norway, and then in alliance with the EU – to help stabilize the market, co-invest in infrastructure (pipelines and ships for transporting CO_2), and allow a firm that is highly motivated to be a first mover to deploy a game-changing suite of technologies. The same story is playing out in nearly every industry where first movers are mobilizing: in steel, cement, plastics, long-distance shipping, electrification of aircraft, and so on.[25]

An XG industrial policy must combine sticks and carrots as incentives. Most of the theory around XG emphasizes sticks – big hammers – that convince incumbent firms and governments to work together to solve problems that require joint action. Government and many elements of civil society can also offer carrots. These include preferential access to markets: for example, by using trade policy (border adjustments) to protect low-emission products from more polluting rivals. The exact methods for calculating the level and type of border adjustment remain a subject of contestation, which is why a variety of methods must be tested and the best, through experimentation, refined.[26] In some cases, deep-pocketed NGOs and public interest organizations can offer rewards – the series of X-prizes, for example – to encourage risky experimentation by an array of actors that might otherwise not be focused on the challenge.[27] There is a big role, as well, for direct subsidy of various forms, including cost-sharing for novel technologies and loan guarantees that lower the financing costs of demonstration projects.

Market-based strategies can play a big role paying for these costs – a topic we explored in chapter 4 (where we showed that well-functioning market-based systems allocate large fractions of the funds they raise to green spending) and chapter 7 (where we outlined a strategy that would lead to more effective green spending that included attention to transformative technological investments). That said, the volume of expenditure must be kept in perspective. Globally, all forms of carbon market policies – cap-and-trade and carbon taxes – raise less than $50 billion per year and allocate about $25 billion per year in green spending (see Figure 4.2). The scale of investment needed in new technologies is hard to pin down, but it is likely that right now the global leaders on climate policy could effectively scale to spend on the order of $100 billion per year on innovation, testing, and early-stage deployment of deep decarbonization technologies – with rapid scaling to higher levels with learning. For comparison, the debate over the European Green Deal – a multi-dimensional effort to transform and decarbonize the European economy – aims to mobilize at least €1 trillion in new investment over the coming decade, with the public portion of that expenditure at possibly about half. The new seven-year EU budget aims to allocate one-quarter of expenditure to climate change, which extrapolates to about €500 billion over the decade-long European Green Deal (plus maybe €100 billion of additional member state funding, although those national numbers may grow as more European countries expand their ambitions).[28]

As these numbers illustrate, there is a huge mismatch between funds that can be readily appropriated from market mechanisms and the level of expenditure needed. Filling that gap will require richer market mechanisms and also direct government spending from the tax base – alongside leverage that can multiply these resources through private capital. This same mismatch is seen everywhere that is experiencing a rise in political seriousness about climate change and a struggle to turn that political pressure into action. In the RGGI system of the northeastern United States – the cap-and-trade system whose design is most purely oriented around generating and spending revenue – the State of New York (the biggest revenue raiser) has mobilized just $100 million per year for green spending.[29] By contrast, the State of California has been spending several hundred million per year through the California Energy Commission – an organization whose main mission is direct support for transformation of the state's energy system aligned with the goal of deep decarbonization.[30]

If all this sits uncomfortably for readers who are skeptical that government has the skills to gather the needed information, it is worth noting that a more market-oriented approach would be no less demanding. That's because the task at hand for decarbonizing most sectors involves creating incentives for learning about radical transformation – big shifts in behavior. Long ago, Nobel-prize-winner Tom Schelling looked closely at how to design markets that would require transformative reductions in airport noise – a task similar to decarbonization in that lots of firms would need to adjust behavior in complex ways, with local details that were enormously variable (depending, in that case, on aircraft routing, pilot behavior, and onboard equipment). The information needed by government administrators to make a market perform that function was roughly equivalent to more direct administrative action.[31]

Decarbonization as an international strategy[32]

Getting serious about climate change means getting serious about creating and then diffusing widely a series of technological revolutions in low-carbon energy supply, industry, and agriculture. And this must eventually be done globally because the activities that cause warming pollution exist globally and the firms that must make potentially costly reductions compete in global markets.

While it is axiomatic that global cooperation will be needed, what is not so clear is how the needed forms of cooperation will emerge. Advocates for emissions trading and other market-based strategies see cooperation emerging through markets. In chapters 5 and 6, we showed that those visions have failed in practice. Offsets (chapter 5) have created the illusion of cross-border links, yet they have primarily served to undermine the ability of markets to create strong incentives to control pollution. Direct links between markets (chapter 6) are rare, thin, and fragile – and they tend to connect like markets rather than create incentives for expansion and deepening of efforts via gains from trade with unlike markets.

Making international cooperation effective requires understanding the nature of the problem at hand. It is useful to distinguish problems along two dimensions. One dimension is whether the nature of actions needed to address a problem is understood – are the policies, technologies, and business models needed to address the problem known, including their cost? The other dimension is whether the key players agree on the level of effort needed and how to allocate the burdens and benefits of cooperation.[33]

This "understanding vs. consensus" matrix, shown in Figure 8.2, helps to map the ways that cooperation can affect technological transitions and, ultimately, solve environmental problems.

Cooperation can help solve problems marked by low understanding and limited agreement (upper left corner) through experimentation, trial projects, puzzling, and learning. In this mode, cooperation does not require widespread agreement or understanding – just a motivation in enough political jurisdictions and firms to jump-start the process of experimentation and testing of ideas in niches. The watchwords for governance are experimentation and learning.[34] In these early stages, the raw information needed for learning and wider understanding emerges. Learning from these niche experiments is not an automatic process – it requires institutions that can review the lessons from experiments and figure out what's working (and what isn't). Often those institutions are technical bodies – such as industry associations and regulators and expert bodies set up by treaties – that help frame the policy options for further effort. Often, experimentation is costly and requires direct incentives so that firms and other key actors, such as research laboratories, will test new ideas. Firms can be motivated to provide those incentives by penalty defaults. And governments can supplement

		Degree of Consensus About Actions	
		Low	High
Degree of Understanding About the Problem at Hand	Low	**Experimentalist learning:** Experimentation and learning in *niches* can help identify superior solutions and political supporters.	**Coordinated diffusion:** Scaling up of effort as more parties agree that action is needed; *diffusion* of lessons from motivated early movers that understand the problem to other sectors and countries.
	High	**Gridlock:** Parties know what they want individually, but collective action is infeasible.	**Contracting:** Specific agreements around specific solutions, so that each party knows what it must do and what to expect from others. Reconfiguration of a technology system involves changing the behavior of all actors.

Figure 8.2   Strategies for international cooperation

Source: Figure reprinted with permission from David G. Victor, Frank W. Geels, and Simon Sharpe, "Accelerating the Low Carbon Transition: The Case for Stronger, More Targeted and Coordinated International Action," BEIS, Energy Transitions Commission, and Brookings Institution (Nov. 2019), at 131, *http://www.energy-transitions.org/content/accelerating-low-carbon-transition.*

those resources with programs designed to spend effectively the revenues that are raised through auctioning of emission credits, a topic we explored in chapters 4 and 7.

With experience and deeper understanding of the nature of the technology and policy transitions, a wider array of niches with successful new industries can emerge. These applications help build experience with the relevant technologies, and allow the creation of infrastructures and rules that facilitate even larger market shares. As firms, governments, and their political supporters discover tangible information about the costs and benefits, they become more powerful politically because they have revenues and other resources that flow from deployment and they have concrete information about what works. All else being equal, this diffusion process will happen faster and with greater impact if the markets where the technology takes off are larger and more numerous. The watchwords for international cooperation, here, are coordinated creation of markets for low-carbon products, joint procurement, and coordination of deployment.

Finally, as diffusion proceeds and the industrial base anchored in the transition economy grows, the underlying interests shift. Interests reconfigure to support further action, and detailed knowledge about the industries and policies needed grows quickly. Here, the watchword for governance is contracting: that is, detailed agreements around known solutions that address known barriers to further application. (Much of the formal literature on international cooperation has emphasized, in various ways, contracting approaches. That's because many scholars start with the assumption that collective action is hard to achieve because even when there are potential joint gains from cooperation, the self-interest of countries leads them to focus more narrowly on protecting just their individual interests.) Joint action does not happen unless there is confidence that collective solutions will be followed.[35] Our approach here emphasizes the roles of uncertainty and learning in the early stages and then discovery of places where, indeed, contracting will be needed.

This framework offers two related insights into how cooperation can usefully contribute to deep decarbonization.

First, cooperation leads to successful problem-solving by performing different functions that lead clockwise around Figure 8.2: from the upper left to the lower right. Cooperation is not magic, and it does not always work. Badly designed, early efforts can lead to gridlock, if parties, as they learn, don't also create a transition in political consensus on the need for action (lower left corner). This danger of gridlock is why it is so important that efforts at cooperation be informed closely by insights into how pervasive transitions in technologies, infrastructures and industries actually happen.[36]

Second, understanding the best modes for cooperation requires looking at the underlying nature of the problem at hand. Most sectors in the world today are in their early stages of decarbonization – where experimentalism is the most important mode of action. This helps to explain why market-based strategies have not been that relevant – because they don't, by themselves, create sufficient incentive for experimentation. Moreover, the geometry of cooperation in these early stages is different from in later phases. In early phases, the role of cooperation is to create a critical mass of first-mover nations and firms, so that reliable incentives for experimentation exist and so that road-mapped technology pathways can be tested. By contrast, today, much of the policy focus on cooperation is on the Paris Agreement, which is an intergovernmental agreement that involves all nations. Paris has the wrong geometry for experimentation and also does not centrally involve industry. Success requires looking far beyond (and within) Paris to much smaller and more focused agreements between key first-mover countries and industry groups. Market policies – if designed to create effective incentives – can be more useful in the later stages of diffusion and reconfiguration. In those stages, uncertainty is lower (thanks to experimentation) and the suites of technologies and business practices are better known, as are the costs. Market incentives within countries can be designed to encourage more widespread adoption of these new technologies. But the suite of incentives will need to include many others – including, most likely, border measures that help ensure that countries and firms that adopt low-emission technologies do not suffer in global competition.[37]

Rethinking leadership

The logic outlined above is particularly well suited for the early stages of transforming the industrial and agricultural activities that cause emissions. Although scholars often call this a "transition," the needed changes are actually much more transformative and radical – they are, in many sectors, complete revolutions in production methods, investment patterns, and probably also the identities of dominant firms. The risks are massive, which is why success requires highly targeted policy strategies in which government and business work together and policy is geared to promote experimentation and to protect markets where new products and services are emerging. Simple price signals – especially from Potemkin markets that have limited coverage – won't achieve that outcome. But strategic industrial policy can yield the needed changes in technology along with demonstrations that help improve performance and create new interest groups that are keen to push the process of decarbonization further.

Realistically, this is a process that will be driven by leaders – by jurisdictions that are willing to regulate and tax themselves to address a global problem. Indeed, there are the green shoots of leadership evident everywhere: in cities, states, and many countries, notably in the EU. The challenge is that leaders, by themselves, can't solve the climate problem. By our estimate, shown in chapter 1, at best about one-fifth of global emissions today come from these leader jurisdictions: in the EU, the United Kingdom, Norway, a swath of the United States located mainly on the coastlines, New South Wales, New Zealand, and perhaps a few others.

Understanding how leadership can be effective will be the central strategic challenge in climate policy for the coming decades. At best, the number of jurisdictions willing to be reliable leaders will increase modestly as experience with decarbonization progresses and concern about climate dangers grows. Yet the more that these leaders do to control their emissions, the less relevant they will become to the underlying problem of climate change. Ironically, the more conspicuous the leadership, the smaller the emissions from these jurisdictions – and the tinier the direct leverage on global emissions. Over time, climate leadership will matter less in terms of reductions at home and more in terms of governments' ability to influence outcomes abroad.

Thus every leadership effort must be designed with an eye to followership: to how success in creating and testing new technologies and market designs makes these building blocks for deep decarbonization more likely to be adopted elsewhere. Followership might happen automatically, as is occurring now in many parts of the renewable energy industry.[38] New technologies pioneered with investments originally in Japan, the United States, Germany, China, and some other countries are spreading rapidly and globally because, often, they are cheaper than more polluting rivals. (The diffusion is not just technological: lessons about policy design and evolution, such as from feed-in-tariffs to auctions, are also diffusing alongside the technology.) In most cases, followership won't be automatic. Testing and deployment of new technologies and policies by leaders will help demonstrate performance and attributes and thus lower risk, but new low-emission technologies won't be automatically cheaper: green steel as a commodity, for example, might be double the cost of higher-emission alternatives. In these cases, followership will require incentives, such as a push from border carbon adjustments and requirements that all countries adopt more active emission control policies.

Through the lens of followership, it is possible to identify some attributes that leaders must keep in mind as they pursue policies with an eye to eventual global transformation of agriculture and industry. These include the following:

- **Deprioritize actions that don't scale.** For example, many leadership jurisdictions are exploring how to cut emissions from natural gas – a fossil fuel that is a lot cleaner than coal, but which still has significant emissions of CO_2. (Natural gas systems that are not well managed also leak emissions of methane into the atmosphere, a potent greenhouse gas.) One option is to require switching of conventional natural gas to biomethane – an option attractive to natural gas companies because it allows lower emissions without any material changes in the gas pipeline and delivery infrastructure. However, if sustainable biomethane supplies are quickly exhausted by leaders, then this option can't yield much followership. Similar concerns arise for many other kinds of bioenergy resources, which tend to compete with food production and wild lands in addition to their lack of truly global scaling potential.

- Seek actions that are likely to align with interests and capabilities of followers. All else being equal, followers will be highly sensitive to costs and risk. They will also favor technologies and policies that align with local interests. Options that explore how to integrate massive quantities of renewables on a grid or utilize fossil fuel and geologic pore space resources through CCS are likely to engender followership because they allow expansion of existing industries in greener ways. For example, Denmark has spent handsomely to cut emissions at home, notably through expansion of wind power. Because Denmark is small and already quite clean, the efforts had modest leverage at home. But when Danish grid operators shared what they learned about wind integration on the grid with Chinese grid operators, they multiplied massively the global impact of their leadership. While China isn't much focused on the problem of global warming, its wind expansion program had created challenges similar to the ones that the Danish grid had solved.[39]

- Focus not just on technologies but also on demonstrating regulatory systems and other policy incentives needed to make those technologies scale. For example, there have been decades of efforts to test and promote CCS technologies – most of which have failed to scale in part because there haven't been reliable incentives needed for long-term investment, including investment in the infrastructure of CO_2 pipelines and disposal systems needed for cost-effective CCS. Several new examples are emerging that could fix that: for example, the Teesside Collective[40] in the United Kingdom and the above-mentioned Northern Lights project in the North Sea.[41] These examples combine initiatives led by industry alongside interventions by government – with funding, regulatory policy, and actions to improve the credibility of the policy and investment environment.

- Create incentives to encourage followership. Those incentives probably take at least two forms. One form is institutional: to help follower jurisdictions gather information, adjust to local circumstances, and learn the state of the art. Those kinds of programs, often called "capacity-building," are essential to building a broader constituency of informed followers. The other form is financial: for example, direct subsidy or investment programs needed to deploy new technologies. Nearly all multilateral development banks and many bilateral development assistance programs, including those sponsored by Norway, Germany, and the United Kingdom, already offer these kinds of programs. In time, it will be important also to adopt trade measures so that all countries see a credible signal that high-emission practices will need to be curtailed.

Conclusion

If it were feasible to create a credible, high, and reliably rising price on carbon that applied to all economies, then the problem of tackling climate change would be a lot easier. Incentives would be aligned in all countries, at least to deploy mature technologies with known performance. The problem of leakage would be diminished, and resources from auctions used to sell emission credits (or taxes paid) would be massive, and firms – incumbents and new entrants alike – would be more focused on innovation and transformation. Big new resources could fund a variety of worthy governmental purposes, including large research, development, and demonstration schemes that could address the fact that innovation and testing of new technologies is a public good – a benefit to all yet hard for any individual firm or society to appropriate sufficiently to make the needed investment. That would be an interesting, ideal world for solving the climate problem. But that magical world does not exist.

In the real world, the role for market-based polices is much smaller. Other approaches – notably, regulation and other elements of industrial policy – will do more of the work of cutting emissions. Those interventions must be adaptive to new information. And they must be embedded within an international cooperation strategy that links government and business and looks far beyond the UN Paris Agreement – beyond what is agreeable by consensus to a large number of countries operating under consensus decision-making rules.

As the world begins to look not just to superficial efforts to reduce emissions, but eventually to paths to deep decarbonization, there is an opportunity to adjust. At this early stage, the policy instruments available to the pioneer governments and firms – those that are willing to spend substantial resources to address the need for deep decarbonization – are well aligned with the need to test technologies and policies. An industrial policy strategy rooted in adaptive regulation and investment stands to benefit from carbon pricing that sends a clear signal to the marketplace, but the nature of the risks involved for firms and the level of carbon pricing available are mis-aligned. Direct intervention into the market is also needed – including subsidies financed, in part, by revenues raised from low-price markets – and cooperation across borders can help by creating larger and more stable buyers for new low-emission products and services. As this early, experimentalist approach to industrial and agricultural transformation gains success, then broader diffusion and reconfiguration of whole markets can spread the deep decarbonization more widely. And if successful, it is possible that transformative technological change will bring with it a fundamental reorganization of the political forces constraining the use of market-based policies today.

9

Conclusion

The debate over climate policy strategy has been off course for decades. Well-intentioned policy advocacy has focused on market-based policies – cap-and-trade, especially – as a mechanism that could generate greater support for controlling climate pollution, greater flexibility to lower costs, and greater incentives for effective policy to expand and deepen around the world. But market instruments have failed to deliver on each of these fronts. That failure, we argue, is rooted in a simple but powerful theory about how political pressures are organized and shape the real-world implementation of carbon markets.

The central problem is not that policymakers are uninformed about the potential gains of economically efficient policy instruments. Rather, the core challenge is that the very features of these programs that promise economic gains – transparency and fungibility of effort across sectors – invariably lead to enormous political liabilities. These structural problems will remain even with mounting political pressure to act on the climate problem. Despite proponents' well-meaning hopes, market-based strategies are not sitting ready on the shelf ready to be used much more effectively once governments finally get serious about the climate crisis. Rather, at best, they will modestly complement other policy instruments – chiefly, industrial policy – which must do most of the work to create deep decarbonization.

The primary problem with market-based strategies, nearly everywhere that they have been used, is ambition. Policymakers and the public have revealed that they are willing to do much more than the prices in carbon markets suggest – as evidenced by the fact that markets are always deployed alongside other regulatory policies that are better designed to navigate around political opposition and deliver greater environmental benefits. When the effort under these parallel efforts can be observed closely and quantified, market-based approaches do a lot less of the real work to cut emissions. In California, for example, the state's multi-sector emissions trading system runs alongside other, more specialized programs to cut emissions from transportation fuels – with the latter yielding ten times the effort (measured as marginal cost) of the former.

Policymakers rely on regulation and other forms of industrial policy because they know that the costs of regulation are less visible to voters and that extensive regulation makes it easier to shift costs and benefits as needed to address political opposition. As a result of these forces, cap-and-trade systems end up trading only the residual reductions that are needed after regulations do the bulk of the work of controlling climate pollution. Prices are low by design because the residual exists after other, more consequential policies do most of the work.

We call these outcomes Potemkin markets because they create the impression that a government is pursuing low-cost, market-based climate policies when in fact these programs serve as window dressing that bears little relationship to the strategies creating emission reductions.

Throughout this book, we have contrasted the idealized theory of market-based policies with the systematic political forces that explain the outcomes we observe in the real world. In addition to ambition – where textbook theory suggests market systems can be designed to reflect the real willingness of societies to decarbonize, but political forces create Potemkin outcomes – there is a big mismatch with regard to the sectoral scope of markets. The scope of most real-world markets has been narrow because there are only a few sectors in the economy where governments can reliably manage the political requests from vocal stakeholders that are harmed by carbon pricing. In transportation, the cost of carbon pricing is highly visible to the broad voting public; in industry, the same cost is highly visible to organized industries competing in international markets. Only in electricity is the task relatively straightforward – often because many of the firms that are affected are in highly regulated industries where regulatory action can help manage risk and allocate costs in politically sustainable ways. Fortuitously, the technologies for decarbonization are also most mature in that sector. (For the same reasons, aggressive carbon taxes are usually found only in the electricity sector.)

Unfortunately, most of the technologies needed for deep decarbonization are in their infancy nearly everywhere else. Pushing early-stage technologies requires efforts tailored to each sector – something that is hard to do with market-based instruments that cover all sectors with a single carbon price determined by the opposition of the most entrenched sector.

One of the chief virtues of market-based approaches to pollution control is that they can raise revenues – and possibly even massive amounts. We have shown that, in the real world, the fact that most programs are Potemkin markets with narrow sectoral coverage and generous free allocation of pollution rights means that public revenues have been much more modest. Every carbon market and many carbon taxes create special funds aimed at promoting worthy environmental and political goals – what we call green spending. But with little oversight, these resources get channeled in ways that often fall far short of worthy greenery – becoming pork of many colors instead. Precious funds get squandered on projects that deliver relatively cost-inefficient benefits to public goods or improved political support for the market as a whole. Spending programs do not make up for lost ambition in carbon pricing and have not yet delivered major investments in potentially transformative technological change because the interest groups lining up at the trough have other, typically more short-term goals in mind.

Political forces also help explain why it has proven difficult to use market instruments to entice expanded geographical coverage. One mechanism that, in theory, could have allowed international expansion of market forces is offsets. We have shown, however, that offsets have instead been a major source of degradation in the quality of market-based approaches to controlling carbon pollution. The experience with carbon offsets has been universally abysmal because the proper calculation of credited reductions turns on highly technical concepts that can only be estimated, never observed. Projects have to establish that they are additional (meaning that but for the carbon credit investment they would not occur) and that they fully account for emissions leakage (meaning the displacement of emissions caused by the project). In theory, an army of government staff, expert scientists, independent watchdogs, and public-minded entrepreneurs could take on this head-spinning challenge. In practice, polluting industries demand high volumes of offsets to keep costs low, and few groups, including program administrators, invest in the meaningful oversight of offset quality. Rather than provide a stepping stone to the geographical expansion of market-based programs, offsets provide polluting industries with a stealthy means of watering down policy ambitions. Worse, offset credits create a perverse incentive for governments to avoid mandatory emission cuts.

Another attractive idea for expanding geographical coverage is to directly link pollution markets together. In theory, direct linkage could encourage international expansion and deepening of efforts to cut pollution. Theory predicts that linked markets will create gains from trade as opportunities are revealed in relatively low-priced markets that allow investment from high-priced markets. Thus, the most important linkages should be forged between markets that are least like each other: that is, where the gains from trade are greatest. Where market links exist, however, they link markets that are most alike – and thus the gains from trade are smallest. The reasons follow from the politics. The process of assembling and retaining the political support needed for a market-based approach to pollution is complex, with different choices in different jurisdictions; allowing markets to trade across borders can readily undo all those local deals. Despite all the talk about the benefits of linking markets, in reality, market links are rare and thin.

Doing better

Our diagnosis is severe and may come as a shock to those who have embraced the orthodoxy on markets. To some, it may be depressing. Still others will see this as vindication: proof that markets were always the wrong way to pursue climate policy and that the efforts to promote markets were a costly diversion. Whatever your brand of catharsis, looking to the future requires grappling with two practical implications of this book.

First, the global conversation on climate policy strategy needs a reset. For decades, markets have been promoted as the solution to climate pollution, both as a means of cost-effectively reducing emissions and as a mechanism to accelerate cooperation on ambitious climate goals. This argument makes sense in theory – at least to many – but falls short in practice. The political economy barriers to effective carbon markets are structural, not ephemeral. They won't go away even if there is more "political will" to tackle climate change: for example, through more public mobilization demanding action and efforts at deeper international cooperation to tackle this global problem.

To be clear, our argument is not that markets are completely irrelevant. Market forces can help to accelerate diffusion of known technologies; they can generate revenues that, if spent well, have constructive roles to play. But those roles will be modest and make sense only as a complement to policies that will do the hard work of deep decarbonization. Chasing markets' promise without the right political and institutional conditions in place only makes it more likely that they will become fragile and fail.

Nor is our view that climate policy should be conducted through opaque efforts that hide costs from the mechanisms of democratic accountability. Our point is that serious climate policy must deal with the world as it is, not as imagined. In that world, there are some sectors where the public is inordinately sensitive to sticker prices (yet demonstrably willing to support other policies), and in every sector political and technological factors vary. Lumping them all together and pretending the market will sort out best marginal efforts is a recipe for inaction overall. Alternative strategies can be transparent in cost, politically responsive, and highly effective – and thus superior strategies for real-world climate policy.

Second, if markets are likely to play only a modest role in the global climate policy response, new strategies will be needed in their place. We have outlined a reform strategy that will rightsize the role of reformed markets and shift policy emphasis to other strategies – industrial policy, writ large – that will have a· bigger impact. Ambition and willingness to invest remain huge challenges. The world is not doing enough to combat climate change today, but with sound policy strategies, it will be easier to channel growing public concern and pressure around climate change into effective action.

The road ahead

In chapters 7 and 8, we have offered a vision for market reforms as well as for the greater use of industrial and foreign policy. This suite of reforms will, we argue, lead to much more effective policy strategies that can, with effort, put the planet on a path to deep decarbonization. To close our story, we explore some of the implications of our arguments for key players in the climate policy process: from governments to environmental advocates, funders of policy analysis and advocacy, scholars, and firms that are on the front lines.

For governments, the core implication of our arguments is that policymakers should not assume that carbon pricing – whether via carbon markets or carbon taxes – can do most of the work in cutting emissions. It has been too easy for leaders in the private and public sectors to say "markets" when pushed for their vision of how the economy should make these cuts. The jurisdictions that are now doing the most to put their economies on the path to deep decarbonization are, for the most part, using other policy instruments. Some, such as the United Kingdom, are cementing those gains by using market incentives to encourage the adoption of known technologies. But the difference between cutting marginal emissions in sectors with commercial technologies and deep decarbonization is smart industrial policy.

An industrial policy perspective on the carbon problem immediately raises the challenge that governments vary enormously in their capacity to design and implement effective industrial policies. The factors that determine those skills – in effect, the skill of state intervention in the economy – are an age-old topic in the study of comparative politics and public administration. One implication of our argument is that the jurisdictions that will play the most central roles in creating conditions for deep decarbonization will be those that marry political willingness to invest in that mission with the skill to utilize those resources effectively. By extension, governments under pressure to act effectively must focus much of their investment on building the skills to prosecute effective industrial policy.

Quality public administration is essential to effective climate policy, but we fear this point has become a blind spot for advocates who have rightly been skeptical of markets for a long time. It's not that market critics are opposed to government capacity-building, but rather that those promoting direct government action haven't sufficiently recognized public-sector competence as a precondition for their preferred theory of change. Consider a core policy element of the United States' Green New Deal and European Green Deal conversations: the emphasis on massive public investment in infrastructure. How should that money be spent wisely and effectively? How will large spending programs avoid the problems of green pork we observe when funds raised from carbon pricing get spent? There has been a lot less effort to answer those questions than to clamor for big government programs. And where the answers have been offered, they have tended to focus on oversight rather than the rest of what matters: effective public administration of massive state intervention in the economy. Government action at the scale the climate problem demands will work if and only if governments themselves work.

For policy advocates, our book offers several suggestions. One is that they must continue to grapple with one of the most important political challenges in deep decarbonization: will incumbent firms and industry associations be part of the political problem, or part of the solution? Many advocacy groups and pundits have offered extreme positions on both sides of this question, but we suggest the community must grapple more centrally with the fact that the answer, often, is unknown. Incumbents will favor incumbent technologies and industrial processes unless they face a strong incentive to change. When forced to change – for example, as many utilities were forced to do in pursuit of early renewable energy policies – many are capable of rapidly deploying solutions at a large scale. One of the most important roles that the environmental advocacy community has played historically is creating the incentives – often, big hammers – that move recalcitrant firms. Ironically, the path to greater cooperation from incumbents may well be paved with the credible threats of advocates who would seek their dissolution.

In writing this book, we were surprised that we did not see a much larger role for environmental policy advocates in the histories of these market mechanisms. A few groups are involved – often on specialized topics, or in broad evangelism – but advocates for the most part have not invested heavily in understanding how these mechanisms work, let alone mobilizing pressure for reform. In some cases, that is because these groups are insiders: they were present at the creation of markets and favor their continued use. For outsiders, these mechanisms are complex and hard to scrutinize without deep expertise. We urge more groups to develop that expertise and to focus on the elements of market systems that are most urgently in need of reform: for example, offsets (which we argue should be eliminated) and green spending regimes (which feature a persistent tendency toward pork that could threaten the success of any public climate investment strategy). Environmental advocates should do what they do best – build coalitions and constituencies that have a strong stake in more effective systems – but arm themselves with a robust theory of how politics affects market operations and deep decarbonization.

On industrial policy, we suggest that there is a new challenge on the horizon. Enormous efforts have gone into building popular support for renewable energy technologies like solar and wind. Environmental groups have been broadly successful in mobilizing popular support around these technologies in the electricity sector, but many lack an agenda for how to replicate their efforts in support of new technologies needed in other industries. Nor is there much of an agenda within the advocacy community for how to design and prosecute effective far-reaching industrial policy.

Our work also suggests a need for rethinking in the philanthropic community. Huge and growing institutional resources are being put into the climate crisis on the sound logic that this is one of the most pressing problems of modern humanity; some newer entrants in the world of climate philanthropy approach their goals like a venture capital investor scouting promising new ideas. Yet much too little of that investment is devoted to figuring out what really works. There needs to be at least modest evaluation of the efficacy of current policy strategies that incorporates a range of strategic perspectives and is conducted by subject matter experts, not only by general-interest philanthropic program evaluators. Overall, today's funding portfolios seem overly tilted toward advocacy without a close enough look at the key question: advocacy of what?

For researchers, we have, throughout this book, identified a large number of questions around policy analysis that need attention: for example, questions around how variation in institutional designs might explain variations in the level of revenues raised by market systems and how those revenues are spent. But here we highlight what is probably the most important topic for the scholarly community to debate: what is the right political theory of change?

We have outlined a simple model of politics that we have argued is useful for explaining the political evolution of market-based climate policies. We have suggested in chapter 7 that the same theory is a useful guide for prioritizing market reforms, and in chapter 8 we have looked to the same political groups and institutions to explain how an industrial policy could provide the backbone of a more effective sector-by-sector industrial strategy for deep decarbonization. We welcome vigorous debate around what our theory leaves out, along with alternative theoretical articulations. Academic research should test these political economy approaches to understanding climate policy more vigorously with evidence, which is mounting but remains largely unorganized and in need of comprehensive explanations. Researchers should apply the full arsenal of tools in their toolkit, including formal models, simulations, comparative political assessments, and many others. Interdisciplinary dialog will be especially important to connect technically complex areas of business and policy with theories and methods rooted in the social sciences.

Finally, we close by exploring the implications of our thinking for the actors whose behavior ultimately matters most: big emitters. Our book underscores what many of these firms already know. Deep decarbonization in most sectors will be difficult, expensive, but – we believe – ultimately essential for the planet as a whole. Some of the easy solutions now surging in popularity – such as offsets, especially low-cost efforts targeting forests and soils under the umbrella of "natural climate solutions" – probably won't work in isolation and likely don't work at the global scale that deep decarbonization demands. Big emitters should not count on finding a silver bullet to offset their own emissions. Instead, using approaches such as red team exercises, where analysts are charged with finding flaws in competing strategies, they must look closely at whether the offsets markets now emerging reflect genuine emission reductions.

Ironically, the renewed enthusiasm for offsets has emerged from what is widely seen as one of the most important and aggressive corporate planning tools: company-wide emission reduction targets, with leading firms pledging "carbon neutrality" or "net-zero emissions" in the near future. We applaud the ambition behind those goals – where that ambition is genuine, as it sometimes is – but we are concerned that the net-zero mindset has amplified interest in offsets and may diffuse attention from what really matters, which is directly reducing emissions through industrial planning and reimagining of corporate strategies. This is most evident today in the aviation sector, where an ambitious sector-wide net-zero goal has, in the hands of the main industry association – the International Civil Aviation Organization – been translated into a giant offsets scheme.

Deep decarbonization in industry won't happen through magical thinking about offsets. Nor will it happen through the creation of grand bargains that see the creation of textbook market-based systems alongside rollbacks of other regulations – because the former doesn't work and the latter is politically impractical. Instead, deep decarbonization will follow an old-fashioned model: it must be earned through industrial policy, investment, experimentation, learning, and scaling. Along the way, many firms and some industries will be lost. Many more will be created. And through all that the planet, in time, will heal.

Notes

Chapter 1 A turn toward markets?

1 A blue-ribbon panel of experts recommended that 2020 carbon prices need to be between $40 and $80 per ton of CO_2-equivalent in order to be consistent with countries' pledges under the United Nations' Paris Agreement. High-Level Commission on Carbon Prices, "Report of the High-Level Commission on Carbon Prices," World Bank (2017).

2 Akshat Rathi, "A carbon tax killed coal in the UK. Natural gas is next," *Quartz* (Feb. 1, 2018).

3 Many others have also observed the same phenomenon. For a recent and vigorous argument, see Mark Jaccard, *The Citizen's Guide to Climate Success: Overcoming Myths that Hinder Progress* (Cambridge University Press, 2020). In an earlier example, from 2013, several leading analysts and proponents of market-based policy concluded that "[f]ifteen years after the signing of the Kyoto Protocol and the creation of the first major platform for carbon markets, the prospect for a unified global carbon trading system in the foreseeable future is essentially finished." Richard G. Newell, William A.

Pizer, and Daniel Raimi, "Carbon markets 15 years after Kyoto: lessons learned, new challenges," *Journal of Economic Perspectives* 27(1) (2013): 123–46.

4 For more on leadership and followership, see chapter 8.

5 Monica Crippa et al., "Fossil CO_2 and GHG Emissions of All World Countries – 2019 Report" (2019), *https://edgar.jrc.ec.europa.eu/overview.php?v=booklet2019*.

6 Nicholas Stern, *The Economics of Climate Change: The Stern Review* (Cambridge University Press, 2007); Leon Clarke et al., "Assessing transformation pathways," Chapter 6 in *Climate Change 2014: Mitigation of Climate Change, Contribution of Working Group III to the Fifth Assessment Report of the IPCC* (Cambridge University Press, 2014), *https://www.ipcc.ch/report/ar5/wg3/*.

7 This is a big and growing topic, especially among the political scientists who are now focused on climate change politics. See, e.g., Leah C. Stokes, *Short Circuiting Policy: Interest Groups and the Battle Over Clean Energy and Climate Policy in the American States* (Oxford University Press, 2020); Matto Mildenberger, *Carbon Captured: How Business and Labor Control Climate Policies* (MIT Press, 2020); Jørgen Wettestad and Lars H. Gulbrandsen (eds.), *The Evolution of Carbon Markets: Design and Diffusion* (Routledge, 2018); Barry G. Rabe, *Can We Price Carbon?* (MIT Press, 2018); Jessica Green, *Rethinking Private Authority: Agents and Entrepreneurs in Global Environmental Governance* (Princeton University Press, 2014); Jonas Meckling, *Carbon Coalitions: Business, Climate Politics, and the Rise of Emissions Trading* (MIT Press, 2011). We also note with appreciation that the few review studies published on carbon pricing policies highlight the divergence of policy designs and challenges these instruments face: e.g. Easwaran Narassimhan et al., "Carbon pricing in practice: a review of existing emissions trading systems," *Climate Policy* 18(8) (2018): 967–91.

8 This argument is perhaps best associated with Canadian energy economist Mark Jaccard, who has advocated for

flexible, sector-by-sector regulations in place of explicit and politically challenging carbon pricing policies. See, e.g., Mark Jaccard, "Want an effective climate policy? Heed the evidence," *Policy Options* (Feb. 2, 2016); Mark Jaccard, "The political acceptability of carbon taxes: lessons from British Columbia," in Jane E. Milne and Mikael S. Andersen (eds.), *Handbook of Research on Environmental Taxation* (Edward Elgar, 2012).

9 Victor et al., *supra* Figure 1.2.

10 Lots of research shows the power of incumbents to block change through various modes of action. For example, see Mildenberger, *supra* note 7; Matthew H. Goldberg et al., "Oil and gas companies invest in legislators that vote against the environment," *Proceedings of the National Academy of Sciences* 117(10) (2020): 5111–12.

11 Fewer studies have looked closely at the relative power of incumbents and new entrants. But encouraging work along these lines includes, e.g., Michael Pahle et al., "Sequencing to ratchet up climate policy stringency," *Nature Climate Change* 8(10) (2018): 861–7; Jonas Meckling et al., "Winning coalitions for climate policy," *Science* 349 (2015): 1170–1.

12 There are a growing number of sympathetic voices on this front. See, e.g., Gernot Wagner, "Carbon Taxes Alone Aren't Good Climate Policy," *Bloomberg Green* (Feb. 6, 2020); Jonas Meckling, Thomas Sterner, and Gernot Wagner, "Policy sequencing toward decarbonization," *Nature Energy* 2 (2017): 918–22.

13 We note with appreciation that many leading proponents of market-based policies are now attuned to these issues. For example, Harvard environmental economist Robert Stavins says in a fresh analysis of the experience with markets that scholars must focus more on positive political economy, which governs the probability that any particular policy scheme is actually adopted and how it is implemented. Robert N. Stavins, "The future of US carbon-pricing policy," *Environmental and Energy Policy and the Economy* 1 (2020): 8–64; see

also Susanne A. Brooks and Nathaniel O. Keohane, "The political economy of hybrid approaches to a US carbon tax: a perspective from the policy world," *Review of Environmental Economics and Policy* 14(1) (2020): 67–75; Nathaniel O. Keohane, Richard L. Revesz, and Robert N. Stavins, "The choice of regulatory instruments in environmental policy," *Harvard Environmental Law Review* 22(2) (1998): 313–67.

14 World Bank Group, *"State and Trends of Carbon Pricing 2019"* (2019).

15 David G. Victor, "The problem with cap and trade," *MIT Technology Review* (June 23, 2009), *https://www.technologyreview.com/s/414025/the-problem-with-cap-and-trade/.*

16 See, e.g., Thomas Sterner & Gunnar Köhlin, "Pricing carbon: the challenges," in Scott Barrett, Carlo Carraro, and Jaime de Melo (eds.), *Towards a Workable and Effective Climate Regime* (CEPR Press, 2015); Dallas Burtraw and Amelia Keyes, "Recognizing gravity as a strong force in atmosphere emissions markets," *Agricultural and Resource Economics Review* 47(2) (2018): 201–19; Severin Borenstein et al., "Expecting the unexpected: emissions uncertainty and environmental market design," *American Economic Review* 109(11) (2019): 3953–77.

17 Put differently, we see these revenues as a key element to solving the market failure of innovation and testing new ideas. The market, left to its own incentives, will lead to under-investment in risky ideas because the new knowledge generated is a public good. The standard prescription from environmental economics sees this as an economic market failure. See Adam B. Jaffe, Richard G. Newell, and Robert N. Stavins, "A tale of two market failures: technology and environmental policy," *Ecological Economics* 54 (2004): 164–74. We see this, as well, as a political market failure: the failure to invest in activities that will create political support for accelerating deep decarbonization.

18 See, e.g., Jesse D. Jenkins, "Political economy constraints on carbon pricing policies: what are the implications for economic efficiency, environmental efficacy, and climate policy design?," *Energy Policy* 69 (2014): 467–77; Gernot Wagner et al., "Push renewables to spur carbon pricing," *Nature* 525 (2015): 27–9; Jesse D. Jenkins and Valerie Karplus, "Carbon pricing under political constraints," in Doug Arent et al. (eds.), *The Political Economy of Clean Energy Transitions* (Oxford University Press, 2017); Daniel Rosenbloom et al., "Opinion: Why carbon pricing is not sufficient to mitigate climate change – and how 'sustainability tranisiton policy' can help," *Proceedings of the National Academy of Sciences* 117(16) (2020): 8664–8. A relatively new empirical social science literature studying carbon markets also shows how the political barriers we address in this book lead to divergence in market designs. See Katja Biedenkopf et al. (eds.), "Special Issue: Global Turn to Greenhouse Gas Emissions Trading? Experiments, Actors, and Diffusion," *Global Environmental Politics* 17(3) (2017); Wettestad and Gulbrandsen, *supra* note 7.

19 The tradition of exposing market failure in the Clean Development Mechanism (CDM) and other carbon offset programs is long and has its roots in academic analysis. See, e.g., Michael Wara, "Is the global carbon market working?," *Nature* 445 (2007): 595–6 (2007); Martin Cames et al., "How Additional Is the Clean Development Mechanism? Analysis of the Application of Current Tools and Proposed Alternatives," Öko-Institut (2016). For more contemporary reporting on the challenges with market-based climate policies, see Jeffrey Ball, "Why carbon pricing isn't working," *Foreign Affairs* (July/Aug. 2018); Julie Cart, "Checking the math on cap-and-trade, some experts say it's not adding up," *CalMatters* (May 22, 2018); David Roberts, "California's cap-and-trade system may be too weak to do its job," *Vox* (Dec. 13, 2018); Herman K. Trabish, "California may be a climate leader, but it could be a century behind on its carbon

goals: study," *Utility Dive* (Oct. 29, 2019); Lisa Song, "Cap and trade is supposed to solve climate change, but oil and gas company emissions are up," *ProPublica* (Nov. 15, 2019).

20 See, e.g., Rhiana Gunn-Wright and Robert Hockett, "The Green New Deal: mobilizing for a just, prosperous, and sustainable economy," *New Consensus* (Jan. 2019); Kate Aronoff et al., *A Planet to Win: Why We Need a Green New Deal* (Verso, 2019); Parrish Bergquist, Matto Mildenberger, and Leah Stokes, "Combining Climate, Economic, and Social Policy Builds Political Support for Climate Action in the US," *Environmental Research Letters* 15 (2020): 054019; Jessica F. Green, "It's time to abandon carbon pricing," *Jacobin* (Sept. 24, 2019).

21 European Commission, "Communication on the European Green Deal," COM(2019) 640 final, *https://ec.europa. eu/info/publications/communication-european-green-deal_en*.

22 See, e.g., Richard Schmalensee and Robert N. Stavins, "Policy evolution under the Clean Air Act," *Journal of Economic Perspectives* 33(4) (2019): 27–50; Joseph E. Aldy, "The Political Economy of Carbon Pricing Policy Design," Harvard Project on Climate Agreements, Discussion Paper ES 17-7 (2017).

23 See generally George Mason University Center for Climate Change Communication, Climate Change in the American Mind Report Series, *https://www.climatechangecommuni cation.org/climate-change-in-the-american-mind-reports/*.

24 While factors influencing voter mobilization are hard to pin down, a recent survey effort provides a useful illustration: Joanna Piacenza, "What is the 2020 election about? We gave 4,400 people a blank space to tell us," *Morning Consult* (Feb. 4, 2020), *https://morningconsult. com/2020/02/04/what-is-the-2020-election-about-we-gave-4400-people-a-blank-space-to-tell-us/*.

25 This focus on what voters notice reflects the best political science pulsing of public opinion, which finds that while voters say they want lots of things from better energy

policy (and, by extension, industrial policy aimed at decarbonization), they also don't want those policies to affect visible energy prices. This careful spadework is most advanced in the study of US populations. Stephen Ansolabehere and David Konisky, *Cheap and Clean: How Americans Think About Energy in the Age of Global Warming* (MIT Press, 2014).

26 The preference for visible benefits from policy and invisible costs is axiomatic to politics. Among the many studies on this topic, see Matthew McCubbins and Terry Sullivan, "Constituency influences on legislative policy choice," *Quality and Quantity* 18 (1984): 299–319. We note that this argument about visible costs is often made in tandem with discussing carbon tax systems, although our view is that it is more universal and applies, as well, to cap-and-trade if that policy were allowed to generate high visible costs (an outcome, of course, that political forces help prevent). See Steafno Carattini, Maria Carvalho, and Sam Fankhauser, "How to Make Carbon Taxes More Acceptable," Grantham Research Institute on Climate Change, London School of Economics and Political Science (2017); Stefano Carattini, Greer Gosnell, and Alessandro Tavoni, "How developed countries can learn from developing countries to tackle climate change," *World Development* 127 (2020): 104829.

27 Because most of this book is about what occurs in the parts of the world where governments and firms face the strongest pressures to act on climate change, we will use the language of democratic accountability – and thus we consider voters. However, it is a small step to extend the logic to other "selectorates" that have an impact on the incentives for governments (and firms) to change policy, such as the mass (non-voting) public. Our point is that what really defines how this broad-based interest group conveys its interests is rooted in the visibility of some policy interventions for things the mass, often unorganized public cares about – like fuel prices. Studies on a wide array of energy policy

reforms make the same point: e.g. the research on the political economy of energy subsidy reform. See generally Gabriela Inchauste and David G. Victor, "The Political Economy of Energy Subsidy Reform," The World Bank Group (2017), *http://documents.worldbank. org/curated/en/745311489054655283/The-political- economy-of-energy-subsidy-reform.*

28 The ease of political organization in small groups where the benefits of collective action are concentrated is one of the bedrock concepts in political economy. See Mancur Olson, *The Logic of Collective Action* (Harvard University Press, 1965).

29 Climate policy cognoscenti call these players "energy-intensive, trade-exposed industries," but we use a simpler term here.

30 Staffan Jacobsson and Volkmar Lauber, "The politics and policy of energy system transformation – explaining the German diffusion of renewable energy technology," *Energy Policy* 34 (2006): 256–76. On the tendency to underestimate how powerful politically fledgling new industrial groups can become, see Leah C. Stokes and Hanna L. Breetz, "Politics in the US energy transition: case studies of solar, wind, biofuels and electric vehicles policy," *Energy Policy* 113 (2018): 76–86.

31 For more, see Bruce Bueno de Mesquita et al., *The Logic of Political Survival* (MIT Press, 2003).

32 This idea of mediation is one of the foundations of political science – it is how varied interests are amalgamated into policies in the legislative process and helps to explain whether political systems are biased to favor status quo or new interests.

33 For a proponent's perspective, see Nathaniel Keohane, "COP 25: The mess in Madrid – and how international carbon markets can still drive ambition despite it," Environmental Defense Fund Climate 411 (Dec. 16, 2019), *http://blogs.edf.org/climate411/2019/12/16/ cop-25-international-carbon-markets-can-still-drive- ambition-despite-lack-of-article-6-rules/.*

34 Allen V. Kneese and Charles L. Schultze, *Pollution, Prices, and Public Policy* (Brookings Institution, 1975).

35 Brad Plumer, "Why has climate legislation failed? An interview with Theda Skocpol," *Washington Post* (Jan. 16, 2013), *https://www.washingtonpost.com/news/wonk/wp/2013/01/16/why-has-climate-legislation-failed-an-interview-with-theda-skocpol/*.

36 Some work is emerging along these lines. For example, see this study that looks at how national political institutions aggregate interests and affect the incentives of policy elites: Jared J. Finnegan, "Institutions, Climate Change and the Foundations of Long-Term Policymaking," Centre for Climate Change Economics and Policy Working Paper No. 353; Grantham Research Institute on Climate Change and the Environment Working Paper No. 321, London School of Economics and Political Science (2019).

37 One notable irony is that the United States under President Clinton was a strong advocate for the Kyoto Protocol, and specifically the use of market-based compliance strategies, which the EU initially opposed. For more on the history of the EU's market, see Jos Delbeke and Peter Vis (eds.), *EU Climate Policy Explained* (Routledge, 2015); A. Denny Ellerman, Frank J. Convery, and Christian de Perthuis (eds.), *Pricing Carbon: The European Union Emissions Trading Scheme* (Cambridge University Press, 2010); A. Denny Ellerman, Barbara K. Buchner, and Carlo Carraro (eds.), *Allocation in the European Emissions Trading Scheme* (Cambridge University Press, 2007).

38 Jørgen Wettestad and Torbjørg Jevnaker, "EU emissions trading: frontrunner – and 'black sheep'?," in Wettestad and Gulbrandsen, *supra* note 7; Jørgen Wettestad and Torbjørg Jevnaker, *Rescuing EU Emissions Trading: The Climate Policy Flagship* (Palgrave Macmillan, 2015).

39 California Air Resources Board, "California's 2017 Climate Change Scoping Plan" (Nov. 2017) at 26–31, *https://ww3.arb.ca.gov/cc/scopingplan/scoping_plan_2017.pdf*.

40 For an overview, see Hyungna Oh, Junwon Hyon, and

Jin-Oh Kim, "Korea's approach to overcoming difficulties in adopting the emission trading scheme," *Climate Policy* 17(8) (2017): 947–61; Sunhee Suk, SangYeop Lee, and Yu Shim Jeong, "The Korean emissions trading scheme: business perspectives on the early years of operations," *Climate Policy* 18(6) (2018): 715–28; Asian Development Bank, "The Korean Emissions Trading Scheme: Challenges and Emerging Opportunities" (Nov. 2018); Katja Biedenkopf and Jørgen Wettestad, "South Korea: East Asian pioneer learning from the EU," in Wettestad and Gulbrandsen, *supra* note 7.

41 Catherine Leining, Suzi Kerr, and Bronwyn Bruce-Brand, "The New Zealand Emissions Trading Scheme: critical review and future outlook for three design innovations," *Climate Policy* 20(2) (2020): 246–64; Tor Håkon Jackson Inderberg, Ian Bailey, and Nichola Harmer, "Adopting and designing New Zealand's emissions trading scheme," in Wettestad and Gulbrandsen, *supra* note 7.

42 There are quite a few modeling-based economics studies of China's nascent carbon markets, but few empirical studies of program design or performance. See, e.g., Lawrence H. Goulder et al., "China's Unconventional Nationwide CO_2 Emissions Trading System: The Wide-Ranging Impacts of an Implicit Output Subsidy," Resources for the Future Working Paper 20-02 (2020); Gørild Heggelund et al., "China's development of ETS as a GHG mitigating policy tool: a case of policy diffusion or domestic drivers?," *Review of Policy Research* 36(2) (2019): 168–94; Valerie J. Karplus, "Institutions and emissions trading in China," *American Economic Review Papers & Proceedings* 108 (2018): 468–72.

Chapter 2 Ambition

1 Leading environmental economists have long recognized the effect of strong regulations in reducing demand for

allowances. See, e.g., Richard Schmalensee and Robert N. Stavins, "The SO_2 Allowance Trading System: the ironic history of a grand policy experiment," *Journal of Economic Perspectives* 27(1) (2013): 103–22.

2 This dynamic has been prominent in market debates for years, but was only recently described with comprehensive rigor in the academic literature by Severin Borenstein et al., "Expecting the unexpected: emissions uncertainty and environmental market design," *American Economic Review* 109(11) (2019): 3953–77.

3 Andy Coghlan and Danny Cullenward, "State constitutional limitations on the future of California's carbon market," *Energy Law Journal* 37(2) (2016): 219–63.

4 Adam B. Jaffe, Richard G. Newell, and Robert N. Stavins, "A tale of two market failures: technology and environmental policy," *Ecological Economics* 54 (2004): 164–74.

5 Stephen Ansolabehere and David M. Konisky, *Cheap and Clean: How Americans Think about Energy in the Age of Global Warming* (MIT Press, 2014). The empirical evidence for the points we make here is strongest in the United States and less well understood elsewhere. And clearly the "cheap and clean" hypothesis applies only to varying degrees, depending on the broader degree of mobilization of the public and relevant interest groups. Our point is one of directionality: that for a given level of public concern and willingness to act, conspicuous clarity on costs reduces interest and also makes it easier for opponents to organize.

6 US Environmental Protection Agency, "California State Motor Vehicle Pollution Control Standards; Notice of Decision Granting a Waiver of Clean Air Act Preemption for California's 2009 and Subsequent Model Year Greenhouse Gas Emission Standards for New Motor Vehicles," *Federal Register* 74 (July 28, 2009): 32744–84; US Environmental Protection Agency, "California State Motor Vehicle Pollution Control Standards; Notice of Decision Granting a Waiver of Clean Air Act Preemption

for California's Advanced Clean Car Program and a Within the Scope Confirmation for California's Zero Emission Vehicle Amendments for 2017 and Earlier Model Years," *Federal Register* 78 (Jan. 9, 2013): 2112–45.

7 President Donald J. Trump, "Executive Order 13783 of March 28, 2017," *Federal Register* 82 (2017): 16093–7.

8 California Air Resources Board, Ford Motor Company, American Honda Motor Co., Inc., Volkswagen Group of America, Inc., and BMW of North America, LLC, "Terms for Light-Duty Greenhouse Gas Emissions Standards," *https://ww2.arb.ca.gov/news/ california-and-major-automakers-reach-groundbreaking- framework-agreement-clean-emission*. Subsequently, a coalition of other automakers, led by General Motors, Toyota Motor Company, and Fiat Chrysler Automobiles, announced they would back the Trump Administration's legal position that federal law pre-empts California from setting its own vehicle pollution standards. Hiroko Tabuchi, "General Motors sides with Trump in emissions fight, splitting the industry," *The New York Times* (Oct. 28, 2019).

9 US Environmental Protection Agency, "Oil and Natural Gas Sector: Emission Standards for New, Reconstructed, and Modified Sources: Final Rule," *Federal Register* 81 (June 3, 2016): 35824–942.

10 A. Denny Ellerman, Frank J. Convery, and Christian de Perthuis, *Pricing Carbon: The European Union Emissions Trading Scheme* (Cambridge University Press, 2010) (see Chapter 2).

11 A. Denny Ellerman, Claudio Marcantonini, and Aleksandar Zaklan, "The European Union Emissions Trading System: ten years and counting," *Review of Environmental Economics and Policy* 10(1) (2016): 89–107. Prices for market futures didn't crash, however, because market participants correctly anticipated the view that the program's second phase would not be similarly overallocated.

12 Coghlan and Cullenward, *supra* note 3.

13 California Chamber of Commerce v. California Air Resources Board, 10 Cal. App. 5th 604 (Cal. Ct. App. 2017), *http://climatecasechart.com/case/california-chamber-of-commerce-v-california-air-resources-board/*.

14 Danny Cullenward and Andy Coghlan, "Structural oversupply and credibility in California's carbon market," *Electricity Journal* 29 (2016): 7–14. Some market participants assert that the auction collapse was driven more by a reaction to the lawsuit challenging the validity of the government's allowance auctions. See Coghlan and Cullenward, *supra* note 3. Those concerns may well have contributed to the scale of the collapse, but the explanation seems wanting in the face of persistently anemic auction demand that cleared up only once a market extension bill eliminated legal uncertainty for the program's post-2020 future.

15 Kate Aronoff, "California Gov. Jerry Brown is backing a climate bill full of giveaways to polluters," *In These Times* (July 14, 2017); Julie Cart, "Checking the math on cap-and-trade, some experts say it's not adding up," *CalMatters* (May 22, 2018); David Roberts, "California's cap-and-trade system may be too weak to do its job," *Vox* (Dec. 13, 2018); Lisa Song, "Cap and trade is supposed to solve climate change, but oil and gas company emissions are up," *ProPublica* (Nov. 15, 2019); Jacques Leslie, "Why California's climate solution isn't cutting it," *Los Angeles Times* (Jan. 2, 2020).

16 Coghlan and Cullenward, *supra* note 3.

17 Oregon H.B. 2020 B, 2019 Regular Session, *https://olis.leg.state.or.us/liz/2019R1/Measures/Overview/HB2020*; Julie Turkewitz, "Oregon climate walkout left Republicans in hiding, statehouse in disarray," *The New York Times* (June 28, 2019).

18 Danny Cullenward, "California's foreign climate policy," *Global Summitry* 3(1) (2017): 1–26.

19 David V. Wright, "Cross-border constraints on climate change agreements: legal risks in the California–Quebec

cap-and-trade linkage," *Environmental Law Reporter* 46(10) (2016): 478–95 (2016); see also Sharmila Murthy, "The constitutionality of state and local 'norm sustaining' actions on global climate change: the foreign affairs federalism grey zone," *University of Pennsylvania Journal of Law & Public Affairs* (forthcoming, 2020).

20 That agreement was updated when Ontario joined the WCI. See "California-Ontario-Québec Agreement on the Harmonization and Integration of their Cap-and-Trade Programs" (Sept. 2017), *https://ww3.arb.ca.gov/cc/capandtrade/linkage/linkage.htm*. In 2019, the Trump Administration sued California, claiming this linking agreement and the domestic California regulations that implement it interfere with the US Government's rightful authority. Anna M. Phillips, Alexa Díaz, and Tony Barboza, "Trump Administration sues California over cap-and-trade agreement with Canada," *Los Angeles Times* (Oct. 23, 2019).

21 David V. Wright, "Enforcement and Withdrawal under the California–Quebec (and not Ontario) Cap-and-Trade Linkage Agreement," Canadian Institute of Resources Law, University of Calgary (Oct. 2018), *https://cirl.ca/symposiums/oct-2018*.

22 In re: Regional Greenhouse Gas Initiative (RGGI), Case No. A-4878-11T4 (N.J. Sup. Ct. App. Div. Mar. 25, 2014).

23 H.J. Mai, "New Jersey adopts rules to rejoin RGGI, heading to 100% clean energy by 2050," *Utility Dive* (June 18, 2019).

24 David G. Victor, "The problem with cap and trade," *MIT Technology Review* (June 23, 2009), *https://www.technologyreview.com/s/414025/the-problem-with-cap-and-trade/*.

25 Leslie McAllister, "The Overallocation problem in cap-and-trade: moving toward stringency," *Columbia Journal of Environmental Law* 34(2) (2009): 395–445; Dallas Burtraw and Amelia Keyes, "Recognizing gravity as a strong force in atmosphere emissions markets,"

Agricultural Resource Economics Review 47(2) (2018): 201–19.

26 Michael Wara, "Instrument choice, carbon emissions, and information," *Michigan Journal of Environmental & Administrative Law* 4(2) (2015): 261–301.

27 Paul Craig, Ashok Gadgil, and Jonathan G. Koomey, "What can history teach us? A retrospective examination of long-term energy forecasts for the United States," *Annual Review of Energy and the Environment* 27 (2002): 83–118; Evan D. Sherwin, Max Henrion, and Inês M.L. Azevedo, "Estimation of the year-on-year volatility and the unpredictability of the United States energy system," *Nature Energy* 3 (2018): 341–6.

28 Borenstein et al., *supra* note 2.

29 Unfortunately, the EU may not have learned its own lesson, at least not right away. We discuss in chapter 5 how it imported a massive number of low-quality offsets that contributed substantially to a second oversupply problem in the 2010s. In response to growing awareness about poor offset quality, EU regulators announced major cutbacks in offset use beginning in phase 3. Emitting industries responded by spiking their use of offsets in phase 2 and banked a massive number of allowances into phase 3 instead. It would take additional reforms and almost ten years for the EU to get a successful handle on the whack-a-mole problems that cap-and-trade creates – and all because allowance banking propagates the errors in one trading period into the others.

Chapter 3 Coverage and allocation

1 Jesse Jenkins, "Why Carbon Pricing Falls Short and What to Do About It," Kleinman Center for Energy Policy, University of Pennsylvania (Apr. 24, 2019).

2 Geoffroy Dolphin, Michael G. Pollitt, and David M. Newbery, "The political economy of carbon pricing: a

panel analysis," *Oxford Economic Papers* 72(2) (2020): 472–500.

3 Here we are focused on this story through the lens of political responsiveness. We are mindful that other factors are at work as well, of course, such as the administrative feasibility of measuring and taxing/trading emissions in some sectors, as well as the economic impacts of the point of incidence of a carbon pricing program. See Erin T. Mansur, "Upstream versus downstream implementation of climate policy," in Don Fullerton and Catherine Wolfram (eds.), *The Design and Implementation of US Climate Policy* (University of Chicago Press, 2012); see also Hal Harvey, Robbie Orvis, and Jeffrey Rissman, *Designing Climate Solutions: A Policy Guide for Low-Carbon Energy* (Island Press, 2018), at 263–4.

4 Management of so-called "international bunker fuels" from international shipping and international aviation is explicitly delegated by broad-based, multilateral treaties to the World Maritime Organization and the International Civil Aviation Organization, respectively. Thus, neither subnational nor national governments have the legal authority to regulate these important emission categories.

5 See, e.g., Carolyn Fischer and Alan K. Fox, "Output-based allocation of emissions permits for mitigating tax and trade interactions," *Land Economics* 83(4) (2007): 575–99; Meredith Fowlie, "Updating the allocation of greenhouse gas emissions permits in a federal cap-and-trade program," in Fullerton and Wolfram, *supra* note 3.

6 We will focus on the core political drivers of how industry organized for free allowance allocations. However, there are other nuanced forces at work as well. They include firms' private cost of capital, which can be significant and therefore present financial barriers to incorporating the option value of allowances into decision-making. If a firm could plausibly pursue emission reductions at a cost that is lower than the value of allowances, it might well make a profit doing so and selling those allowances – but only if the firm's ability to deploy capital is cheap enough to

enable these potential profits. That problem is worsened because many firms conceive of cap-and-trade programs primarily as a compliance expense to be minimized, not optimized, when the firm's profits flow largely from other, especially capital-intensive activities. Few firms receive complete free allocation; more common is that sensitive industries receive most, but not all, of the allowances they need to comply with program rules. Under these conditions, there is some theoretical incentive to reduce emissions and recognize the opportunity cost of hoarding valuable free allowances, but regulatory compliance teams are more likely to be focused on acquiring the remaining allowances needed rather than cost-optimizing across a large company's operations.

7 See, e.g., Meredith Fowlie and Mar Reguant, "Challenges in the measurement of leakage risk," *American Economic Review Papers and Proceedings* 108 (2018): 124–9.

8 See Meredith Fowlie and Danny Cullenward, "Emissions leakage and resource shuffling," chapter 4 in the 2018 Annual Report of the Independent Emissions Market Committee (October 2018), *https://calepa.ca.gov/climate/iemac-independent-emissions-market-advisory-committee/*.

9 According to California program data, the oil and gas industry's midstream (refining) and upstream (production) segments received 22.1 million and 7.8 million allowances, respectively, for a total of about 70% of the 43.1 million allowances given freely to industrial emitters in 2019. See California Air Resources Board, "Cap-and-Trade Program Vintage 2019 Allowance Allocation Summary" (Dec. 18, 2018), *https://ww3.arb.ca.gov/cc/capandtrade/allowanceallocation/v2019allocation.pdf*.

10 For a discussion of just a few of the practical challenges border carbon adjustments would raise, see Adele C. Morris, "Making Border Carbon Adjustments Work in Law and Practice," Urban Institute and Brookings Institution Tax Policy Center Report (July 26, 2018), *https://www.brookings.edu/research/*

making-border-carbon-adjustments-work-in-law-and-practice/.

11 Jim Bacchus, *The Willing World: Shaping and Sharing a Sustainable Global Prosperity* (Cambridge University Press, 2018).

12 Foreign affairs issues are discussed in more detail in chapter 6. In the United States, subnational governments face additional barriers under a legal doctrine known as the dormant commerce clause, which may restrict efforts to manage cross-border emissions flows. For a brief overview, see Danny Cullenward and David Weiskopf, "Science advocacy and the legal system: is life cycle assessment unconstitutional?," in J.L. Drake et al. (eds.), *New Trends in Earth-Science Outreach and Engagement* (Springer, 2014).

13 Stefan U. Pauer, "Border Carbon Adjustments in Support of Domestic Climate Policies: Explaining the Gap between Theory and Practice," Smart Prosperity Institute Clean Economy Working Paper 19-05 (Oct. 2019), *https://institute.smartprosperity.ca/library/research/border-carbon-adjustments-support-domestic-climate-policies-explaining-gap-between*.

14 Bruce Huber, "How did RGGI do it? Political economy and emissions auctions," *Ecology Law Quarterly* 40 (2013): 59–106; Jonathan L. Ramseur, "The Regional Greenhouse Gas Initiative: Background, Impacts, and Selected Issues," Congressional Research Service Report #R41836 (July 16, 2019), *https://fas.org/sgp/crs/misc/R41836.pdf*.

15 European Commission, "Transitional Free Allocation to Electricity Generators," *https://ec.europa.eu/clima/policies/ets/allowances/electricity_en*; see also A. Denny Ellerman, Barbara K. Buchner, and Carlo Carraro (eds.), *Allocation in the European Emissions Trading Scheme* (Cambridge University Press, 2007); Karsten Neuhoff, Kim Keats, and Misato Sato, "Allocation, incentives and distortions: the impact of EU ETS emissions allowance

allocations to the electricity sector," *Climate Policy* 6(1) (2006): 73–91.

16 For more details on the political economy of free allocation and carbon pricing in California's electricity sector, see Danny Cullenward, "Leakage in California's carbon market," *Electricity Journal* 27(9) (2014): 36–48; Guri Bang, David G. Victor, and Steinar Andresen, "California's cap-and-trade system: diffusion and lessons," *Global Environmental Politics* 17(3) (2017): 12–30; Stefan U. Pauer, "Including electricity imports in California's cap-and-trade program: a case study of a border carbon adjustment in practice," *Electricity Journal* 31 (2018): 39–45.

17 Technically, the California Climate Credit is a credit given to each residential customer on the basis of the metered billing unit, rather than the number of people. That is, each meter gets a rebate, whether that household is a single person or a family of four. See California Public Utilities Commission, "California Climate Credit," *https://www.cpuc.ca.gov/climatecredit/*.

18 In recognition of this problem, a proposed carbon market for transportation fuels in the northeastern United States called the Transportation & Climate Initiative includes mechanisms to help compensate low-income customers – but primarily through spending priorities from the revenue collected at auction, a topic we discuss in the next chapter. Transportation & Climate Initiative, "Framework for a Draft Regional Policy Proposal" (Oct. 2019), *https://www.transportationandclimate.org/sites/default/files/TCI-Framework_10-01-2019.pdf*.

Chapter 4 Revenue and spending

1 These perspectives are considered in thoughtful detail by two leading books: Dale W. Jorgenson, Richard J. Gottle, Mun S. Ho, and Peter J. Wilcoxen, *Double Dividend:*

Environmental Taxes and Fiscal Reform in the United States (MIT Press, 2013); Lawrence Goulder and Marc Hafstead, *Confronting the Climate Challenge: US Policy Options* (Columbia University Press, 2017).

2 Climate Leadership Council, "Our Plan" (Sept. 2019), *https://clcouncil.org/our-plan/*; James A. Baker III et al., "The Conservative Case for Carbon Dividends, Climate Leadership Council" (Feb. 2017) (the "Baker–Shultz plan"), *https://www.clcouncil.org/media/2017/03/The-Conservative-Case-for-Carbon-Dividends.pdf*.

3 See James Boyce, *The Case for Carbon Dividends* (Polity, 2019); George Akerlof et al., "Economists' Statement on Carbon Dividends, Climate Leadership Council" (2019), *https://www.clcouncil.org/economists-statement/*. As a representative example of ideological diversity among elite actors favoring climate dividends, see Citizens' Climate Lobby Advisory Board, *https://citizensclimatelobby.org/about-ccl/advisory-board/*.

4 Jonathan L. Ramseur, "Market-Based Greenhouse Gas Emission Reduction Legislation: 108th through 116th Congresses," Congressional Research Service Report #R45472 (2020), *https://crsreports.congress.gov/product/details?prodcode=R45472*.

5 US Government Interagency Working Group on the Social Cost of Greenhouse Gases, "Technical Support Document: Technical Update of the Social Cost of Carbon for Regulatory Impact Analysis Under Executive Order 12866 (August 2016)" (using 3% average discount rate in 2015), *https://19january2017snapshot.epa.gov/climatechange/social-cost-carbon_.html*. We note that there is a broad debate about the use and construction of these numbers. A number of newer studies suggest that actual climate impacts may be much higher, especially when equity or long-term growth effects are considered. See, e.g., Frances C. Moore and Delavane Diaz, "Temperature impacts on economic growth warrant stringent mitigation policy," *Nature Climate Change* 5(2) (2015): 127–31; Matthew Adler et al., "Priority for the

worse-off and the social cost of carbon," *Nature Climate Change* 7(6) (2017): 127–31.

6 European Environment Agency, "Total Greenhouse Gas Emission Trends and Projections," *https://www.eea.europa.eu/data-and-maps/indicators/greenhouse-gas-emission-trends-6/assessment-3.*

7 European Commission, "Analysis of the Use of Auction Revenues by Member States" (March 2017), at 16, *https://ec.europa.eu/clima/sites/clima/files/ets/auctioning/docs/auction_revenues_report_2017_en.pdf.*

8 See Sandbag, "Carbon Price Viewer," *https://sandbag.org.uk/carbon-price-viewer/.*

9 Damien Meadows, Yvon Slingenberg, and Peter Zapfel, "EU ETS: pricing carbon to drive cost-effective reductions across Europe," in Jos Delbeke and Peter Vis (eds.), *EU Climate Policy Explained* (Routledge, 2015), at 34.

10 International Carbon Action Partnership, "Emissions Trading Worldwide: Status Report 2019" (2019), at 106–7. According to ICAP, however, the share of free allocation is intended to decrease significantly in the market's post-2020 period.

11 This view is rarely committed to print, owing to the rhetorical commitment to cap-and-trade programs as environmental controls rather than a source of revenue, but the suggestion arises in an important book that makes the case for a regulation-first climate strategy: Hal Harvey, *Designing Climate Solutions: A Policy Guide for Low-Carbon Energy* (Island Press, 2018). Harvey and colleagues note, however, that some revenues may need to be recycled to address equity issues and/or political resistance to carbon pricing.

12 See, e.g., Lawrence H. Goulder and Stephen H. Schneider, "Induced technological change and the attractiveness of CO_2 abatement policies," *Resource and Energy Economics* 21 (1999): 211–53.

13 A growing number of political observers and analysts are making arguments about the potential to use carbon revenues to expand political coalitions that support

additional policy ambition. Jonas Meckling et al., "Winning coalitions for climate policy," *Science* 349 (2015): 1170–2; Gernot Wagner et al., "Push renewables to spur carbon pricing," *Nature* 525 (2015): 27–9; Jonas Meckling et al., "Policy sequencing toward decarbonization," *Nature Energy* 2 (2017): 918–22; Michael Pahle et al., "Sequencing to ratchet up climate policy stringency," *Nature Climate Change* 8 (2018): 861–7. However, this important literature does not dwell much on the potential for climate funds to be spent ineffectively.

14 The touchstone study comes from Jeremy Carl and David Fedor, "Tracking global carbon revenues: a survey of carbon taxes versus cap-and-trade in the real world," *Energy Policy* 96 (2016): 50–77. Since then, we know of just one other comprehensive assessment: Sébastian Postic and Clément Métivier, "Global Carbon Account 2019," Institute for Climate Economics (May 2019). This study was subsequently updated and included in a World Bank report on revenue use: World Bank, "Using Carbon Revenues," Partnership for Market Readiness Technical Note 16 (Aug. 2019).

15 Jonathan L. Ramseur, "The Regional Greenhouse Gas Initiative: Background, Impacts, and Selected Issues," Congressional Research Service Report #R41836 (July 16, 2019), at 10–11, *https://fas.org/sgp/crs/misc/R41836.pdf*.

16 Andy Coghlan and Danny Cullenward, "State constitutional limitations on the future of California's carbon market," *Energy Law Journal* 37(2) (2016): 219–63.

17 California Health & Safety Code § 39712(a)(2); see also Coghlan and Cullenward, *supra* note 16.

18 California Air Resources Board, "California Climate Investments: 2020 Annual Report" (Mar. 2020), *http://www.caclimateinvestments.ca.gov/annual-report*.

19 California Legislative Analyst's Office, "Administration's Cap-and-Trade Report Provides New Information, Raises Issues for Consideration" (Apr. 15, 2016), *https://lao.ca.gov/Publications/Report/3445*.

20 California Air Resources Board, *supra* note 18, at xvi (reporting portfolio-wide emission reductions of 44.7 million tCO₂e from green spending programs); ibid., at 121 (reporting total project costs of $21.4 billion for green spending programs).

21 For context on state-level programs and the challenges with projecting costs and benefits, see Ian Hoffman et al., "The Cost of Saving Electricity Through Energy Efficiency Programs Funded by Utility Customers: 2009–2015," Lawrence Berkeley National Laboratory (June 2018), *https://emp.lbl.gov/publications/cost-saving-electricity-through*.

22 The most recent comprehensive analysis of EU member state revenue use comes from 2017 and applies to the period 2013–15. See European Commission, *supra* note 7. Some additional information is released in technical reports, as shown in Figure 4.5, but otherwise very little information appears to be publicly available. For an overview of available data, see Andrei Marcu et al., "2020 State of the EU ETS Report" (2020), *https://ercst.org/publication-2020-state-of-the-eu-ets-report/*.

Chapter 5 Offsets

1 There are a few important exceptions to this rule. Fossil fuel emissions are often associated with aerosol emissions, which have atmospheric lifetimes measured in days and which produce highly variable cooling effects depending on where they occur. Geeta G. Persad and Ken Caldeira, "Divergent global-scale temperature effects from identical aerosols emitted in different regions," *Nature Communications* 9 (2018): 3289. And while CO₂ is a globally well-mixed greenhouse gas that remains in the atmosphere for hundreds and even thousands of years, higher local concentrations can build up near emission sources and lead to exacerbated air quality

concerns. Mark Z. Jacobson, "Enhancement of local air pollution by urban CO_2 domes," *Environmental Science & Technology* 44 (2010): 2497–502.

2 Technically, there are two broad approaches to offsets. The initial Clean Development Mechanism program established for international offsets under the Kyoto Protocol set up a process where individual projects would propose project-specific calculations for emission reductions. This led to significant transaction costs because each project would have to substantiate complex technical claims about counterfactual and observed emission projections. It also led to gaming, where projects could make outlandish claims, such as inflating baseline emissions to earn more credits. In response to these concerns, the CDM and the California offsets programs developed a protocol-level or standardized approach to offset crediting. Under this second approach, projects that meet protocol eligibility criteria earn offsets according to a standard set of predetermined formulas. Although this approach provides some benefits, it largely concentrates the uncertainty and risks in the design of the protocols, rather than the individual project calculations. See Barbara Haya et al., "Managing uncertainty in carbon offsets: insights from California's standardized approach," *Climate Policy* (forthcoming, 2020).

3 The "where" is of great importance, even if offsets are executed to perfection. Environmental justice interests remain opposed to offsets because offsets enable incumbent emitters – which are disproportionately located in low-income communities of color – to avoid making major changes to their own emissions. Since local air pollution is often correlated with greenhouse gas emissions, the location of pollution reduction matters to environmental justice communities. Offsets shift the "where" of reductions away from covered sources and therefore can exacerbate, or at least perpetuate, environmental inequities. See Lara Cushing et al., "Carbon trading, co-pollutants, and environmental equity: evidence

from California's cap-and-trade program (2011–2015)," *PLoS Medicine* 15(7) (2018): e1002604.

4 Technically, what really matters is not perfection, but conservative accounting that avoids over-crediting with very high confidence. If an offset project generates more emission reductions than the offset credits it earns, then it has no negative impacts on the quality of the overall carbon market – even though the accounting in this hypothetical is imperfect.

5 See, e.g., California Air Resources Board, "2017 Scoping Plan, Appendix A: AB 32 Environmental Justice Advisory Committee (EJAC) Recommendations" (Nov. 2017), *https://ww3.arb.ca.gov/cc/scopingplan/2030sp_appa_ejac_final.pdf*.

6 Jason Gray, who manages the offsets team as Branch Chief of the Climate Change Program Evaluation Branch at the California Air Resources Board, conveyed this information directly to one of us (Cullenward) in Sacramento, California, in August 2019.

7 As of this writing, California has six offset protocols approved for use in its cap-and-trade program and a seventh, the Tropical Forest Standard, that is approved for others' use but which is overseen, in theory, by the California Air Resources Board. In the United States, trona is mined as the primary source of sodium carbonate, also called soda ash, which is used in the manufacture of various products, including glass, paper, rayon, and detergents.

8 A slightly older, but well-established study put the cost at $600/tCO$_2$. American Physical Society, "Direct Air Capture of CO$_2$ with Chemicals" (Robert Socolow et al. eds., 2011). A group of scientists who work for one the companies pursuing this technology more recently put the cost at much lower levels, but debate continues within the field about how realistic these lower estimates are. David W. Keith et al., "A process for capturing CO$_2$ from the atmosphere," *Joule* 2(8) (2018): 1573–94.

9 For an overview, see Michael Wara, "Is the global

carbon market working?" *Nature* 445 (2007): 595–6; see also Michael Wara, "Measuring the Clean Development Mechanism's performance and potential," *UCLA Law Review* 55 (2008): 1759–803.

10 Lambert Schneider and Anja Kollmuss, "Perverse effects of carbon markets on HFC-23 and SF_6 abatement projects in Russia," *Nature Climate Change* (2015) 5: 1061–3.

11 A. Denny Ellerman, Claudio Marcantonini, and Aleksandar Zaklan, "The European Union Emissions Trading System: ten years and counting," *Review of Environmental Economics and Policy* 10(1) (2016): 89–107.

12 Martin Cames et al., "How Additional is the Clean Development Mechanism? Analysis of the Application of Current Tools and Proposed Alternatives," Öko-Institut e.V. study prepared for DG CLIMA (Mar. 2016), at 11, *https://ec.europa.eu/clima/sites/clima/files/ets/docs/clean_dev_mechanism_en.pdf*.

13 European Commission, DG-Climate Action, "Use of International Credits," *https://ec.europa.eu/clima/policies/ets/credits_en* ("The EU has a domestic emissions reduction target and does not currently envisage continuing use of international credits after 2020").

14 Jonathan L. Ramseur, "The Regional Greenhouse Gas Initiative: Background, Impacts, and Selected Issues," Congressional Research Service Report #R41836 (July 16, 2019), *https://fas.org/sgp/crs/misc/R41836.pdf*.

15 Haya et al., *supra* note 2.

16 California Air Resources Board, "Compliance Offsets Program" (May 27, 2020), *https://ww3.arb.ca.gov/cc/capandtrade/offsets/offsets.htm*.

17 Barbara Haya, "Policy Brief: The California Air Resources Board's US Forest Offset Protocol Underestimates Leakage," UC Berkeley Goldman School of Public Policy Working Paper (May 2019), *https://gspp.berkeley.edu/research/working-paper-series/policy-brief-arbas-us-forest-projects-offset-protocol-underestimates-leaka*.

18 A copy of the exchange can be found on the website of the

Pacific Forest Trust, an organization that advocates for carbon offsets: *https://www.pacificforest.org/wp-content/uploads/2019/07/Wieckowski-letters-2019.pdf*.

19 This concern was raised prominently by the Environmental Commissioner of Ontario, Ontario's former environmental watchdog agency, which was subsequently shut down when a conservative government came into power and withdrew Ontario from the WCI market. See Environmental Commissioner of Ontario, "Ontario's Climate Act: From Plan to Progress, Chapter 4: Offsets" (Jan. 2018), at 141–9, *https://eco.auditor.on.ca/reports/2017-from-plan-to-progress/*. California's Independent Emissions Market Advisory Committee (on which Cullenward serves) reviewed this issue and recommended CARB evaluate and justify its choice of leakage factor. Independent Emissions Market Advisory Committee, "2018 IEMAC Annual Report" (Oct. 2018), at 47, *https://calepa.ca.gov/climate/iemac-independent-emissions-market-advisory-committee/*.

20 *Amicus Curiae* Brief of The Nature Conservancy in Support of Defendants' Motion for Summary Judgment, United States v. California et al., Case No. 2:19-cv-02142-WBS-EFB (E.D. Cal., Feb. 18, 2020), available at *https://statepowerproject.org/california/#US*.

21 For more on the role of private environmental governance in this area, see Jessica F. Green, "Blurred lines: public–private interactions in carbon regulations," *International Interactions* 43(1) (2017): 103–28; Jessica F. Green, "Order out of chaos: public and private rules for managing carbon," *Global Environmental Politics* 13(2) (2013): 1–25; Lauren Gifford, "'You can't value what you can't measure': a critical look at forest carbon accounting," in press at *Climatic Change* (2020).

22 Hal Harvey, Robbie Orvis, and Jeffrey Rissman, *Designing Climate Solutions: A Policy Guide for Low-Carbon Energy* (Island Press, 2018), at 268.

23 This firm advertises that it was "directly involved" in development of the California coal mine methane

protocol. It also advertises that it "currently develops the US EPA's annual Coal Emissions inventory for all US coal mines." See Ruby Canyon Engineering, "Coal Mine Methane (CMM) Consulting," Overview and US EPA CMOP, respectively, *https://rubycanyoneng.com/what-we-do/cmm-consulting/*.

24 California Air Resources Board, "California Tropical Forest Standard" (Sept. 19, 2019), *https://ww3.arb.ca.gov/cc/ghgsectors/tropicalforests.htm*. For background on the controversy with the Tropical Forest Standard, see Lisa Song, "An even more inconvenient truth: why carbon credits for forest preservation may be worse than nothing," *ProPublica* (May 22, 2019).

25 The Governors' Climate and Forests Task Force was set up in 2008 to explore mechanisms to provide international offset and other financial credits for tropical forests, with California as the anchor non-tropical partner. See Danny Cullenward, "California's foreign climate policy," *Global Summitry* 3(1) (2017): 1–26; see also California Air Resources Board, "International Sector-Based Offset Credits," *https://ww3.arb.ca.gov/cc/capandtrade/sectorbasedoffsets/sectorbasedoffsets.htm*.

26 Carolyn Kormann, "How carbon trading became a way of life for California's Yurok tribe," *The New Yorker* (Oct. 10, 2018), *https://www.newyorker.com/news/dispatch/how-carbon-trading-became-a-way-of-life-for-californias-yurok-tribe*.

27 California Assembly Bill AB 398 (Stat. 2017, E. Garcia) codified limits on projects that do not produce "direct environmental benefits" to California air or water quality. See California Health & Safety Code § 38562(c)(2)(E), *https://leginfo.legislature.ca.gov/faces/billNavClient.xhtml?bill_id=201720180AB398*.

28 Oregon House Bill 2020 B (2019 Regular Session), Section 30(2)(a), *https://olis.leg.state.or.us/liz/2019R1/Measures/Overview/HB2020*.

29 Washington Senate Bill 5981 (2019 Regular Session; Carlyle, Palumbo, and Lovett), Section 13(3), *https://*

*app.leg.wa.gov/billsummary?BillNumber=5981&Initiati
ve=false&Year=2019.*

30 New York Environmental Conservation Law Section
75-0109(4)(h)(ii) (as added by Senate Bill 6599 and
Assembly Bill 8429, 2019-2020 Regular Sessions), *https://
nyassembly.gov/leg/?bn=A08429&term=2019.*

31 See European Commission, *supra*, note 13.

32 Christiana Figueres, "Sectoral CDM: opening the CDM
to the yet unrealized goal of sustainable development,"
McGill Journal of Sustainable Development Law 2(1)
(2006): 5–25, at 12–13.

33 See Haya et al., *supra* note 2, at 17.

34 See, e.g., Iselin Stensdal, Gørild Heggelund, and Duan
Maosheng, "China's carbon market: in it to learn it,"
in Jørgen Wettestad and Lars Gulbrandsen (eds.), *The
Evolution of Carbon Markets: Design and Diffusion*
(Routledge, 2018); see also Coraline Goron and Cyril
Cassisa, "Regulatory institutions and market-based
climate policy in China," *Global Environmental Politics*
17(1) (2017): 99–120.

35 To be clear, the articles exploring connections between
China's efforts to develop market-based policies in the
electricity sector and its early experience with CDM do
not make such exaggerated claims. Instead, they include
these connections in a broader and more sophisticated
analysis of institutional and political drivers of Chinese
policy outcomes.

36 A recent study of Mexico's experience designing carbon
pricing policies – including both a cap-and-trade program
and a carbon tax – affirms that industry opposition to
high carbon prices remains a critical factor, even when
a government receives substantial multilateral support
and the carbon pricing policies help address short-term
budget needs. See Arjuna Dibley and Rolando Garcia-
Miron, "Creating a climate for change? Carbon pricing
and long-term policy reform in Mexico," in World
Bank, First International Conference on Carbon Pricing,

World Bank Working Paper Series, Report No. 141909
(Nov. 2019).

Chapter 6 Market links

1 Jessica F. Green, Thomas Sterner, and Gernot Wagner, "A
  balance of bottom-up and top-down in linking climate
  policies," *Nature Climate Change* 4 (2014): 1064–7.
2 Matthew Ranson and Robert N. Stavins, "Linkage of
  greenhouse gas emissions trading systems: learning from
  experience," *Climate Policy* 16 (2016): 284–300; Michael
  A. Mehling, Gilbert E. Metcalf, and Robert N. Stavins,
  "Linking climate policies to advance global mitigation,"
  Science 359 (2018): 997–8.
3 The coverage of the EU ETS evolved with countries'
  membership in the scheme. The first phase of the EU ETS
  (2005–7) featured the original fifteen EU member states.
  In the second trading phase (2008–12), these were supplemented by twelve new EU states and three non-member
  states (Norway, Iceland, and Lichtenstein). Croatia's
  membership in the EU expanded the list to thirty-
  one total states in phase 3 (2013–20). More recently,
  Switzerland joined on January 1, 2020, bringing the
  total number of participants to thirty-two. At the time of
  writing, the United Kingdom has left the EU but remains
  part of the EU ETS, although the implications of Brexit
  for the United Kingdom's long-term participation in the
  EU ETS are not yet known.
4 Danny Cullenward, "The limits of administrative law as
  regulatory oversight in linked carbon markets," *UCLA
  Journal of Environmental Law & Policy* 33(1) (2015):
  1–41.
5 This story oversimplifies actual market dynamics, of
  course. Where there are risks of de-linking or other
  administrative interventions, markets can and do trade
  instruments at a discount to one another. See, e.g., Judd

Ormsby and Suzi Kerr, "The New Zealand Emissions Trading Scheme De-Link from Kyoto: Impacts on Banking and Prices," Motu Economic and Public Policy Research Working Paper 16-13 (Aug. 16, 2016) (describing divergence in international and domestic offset prices as New Zealand prepared to reduce international offset eligibility); Michael Mastrandrea, Danny Cullenward, and Mason Inman, "Ontario's Exit Exacerbates Allowance Overallocation in the Western Climate Initiative Cap-and-Trade Program," Near Zero Research Note (July 16, 2018) (illustrating how secondary market trading exported Ontario allowances to California and Québec accounts in the run-up to Ontario's 2018 elections); William A. Pizer and Andrew J. Yates, "Terminating links between emission trading programs," *Journal of Environmental Economics and Management* 71 (2015): 142–59 (discussing the economics of linking and de-linking rules). Offsets also typically trade at a discount to allowances, reflecting the potential for regulatory determinations of non-additionality or other reversals to reduce the value of an instrument "worth" the exact same right to pollute on paper. See A. Denny Ellerman, Claudio Marcantonini, and Aleksandar Zaklan, "The European Union Emissions Trading System: ten years and counting," *Review of Environmental Economics and Policy* 10(1) (2016): 89–107 (showing a persistent and growing divergence between CER offset prices and European Union Allowances as Europe prepared to reduce CER eligibility).

6 International Energy Agency, "Towards International Emissions Trading: Design Implications for Linkages," Organization for Economic Co-operation and Development (2002); Robert Marschinski, Christian Flachsland, and Michael Jakob, "Sectoral linking of carbon markets: a trade theory analysis," *Resource and Energy Economics* 34 (2012): 585–606.

7 For an overview, see Daniel M. Bodansky et al., "Facilitating linking of climate policies through the

Paris outcome," *Climate Policy* 16(8) (2016): 956–72; Robert N. Stavins and Robert C. Stowe (eds.), *Market Mechanisms and the Paris Agreement*, Harvard Project on Climate Agreements (2017); see also Lambert Schneider and Stephanie La Hoz Theuer, "Environmental integrity of international carbon market mechanisms under the Paris Agreement," *Climate Policy* 19(3) (2018): 386–400.

8 For context, see David V. Wright, "Cross-border constraints on climate change agreements: legal risks in the California–Quebec cap-and-trade linkage," *Environmental Law Reporter* 46(10) (2016): 478–95.

9 California-Ontario-Québec Agreement on the Harmonization and Integration of Their Cap-and-Trade Programs (Sept. 2017), *https://ww3.arb.ca.gov/cc/capandtrade/linkage/linkage.htm*.

10 See, e.g., Sharmila L. Murthy, "The constitutionality of state and local 'norm sustaining' actions on global climate change: the foreign affairs federalism grey zone," *University of Pennsylvania Journal of Law & Public Affairs* (forthcoming, 2020).

11 David V. Wright, "Enforcement and Withdrawal under the California–Quebec (and not Ontario) Cap-and-Trade Linkage Agreement," Canadian Institute of Resources Law, University of Calgary (Oct. 2018), *https://cirl.ca/symposiums/oct-2018*.

12 California Air Resources Board, Market Notice (June 15, 2018), *https://arb.ca.gov/cc/capandtrade/auction/market-noticejune2018.pdf*; see also Mastrandrea et al., *supra* note 5.

13 California Air Resources Board, Compliance Instrument Report (2019) (see tab "2019 Q2," cell "A43"), *https://ww2.arb.ca.gov/cap-and-trade-program-data*.

14 Regional Greenhouse Gas Initiative, Inc., "Model Rule and MOU Versions" (2019), *https://www.rggi.org/program-overview-and-design/design-archive/mou-model-rule*. To clarify, the RGGI Model Rule is not a legally binding document, but rather a template for

how each participating state can codify the negotiated agreements into domestic law via its administrative law process.

15 See In re Regional Greenhouse Gas Initiative, Docket No. A-4878-11T4 (Sup. Ct. N.J. App. Div., March 25, 2014) (*per curiam*). Technically, the decisions ordered the New Jersey environmental regulator to fix procedural defects in its withdrawal of cap-and-trade regulations, rather than to recognize the Governor's withdrawal, but the court noted that it would not have needed to hear the case if the regulator had properly justified the revocation of its cap-and-trade regulations following the Governor's decision to withdraw. Ibid. at *13.

16 Jonathan L. Ramseur, "The Regional Greenhouse Gas Initiative: Background, Impacts, and Selected Issues," Congressional Research Service Report #R41836 (July 16, 2019), *https://fas.org/sgp/crs/misc/R41836.pdf*.

17 Gilbert E. Metcalf and David Weisbach, "Linking policies when tastes differ: global climate policy in a heterogeneous world," *Review of Environmental Economics and Policy* 6(1) (2012): 110–29.

18 Danny Cullenward, Mason Inman, and Michael D. Mastrandrea, "Tracking banking in the Western Climate Initiative cap-and-trade program," *Environmental Research Letters* 14 (2019): 124037, *https://iopscience. iop.org/article/10.1088/1748-9326/ab50df*.

19 Rachel Becker, "No longer the loneliest? Why Oregon's all-in climate push matters to California," *CalMatters* (June 6, 2019), *https://calmatters.org/economy/2019/06/ oregon-carbon-cap-trade-bill-california-west/*.

20 In responding to a statutory instruction to "evaluate and address concerns related to overallocation," California Health & Safety Code § 38562(c)(2)(D), the California regulator highlighted that the demand for unused California allowances depends on whether or not linked programs would need to purchase these instruments. In fact, this was the first "key factor" policymakers identified in their summary table of forces impacting

the program's supply–demand balance. California Air Resources Board, "2018 Cap-and-Trade Rulemaking, Staff Report: Initial Statement of Reasons," Appendix D: AB 398: "Evaluation of Allowance Budgets 2021 Through 2030" (Sept. 4, 2018), at 18, Table A-1, *https://ww2.arb. ca.gov/rulemaking/2018/cap-and-trade-ghg-2018*.

21 Cullenward et al., *supra* note 18.

22 Jean Chemnick, "Poland celebrates coal as talks start in mining capital," *E&E News Climatewire* (December 6, 2018), *https://www.eenews.net/stories/1060108909*.

23 See, e.g., Torbjørg Jevnaker and Jørgen Wettestad, "Ratcheting up carbon trade: the politics of reforming EU emissions trading," *Global Environmental Politics* 17(2) (2017): 104–24.

24 For an overview of California's history with multilateral climate initiatives, see Danny Cullenward, "California's foreign climate policy," *Global Summitry* 3(1) (2017): 1–26.

25 Stuart Evans and Aaron Wu, "Australia–EU ETS linking – lessons for the post-Paris world," First International Conference on Carbon Pricing, World Bank Working Paper Series (Nov. 2019); Ian Bailey and Tor Håkon Jackson Inderberg, "Australia: domestic politics, diffusion and emissions trading design as a technical and political project," in Jørgen Wettestad and Lars Gulbrandsen (eds.), *The Evolution of Carbon Markets: Design and Diffusion* (Routledge, 2018).

26 Augusta Williams, "Linking across borders: opportunities and obstacles for a joint Regional Greenhouse Gas Initiative–Western Climate Initiative market," *Columbia Journal of Environmental Law* 43 (2018): 227–67.

27 Others have also warned, appropriately, about the potential for market links to propagate the problems of one linked partner to another – a challenge that would be central to any effort to link markets with different prices that can also reflect differences in program quality. See Jessica F. Green, "Don't link carbon markets," *Nature* 543 (2017): 484–6.

Chapter 7 Getting the most out of markets

1 Danny Cullenward, "For insights into climate policy, look to practice – not just theory," *One Earth* 1 (2019): 46–7.

2 For a more diplomatic argument, see Dallas Burtraw and Amelia Keyes, "Recognizing gravity as a strong force in atmosphere emissions markets," *Agricultural and Resource Economics Review* 47(2) (2018): 201–19.

3 See, e.g., Nicholas Koch et al., "Causes of the EU ETS price drop: recession, CDM, renewable policies, or something else?" *Energy Policy* 73 (2014): 676–85.

4 When we criticize the opacity of California's climate policies throughout the book, we focus primarily on the quality of information made available from the state's climate regulator, the California Air Resources Board. Readers from outside California should know that another part of the state government, the non-partisan Legislative Analyst's Office, produces exceptionally clear and helpful information. See, e.g., Legislative Analyst's Office, "Cap-and-Trade Extension: Issues for Legislative Oversight" (Dec. 2017); Legislative Analyst's Office, "Assessing California's Climate Policies – Electricity Generation" (Jan. 2020); Legislative Analyst's Office, "The 2020–21 Budget: Climate Change Proposals" (Feb. 2020), *https://lao.ca.gov/*.

5 Cameron Hepburn et al., "The economics of the EU ETS Market Stability Reserve," *Journal of Environmental Economics and Management* 80 (2016): 1–5.

6 Decision (EU) 2015/1814 of the European Parliament and of the Council, Official Journal of the European Union, L 264 (October 6, 2015), 1–5, *https://eur-lex.europa.eu/eli/dec/2015/1814/oj*; see also Torbjørg Jevnaker and Jørgen Wettestad, "Ratcheting up carbon trade: the politics of reforming EU emissions trading," *Global Environmental Politics* 17(2) (2017): 104–24.

7 For an example of a critical perspective, see Stephen

W. Salant, "What ails the European Union's emissions trading system?" *Journal of Environmental Economics and Management* 80 (2016): 6–19.

8 Some economists continue to argue that low prices are good outcomes, rather than a warning sign that markets aren't doing the real work of deep emission reductions. For an overview, see Sabine Fuss et al., "A framework for assessing the performance of cap-and-trade systems: insights from the European Union Emissions Trading System," *Review of Environmental Economics and Policy* 12(2) (2018): 220–41.

9 The initial transfer was set at 12% of the surplus. See Decision (EU) 2015/1814 of the European Parliament and of the Council, *supra* note 6. The EU subsequently doubled this amount to 24% beginning in 2019 through the end of calendar year 2023, in order to more rapidly draw down the large bank of excess allowances that had accumulated in the previous decade. See Directive (EU) 2018/410 of the European Parliament and of the Council, Official Journal of the European Union, L 76/3 (Mar. 19, 2018), 3–27, *https://eur-lex.europa.eu/eli/dir/2018/410/oj*.

10 See Hepburn et al., *supra* note 5.

11 The Regional Greenhouse Gas Initiative, "Elements of RGGI," *https://www.rggi.org/program-overview-and-design/elements*; see also The Regional Greenhouse Gas Initiative, "RGGI Program Review: Summary of Proposed Changes to RGGI Regional CO_2 Allowance Budget" (Nov. 21, 2013); The Regional Greenhouse Gas Initiative, "Second Control Period Interim Adjustment for Banked Allowances Announcement" (March 17, 2014).

12 The Regional Greenhouse Gas Initiative (2014), *supra* note 11.

13 New York and Illinois (the latter of which is not in RGGI) created the first zero-emission credit (ZEC) subsidy programs for nuclear energy in the United States. See Nuclear Energy Institute, "Zero-Emission Credits" (Apr. 2018). These policies were challenged in court

and ultimately upheld in two parallel cases. Coalition for Competitive Electricity v. Zibelman, 906 F.3d 41 (2nd Cir. 2018) (New York); Electric Power Supply Association v. Star, 904 F.3d 518 (7th Cir. 2018) (Illinois). Following these favorable outcomes, New Jersey (once again part of RGGI) adopted a similar program. Robert Walton, "New Jersey moves ahead on nuke subsidies, approving ZEC application process," *Utility Dive* (Nov. 21, 2018). For an overview of state renewable energy policies, see Galen L. Barbose, "US Renewables Portfolio Standards: 2019 Annual Status Update," Lawrence Berkeley National Laboratory (2019), *https://emp.lbl. gov/projects/renewables-portfolio*.

14 California Air Resources Board, "Proposed Amendments to the California Cap on Greenhouse Gas Emissions and Market-Based Compliance Mechanisms Regulation," Staff Report: ISOR Appendix D, "Evaluation of Allowance Budgets 2021 through 2030" (Sept. 4, 2018); see also Lisa Song, "Cap and trade is supposed to solve climate change, but oil and gas company emissions are up," *ProPublica* (Nov. 15, 2019).

15 California Air Resources Board, "California's 2017 Climate Change Scoping Plan: The Strategy for Achieving California's 2030 Greenhouse Gas Target" (Nov. 2017), at 26 (Table 2); ibid. at 30 (Figure 9).

16 Guri Bang, David G. Victor, and Steinar Andresen, California's "Cap-and-trade system: diffusion and lessons," *Global Environmental Politics* 17(3) (2017): 12–30.

17 Julie Cart, "Checking the math on cap-and-trade, some experts say it's not adding up," *CalMatters* (May 22, 2018); David Roberts, "California's cap-and-trade system may be too weak to do its job," *Vox* (Dec. 13, 2018); Song, *supra* note 14.

18 California Independent Emissions Market Advisory Committee, "2018 Annual IEMAC Report" (Oct. 2018) and "2019 Annual IEMAC Report" (Dec. 2019), *https:// calepa.ca.gov/climate/iemac-independent-emissions-*

market-advisory-committee/; Letter from California Senator Ben Allen et al. to California Air Resources Board Chair Mary Nichols et al. (Mar. 1, 2019), *https:// osf.io/yvqna/*.

19 Letter from California Air Resources Board Chair Mary Nichols and California Environmental Protect Agency Secretary Jared Blumenfeld to California Senator Ben Allen et al. (April 22, 2019), *https://osf.io/ckypn/;* see also Danny Cullenward, Mason Inman, and Michael D. Mastrandrea, "Tracking banking in the Western Climate Initiative cap-and-trade program," *Environmental Research Letters* 14 (2019): 124037, *https://iopscience. iop.org/article/10.1088/1748-9326/ab50df.*

20 Mason Inman, Michael D. Mastrandrea, and Danny Cullenward, "An open-source model of the Western Climate Initiative cap-and-trade programme with supply–demand scenarios through 2030," *Climate Policy* 20(5) (2020): 626–40.

21 Severin Borenstein et al., "Expecting the unexpected: emissions uncertainty and environmental market design," *American Economic Review* 109(11) (2019): 3953–77.

22 Part of the reason for this bimodal outcome is that Borenstein et al. (ibid.) assume conventional but nevertheless pessimistic price elasticities and do not account for price-induced technological change. See Chris Busch, "Analyzing the Likely Impact Of Oversupply on California's Carbon Market Must Consider State's 2030 Emissions Goal and Potential for Clean Tech Breakthroughs" (Jan. 10, 2018), *https://energyinnovation. org/2018/01/10/analyzing-likely-impact-oversupply-californias-carbon-market-must-consider-states-2030-emissions-goal-potential-clean-tech-breakthroughs/.* The assumptions in Borenstein et al. are also significantly more pessimistic than what the California Air Resources Board assumed in its rulemaking. "Near Zero Comment Letter to the California Air Resources Board" (Oct. 22, 2018), *https://www.ghgpolicy.org/s/Near-Zero-comment-letter-Oct-2018.pdf.*

23 Prices listed in real 2018 US dollars.

24 See Roberts, *supra* note 17 (quoting the California Air Resources Board's lead cap-and-trade staff member, Rajinder Sahota); see also California Air Resources Board, *supra* note 14 (describing the Board's official written views).

25 The EU ETS features a fund that does exactly this: 300 million allowances were reserved for sale from the New Entrant Fund (NEF300), with funds appropriated for deploying new technologies like carbon capture and storage projects that would not be economic at prevailing EU ETS market prices. See Damien Meadows, Yvon Slingenberg, and Peter Zapfel, "EU ETS: pricing carbon to drive cost-effective reductions across Europe," in Jos Delbeke and Peter Vis (eds.), *EU Climate Policy Explained* (Routledge, 2015).

26 Steven J. Davis et al., "Net-zero emission energy systems," *Science* 360 (2018): eaas9793.

27 National Academies of Sciences, Engineering, and Medicine, *An Assessment of ARPA-E* (The National Academies Press, 2017).

28 In green spending systems that do not differentiate between achieving the lowest-cost reductions and unlocking transformative investments, higher-than-expected marginal costs can be explained away as transformative investments. This kind of rationale-shifting wouldn't be possible if policymakers had to identify expenditures as belonging to distinct funds.

29 See Bob Wieckowski, "California's cap and trade extension: how Senate Bill 775 envisioned a new path to reduce greenhouse gas emissions," *UC Hastings Environmental Law Journal* 24(1) (2018): 15–20.

30 See, e.g., Christa M. Anderson, Christopher B. Field, and Katherine J. Mach, "Forest offsets partner climate-change mitigation with conservation," *Frontiers in Ecology and the Environment* 15(7) (2017): 359–65.

31 A. Denny Ellerman, Claudio Marcantonini, and Aleksandar Zaklan, "The European Union Emissions

Trading System: ten years and counting," *Review of Environmental Economics and Policy* 10(1) (2016): 89–107.

32 European Commission, "Climate Action, EU ETS: Use of International Credits," *https://ec.europa.eu/clima/policies/ets/credits_en.*

33 The Office of the Auditor General of Norway's investigation of Norway's International Climate and Forest Initiative, Document 3:10 (2017–18).

34 Mariana Lopes, "Bolsonaro's Amazon-sized spat with Germany and Norway threatens Europe–South America trade deal," *Washington Post* (Aug. 20, 2019).

35 See, e.g., California Air Resources Board, "2016 Cap-and-Trade Regulations, Initial Statement of Reasons" (Aug. 2, 2016), at 21, *https://www.arb.ca.gov/regact/2016/capandtrade16/isor.pdf.*

36 California Air Resources Board, "Updated Tropical Forest Standard" (July 30, 2019), at 23 (Section 11.2), *https://www.arb.ca.gov/cc/ghgsectors/tropicalforests.htm.* Technically, the buffer pool must be at least 10%, but given that the Standard was designed for use in Acre and regulators were unwilling to increase the minimum size in response to concerns from academic comments, it seems sensible to consider 10% as a reasonable proxy for what regulators would expect from its first participating jurisdiction. For context, deforestation rates in Acre jumped 73% from 2017 to 2018 – all before President Bolsonaro took office and accelerated deforestation trends. See PRODES Legal Amazon Deforestation Monitoring System, Instituto Nacional de Pesquisas Espaciais, Ministério da Ciência, Tecnologia, Inovações e Comunicações, *http://www.obt.inpe.br/OBT/assuntos/programas/amazonia/prodes.*

37 David V. Wright, "Cross-Border constraints on climate change agreements: legal risks in the California–Quebec cap-and-trade linkage," *Environmental Law Reporter* 46(10) (2016): 478–95.

38 Danny Cullenward, "The limits of administrative law as

regulatory oversight in linked carbon markets," *UCLA Journal of Environmental Law & Policy* 33(1) (2015): 1–41.

39 This view is rarely put to paper, but is occasionally referenced obliquely. See Dallas Burtraw, "Approaches to Adjusting Allowance Supply in California's Cap-and-Trade Program," Presentation to the California Air Resources Board Workshop on Evaluating Allowance Supply (Aug. 16, 2019), at slide 12, *https://www.arb. ca.gov/cc/capandtrade/meetings/20190816/rff_ct_ workshop_16aug2019.pdf*.

Chapter 8 Rightsizing markets and industrial policy

1 Thomas H. Tietenberg, *Emissions Trading: Principles and Practice* (Routledge, 2006).
2 Sustainable Development Solutions Network (SDSN) and the Institute for Sustainable Development and International Relations (IDDRI), "Pathways to Deep Decarbonization" (Dec. 2015), *http://deepdecarbonization.org/wp-content/ uploads/2016/03/DDPP_2015_REPORT.pdf*; Leon Clark et al., "Assessing transformation pathways," in IPCC, *Climate Change 2014: Mitigation of Climate Change* (Cambridge University Press, 2014); IPCC, "Global Warming of 1.5°C" (IPCC, 2018), *https://www.ipcc.ch/ sr15/*; Steven J. Davis et al., "Net-zero emissions energy systems," *Science* 360 (2018): eaas9793.
3 Daniel C. Esty (ed.), *A Better Planet: Forty Big Ideas for a Sustainable Future* (Yale University Press, 2019); Energy Transitions Commission, "Mission Possible: Reaching Net-Zero Carbon Emissions from Harder-to-Abate Sectors by Mid-Century" (Nov. 2018), *http:// www.energy-transitions.org/sites/default/files/ETC_ MissionPossible_FullReport.pdf*; see also David G. Victor, Frank W. Geels, and Simon Sharpe, "Accelerating

the Low Carbon Transition: The Case for Stronger, More Targeted and Coordinated International Action," BEIS, Energy Transitions Commission, and Brookings Institution (Nov. 2019).

4 See Charles F. Sabel and David G. Victor, *Experimentalist Strategies for Governing Global Climate Change* (Princeton University Press, 2021). Early elements of this study were published at: Charles F. Sabel and David G. Victor, "Making the Paris Process More Effective: A New Approach to Policy Coordination on Global Climate Change," Stanley Foundation Policy Analysis Brief (2016), *http://www.stanleyfoundation.org/publications/ pab/Sabel-VictorPAB216.pdf*; Charles F. Sabel and David G. Victor, "Governing global problems under uncertainty: making bottom-up climate policy work," *Climatic Change* 144 (2015): 15–27.

5 See, e.g., Jonas Meckling, Thomas Sterner, and Gernot Wagner, "Policy sequencing toward decarbonization," *Nature Energy* 2(12) (2017): 918–22; Steve Bernstein and Matthew Hoffman, "The politics of decarbonization and the catalytic impact of subnational climate experiments," *Policy Sciences* 51(2) (2018): 189–211; Mark Jaccard, *The Citizen's Guide to Climate Success: Overcoming Myths That Hinder Progress* (Cambridge Core, 2020).

6 Linda Cohen and Roger Noll, *The Technology Pork Barrel* (Brookings Institution, 1991).

7 For example, see the comparisons in the iconic study of emissions trading by Tom Tietenberg and the Project 88 reports, which rightly pointed the government to ways that markets could be used to obtain higher efficiency. Thomas H. Tietenberg, *Emissions Trading: An Exercise in Reforming Pollution Policy* (Resources for the Future, 1985); Robert N. Stavins, "Project 88 – Harnessing Market Forces to Protect Our Environment: Initiatives for the New President," A Public Policy Study Sponsored by Senator Timothy E. Wirth, Colorado, and Senator John Heinz, Pennsylvania (1988).

8 This is true not just for regulatory interventions, which

we will discuss in this chapter in more detail, but also government-oriented R&D programs, where there has been a lot of introspection and learning about how to be effective. See National Research Council, *Funding a Revolution: Government Support for Computing Research* (National Academy Press, 1999); David Hart and Richard Lester, *Unlocking Energy Innovation: How America Can Build a Low-Cost, Low-Carbon Energy System* (MIT Press, 2012).

9 Richard Schmalensee and Robert N. Stavins, "The SO_2 Allowance Trading System: the ironic history of a grand policy experiment," *Journal of Economic Perspectives* 27(1) (2013): 103–22.

10 For more on XG, see Sabel and Victor (2021), *supra* note 4.

11 Charles F. Sabel and Jonathan Zeitlin, "Experimentalist governance," in David Levi-Faur (ed.), *The Oxford Handbook of Governance* (Oxford University Press, 2012).

12 For a fuller discussion of club-based logics, see David G. Victor, *Global Warming Gridlock* (Cambridge University Press, 2011); Sabel and Victor (2021), *supra* note 4.

13 The best research on successful clean industrial transformations has focused on this interplay between technology and political power – through the creation of new interest groups and rewiring the incentives of incumbents. See, e.g., Staffan Jacobsson and Volkmar Lauber, "The politics and policy of energy system transformation – explaining the German diffusion of renewable energy technology," *Energy Policy* 34(3) (2006): 256–76; Daniel Gray and David Bernell, "Tree-hugging utilities? The politics of phasing out coal and the unusual alliance that passed Oregon's Clean Energy Transition Law," *Energy Research and Social Science* 59 (2020): 101288.

14 This three-step approach to radical decarbonization is drawn from the historical study of technological change and outlined in Victor et al., *supra* note 3; see also Frank

W. Geels et al., "Sociotechnical transitions for deep decarbonization," *Science* 357 (2017): 1242–4.

15 *See* Margaret R. Taylor, "Innovation under cap-and-trade programs," *Proceedings of the National Academy of Sciences*, 109(13): 4804-09 (2012).

16 Kai N. Lee, *Compass And Gyroscope: Integrating Science and Politics for the Environment* (Island Press, 1993).

17 Sabel and Zeitlin, *supra* note 11.

18 Ibid.

19 For more on sector approaches applied to climate change, see Victor et al., *supra* note 3.

20 Charles Sabel, Rory O'Donnell, and Larry O'Connell, "Self-Organization under Deliberate Direction: Irish Dairy and the Possibilities of a New Climate Change Regime," Columbia Law School Working Paper (Feb. 2015).

21 Sabel and Victor (2021), *supra* note 4.

22 David G. Victor and Lesley A. Coben, "A herd mentality in the design of international environmental agreements?" *Global Environmental Politics* 5(1) (2005): 24–57; Sabel and Victor (2016), *supra* note 4.

23 Jeffrey Ball, "Why the US should embrace 'Green China Inc.,' not fight it," *Fortune* (May 28, 2019), *https://fortune.com/2019/05/28/trade-war-green-china/*; Evan Osnos, "Green giant: Beijing's crash program for clean energy," *The New Yorker* (Dec. 13, 2009), *https://www.newyorker.com/magazine/2009/12/21/green-giant*.

24 Energy Transitions Commission, *supra* note 3.

25 Victor et al., *supra* note 3.

26 For more on the state of play in border adjustments and experimentalism to learn which methods will work best, see Sabel and Victor (2021), *supra* note 4.

27 Prizes have taken many forms. Jonathan Bays, Tony Goland, and Joe Newsum, "Using Prizes to Spur Innovation, McKinsey" (July 2009), *https://www.mckinsey.com/business-functions/strategy-and-corporate-finance/our-insights/using-prizes-to-spur-innovation*. For public sector prizes such as NSF's innovation prizes,

see National Research Council, "Innovation Inducement Prizes at the National Science Foundation" (2007). And for a rigorous empirical assessment of earlier prizes, see Liam Brunt, Liam, Josh Lerner, and Tom Nicholas, "Inducement prizes and innovation," *Journal of Industrial Economics* 60(4) (2012): 657–96.

28 For more on the European Green Deal, which includes many elements (in part because it must appeal to many supporters), see European Commission, "A European Green Deal," 11.12.2019 COM(2019) 640 final, *https://ec.europa.eu/info/strategy/priorities-2019-2024/european-green-deal_en.* For the investment plan, which focuses on deployment and does not include many of the earlier-stage innovations, yet offers a sense of scale and leverage between public and private portions, see Bhakti Mirchandani, "A €1 trillion opportunity: how to read the EU Green Deal investment plan," *Forbes* (Feb. 3, 2020).

29 RGGI, "The Investment of RGGI Proceeds in 2017" (Oct. 2019), *https://www.rggi.org/investments/proceeds-investments.*

30 The annual budget for the CEC has recently ranged from approximately $400 to $900 million. California Legislative Analyst's Office, "The 2018–19 Budget: Resources and Environmental Protection" (Feb. 14, 2018), *https://lao.ca.gov/Publications/Report/3747;* California Legislative Analyst's Office, "The 2020–21 Budget: Resources and Environmental Protection" (Feb. 25, 2020), *https://lao.ca.gov/Publications/Report/4178.*

31 Thomas C. Schelling (ed.), *Incentives for Environmental Protection* (MIT Press, 1983).

32 This section is based heavily on Victor et al., *supra* note 3.

33 A variety of 2 × 2 matrices around types of cooperation problems are used by political scientists. This one reflects two studies: Robert O. Keohane and David G. Victor, "Cooperation and discord in global climate policy," *Nature Climate Change* 6(6) (2016): 570–5; Robert Hoppe, *The Governance of Problems: Puzzling,*

Powering and Participation (Policy Press, 2010). The emphasis on cognitive understanding of solution sets affecting cooperation reflects, as well, work on experimentalist governance. See Sabel and Zeitlin (2012), *supra* note 11.

34 For a study that emphasizes experimentalist approaches to climate governance, see Sabel and Victor (2021), *supra* note 4.

35 For a summary of the "game theory" strategic logic, see Todd Sandler, *Collective Action: Theory and Applications* (University of Michigan Press, 1992).

36 In this study, we devote little attention to gridlock and concentrate instead on ways to avoid getting stuck in gridlock equilibria. For a larger look at gridlock itself, see Thomas Hale, David Held, and Kevin Young, *Gridlock: Why Global Cooperation Is Failing When We Need It Most* (Polity, 2013).

37 So far there is very little practical experience with border carbon adjustments (BCAs) because policymakers have addressed competitiveness concerns in other ways, such as with free allocations to trade-exposed sectors or reductions in effective tax levels for those sectors. However, there has been extensive analysis of how these BCA systems could be designed to be compatible with the World Trade Organization. For more on variation in the tax levels, see Geoffroy Dolphin, Michael G. Pollitt, and David M. Newbery, "The political economy of carbon pricing: a panel analysis," *Oxford Economic Papers* 72(2) (2020): 472–500. For more on BCAs directly, see Stefan U. Pauer, "Border Carbon Adjustments in Support of Domestic Climate Policies: Explaining the Gap between Theory and Practice," Smart Prosperity Institute Clean Economy Working Paper 19-05 (Oct. 2019).

38 The solar industry is perhaps the best example. See Gregory F. Nemet, *How Solar Energy Became Cheap: A Model for Low-Carbon Innovation* (Routledge, 2019).

39 Danish Energy Agency, "Important Long-Term Energy Cooperation with China," *https://ens.dk/en/our-respon*

sibilities/global-cooperation/country-cooperation/china.

40 Teesside Collective, *http://www.teessidecollective.co.uk/*.
41 Northern Lights Project, "About the project," *https://northernlightsccs.com/en/about*.

Index